The
Good Nanny
Book

We all want to spend as much time as possible with our children. But for many working parents, some kind of formal child care is an absolute necessity. *The Good Nanny Book* is designed to take much of the guesswork out of hiring a qualified child care professional by helping you:

- Determine if nanny care is the right choice for your child
- Know where and how to search
- Decide if you want a live-in or a live-out nanny
- Effectively judge a candidate's qualifications
- Do everything possible to make sure your nanny and your child "get along"
- Prevent a high turnover

Complete with sample job applications and work agreements, interview tips, profiles of "nanny personalities" to avoid, shared parent and nanny child care tips, PLUS over 100 interviews with real-life parents, *The Good Nanny Book* will help you find a loving and capable professional who wants exactly the same thing as you do—the very best for your child.

The Good Nanny Book

How to Find, Hire, and Keep the Perfect Nanny for Your Child

P. Michele Raffin

BERKLEY BOOKS, NEW YORK

THE GOOD NANNY BOOK

A Berkley Book / published by arrangement with
the author

PRINTING HISTORY
Berkley trade paperback edition / March 1996

ISBN: 0-425-15133-6

BERKLEY®
Berkley Books are published by The Berkley Publishing Group,
200 Madison Avenue, New York, New York 10016.
BERKLEY and the "B" design
are trademarks belonging to Berkley Publishing Corporation.

PRINTED IN THE UNITED STATES OF AMERICA

10 9 8 7 6 5 4

This book is dedicated to Tom, to Caroline and Ben who produced him, and to Elizabeth, Ross, Jason, and Nick, the reason we have had nannies come into our lives.

It is also dedicated to the good ones: the nannies who, in partnership with the parents, provide love and nurturing to children.

Acknowledgments

This book would not have been possible without the support given—in multiple ways—by Caroline and Ben Raffin. Thank you Petunia and Louie. I am also grateful to Hillary Cige, Candice Fuhrman, and Suzanne Lipsett for their belief in this project and their assistance in transforming it into a book.

It was Tom who coined the term "Nanny from Hell," who always found humor in child care issues, and who encouraged me to write this book.

Deepest thanks are also due for referrals, comments, suggestions, and editing by Debby Rachleff, Caroline Fromm Lurie, Monica Frei, David Chase, Dave Saxon, and Robin Katzuros. To the peripatetic, consistently amazing advertising ace Joanne Sobel, special thanks. My gratitude also to James Back, San Francisco attorney-at-law, who was the only immigration lawyer I consulted who explained the issues in terms I could easily understand. Thanks to Janine Hecker for friendship, support, and photos. To Mike and Janey J.— thanks for the dinners, stories, and referrals. Chapter 8 would not have been possible without the information Drs. John McNeel and Virginia Price provided. Dr. Deborah Davis, editor of the *National Nanny Newsletter,* has directly and indirectly helped many families and nannies learn how to work and live together effectively. My thanks to her.

To the scores of nannies, nanny employers, nanny placement agencies, children cared for by nannies, and other nanny experts who unselfishly gave me insight into their lives, my deep gratitude. I hope that I have done justice to your experiences.

Contents

Definition: A Good Nanny   xi

Introduction   1

CHAPTER 1   The Nanny Solution: Yes or No?   9

CHAPTER 2   Visualizing a Nanny from Heaven   25

CHAPTER 3   Potential Sources   39

CHAPTER 4   Selecting a Nanny from Heaven   71

CHAPTER 5   A Gallery of Nannies: From Heaven to Hell   101

CHAPTER 6   Setting Up Your Home   155

CHAPTER 7   Managing a Home Employee   167

CHAPTER 8   The Triple-A Approach to Life with Nanny   219

EPILOGUE   248

APPENDIX A   In-Home Child Care Definitions   255

APPENDIX B   The Work Agreement: Worksheet and Sample   257

APPENDIX C   Parents and Nannies Share Child Rearing Tips   262

A Good Nanny

"She rejoices when the child is happy, and feels sorry for the child when he is ill; she picks him up when he falls . . . she washes and cleans him when he is dirty . . . ; she chews the child's meat for him when he has no teeth so that he can swallow profitably, and without danger; she plays with the child to make him sleep."

—Le Grand Propriétaire de toutes choses, très utile et profitable pour tenir le corps en santé, compiled by B. de Glanville, 1556[1]

"A good nanny has a stable and happy disposition coupled with a good sense of humor. She is not subject to intense and obvious mood swings or bouts of unpredictable behavior. . . . She has a good sense of herself, likes herself and knows how to take care of her own needs. . . . She has resolved her relationships with her own family in such a way that she can work professionally in another family. . . . She knows what the role of a nanny is and should be and she is not seesawing back and forth between playing the role of another child in the family or competing with the mother for her position. . . .

". . . The successful nanny is a person who has a strong sense of ethics and responsibility coupled with integrity and honesty. She is kind but firm . . . and is honest and respectful of the privacy of the household in which she is working. . . .

". . . The successful nanny is one who can discuss conflict without ruffling feathers unnecessarily. She can assert her own needs while respecting the other point of view. She operates as a professional from her knowledge and intellect, not from emotion or instinct."

—Diana Forney, NN NNEB RSH (Royal Society of Health),
Consultant, Nanny Training Programs[2]

"I finally decided that what I want in a nanny is someone who is going to be *nice* to my children."

—Parent of four young children, 1995

---

1. Philippe Aries, *Centuries of Childhood: A Social History of Family Life.* New York: Alfred A. Knopf, 1962.
2. *National Nanny Newsletter.* December 1984.

Introduction

MYTH
Only the very rich use nannies.

TRUTH
The middle class uses more nannies and other home child care providers than any other economic group.

There's a child care crisis in America today.

I'm not referring to the proliferation of two-working-parent families or the decline of the extended family system for looking after the children. I'm not referring to the rash of lawbreaking among normally law-abiding citizens who are hiring illegal aliens to provide home child care. Too many prominent individuals have bared their souls to the public on this issue already.

No, I'm speaking about a situation much more serious and closer to the diaper pail: the child care crisis in my own home.

The national child care crisis does not touch us with as much force as when it hits our own homes. This is when it becomes very real. As one mother put it, "Every family should have a back-up plan when their child care fails. Mine is very simple. I quit my job."

THE NANNY SOLUTION

Today, for millions of normal middle-class families—not wealthy or elitist families—home child care is the best and sometimes only solution to their child care problems. Many parents work hours that are incompatible with day care schedules. Some can't get their children into quality day care centers in their area. Families with several children sometimes simply can't afford the cost of day care. And for others, having a day care worker come into the home rather than taking the child away simply seems to be best for the child.

This book looks at "the nanny solution" from every angle. The goal is to help you decide whether home care is for you and, if it is, to provide you with the information you need to hire, manage, monitor, and if necessary fire a home care provider. Much of the information here is concrete and straightforward, but some can only be conveyed through examples. You'll find here many examples drawn from real life. Some are dreams, some are nightmares. All, I hope, will be instructive.

A NOTE ABOUT THE TERMINOLOGY

I've used the term "nanny" to refer to all home child care providers rather than draw distinctions between baby-sitters, mother's helpers, au pairs, and others, even though I am aware that they all pertain to different job descriptions. Appendix A lists the various terms and their definitions. I use "nanny" the way the British do: to refer to someone who cares for children in the children's own home. In England, the women who receive extensive formal child care training (3,000 hours plus) are called "nursery nurses," not nannies.

I also use feminine pronouns when referring to nannies. Even though a growing number of males are now taking child care jobs, the field is still predominantly female.

About my use of the terms "Nanny from Heaven" and "Nanny from Hell": Child care issues are so tension provoking for most of us that being able to laugh about a situation is a great release. In our family, classifying terrible care givers as Nannies from Hell allowed us to be lighthearted as we viewed our experiences with them. When we finally got a good nanny, we automatically referred to her as a Nanny from Heaven.

Speaking about good nannies . . . To begin our investigation of the much ignored and underestimated problem of securing great home child care, I return to the scene of my own awakening to the importance of a fabulous nanny.

OUR FAMILY'S STORY

We've had more nannies than I care to count. Nannies used to stay at our house about as long as the winter flu season. I began to suspect there was a sign of some sort outside the front door that read, in nanny lingo, Vacation Home for Wayward Nannies. Stop Here.

It reached the point where my two-year-old would greet a new nanny by waving "bye-bye" and my five-year-old would say, "Hi, how long are you staying? Will you be here past lunch?"

What was wrong? I offered a competitive salary. I tried to be a sensitive employer. What was the problem? Why was it so hard to find and retain good child care? And why, when they *did* stay, did I usually feel as though our child care providers were other children to look after, children with far more problems and complications than my own had?

There had to be an answer. Either the existence of wonderful home child care was a myth or something was wrong with the way I hired and managed my nannies.

Initially the first premise seemed the most reasonable. Maybe I was disappointed with my child care because I had unrealistic expectations. Maybe great nannies were extinct—or perhaps they never existed at all. After all, Mary Poppins, the epitome of nannies, was herself questionable if you really think about it. True, she only insisted on one day off every two weeks. But she arrived with no references and refused to discuss her past. And on her first afternoon with the family she took the children to meet her friend, a street entertainer, and they all went to a horse race!

"Do you think maybe everyone struggles with child care?" I asked my husband, Tom, after one particularly bad home child care experience. We had just had a nanny "stolen" from us. The nanny had been with us only one chaotic and awful month, but it was enough time for her to wreak havoc. We knew we needed to replace her, but before we had time another parent approached her at the park where she had taken our children. The parent hired her on the spot to start work the next day. Faster than one can say "peekaboo" she was gone. The family who hired her never called to check a reference. They knowingly hired someone who was willing to leave her present job with no notice. They knew very little else about her.

Our home life fell into disarray from this sudden and unplanned-for gap in our child care. Tom missed several important meetings; baths became so infrequent that the dirt, paint, and other debris on the children dried and flaked off; and the sight of macaroni and cheese out of the box—formerly a favorite food— would elicit moans and gagging sounds from everyone.

But we survived. In fact, my initial feeling of outrage at the "theft" ultimately gave way to feelings of sympathy for the family who had acquired our previous nanny. They reminded me of the thieves who stole a truck, only to discover it was from a diaper service, full, and on its way *back* to the cleaning plant.

"It's strange," I mused to Tom. "This other family was pretty desperate to steal our nanny, and she was a Nanny from Hell. If there's such competition for terrible nannies, maybe there's just no such thing as reliable, excellent home child care anywhere. Maybe the problem isn't us."

But when I uttered these words, I realized how hollow they sounded. My many years in business as a personnel vice president had taught me that there is always a great person for every job. You just have to know how to look. The reason we and this other family had the misfortune to experience a Nanny from Hell was that we hadn't done a good hiring job. The problem *was* us.

Nannies from Heaven do exist. In fact, one of my closest friends had one working for her. This nanny got the baby to sleep through the night, toilet trained the toddler and, my friend bragged, even taught her eldest to make his bed—after he had picked up the Legos and other assorted toys under his sheets.

I decided to no longer settle for anything other than *great* child care and to learn how to accomplish this. I vowed never again to keep someone on just because she was a "body." Not only our children but our whole family deserved better. We needed a wonderful nanny, a Nanny from Heaven, and nothing else would do. How was I going to find her? I'd scour the libraries, draw on my business experience, and search out other parents who used home child care to see what I could learn from their experiences. If there was a secret to finding and retaining top-notch child care in the home, I'd find it.

I did, and in the process I learned much, much more than I had ever intended. I even got tips on parenting, from both parents and nannies (see Appendix C)! This book started out as a stack of tapes and several loose-leaf books of notes I took during my self-education on finding and managing excellent home child care. I conducted scores of interviews with the experts—other parents—and listened with amazement to stories from people all over America about their experiences with nannies, au pairs, and baby-sitters. I've included some of them, in condensed but otherwise unaltered form. What impressed me most was the large number of both families and nannies from heaven. Yet often they couldn't find each other. Wonderful families were stuck with less than ideal child care givers and terrific nannies seemed to have a hard time finding the right family. Once I answered affirmatively my first question—Is there a great nanny out there for my family?—I turned to other important issues, such as how to choose the right person and, once hired, how to ensure that relationship would continue to be good.

After finishing my interviews I shared the information I had gathered with friends who needed assistance in resolving child care problems. Word spread and I started to receive phone calls from people I didn't even know asking for help. Many times after I counseled parents about how to find and keep a wonderful nanny, they would encourage me to reach a broader audience. "You should write a book," one parent (a pediatrician) urged me. "Do it for the welfare of the children . . . and to reassure parents that they shouldn't give up until they find excellent child care."

So, let me state unequivocally that home child care can be a wonderful experience for you and for your family. It really is possible! And every parent who decides to use child care in any form should not settle for anything less than the best. Too often, the only stories we hear are the tales of child care gone terribly wrong. Many of us settle for child care that is less than ideal, rationalizing that it isn't as bad as the few horror stories reported by the media. Some of us shy away from home child care altogether from fear that it could really be as bad as those stories suggest.

Admittedly, many of the tales I heard during my research were about bad experiences. They put my own previous experiences with Nannies from Hell into perspective and I felt reassured to know not only that I wasn't alone, but that others had survived even tougher problems. I hope that the troubles others have had (Tom calls these stories "Tales from the Crib[t]"), instead of scaring you off, will reassure you that even in the worst stories, the children seem unharmed, the parents recover, and in most cases, they can now laugh at what happened. If you have had a Nanny from Hell experience and sufficient time has passed since then, perhaps reading about others will help you recognize whatever humor there was in your own situation. Laughter is a wonderful healer.

When I asked my eldest child to describe our Nanny from Heaven in one word, the response was "Awesome." Our youngest responded, "I love her." Even our pets are glad she is in their lives. Your family deserves a wonderful nanny too. A good nanny, a Nanny from Heaven, is out there waiting for you to find her.

Memory Lane

"So, you're writing a story about nannies?" my mom commented during one phone conversation. "Be sure and include the one about the Condado Bandit."

"The Condado Bandit?" I questioned. "Who was that?"

"You don't remember! How could you forget the Condado Bandit?" was the incredulous response from the woman who only remembers if she brushed her teeth in the morning by feeling the toothbrush to see if it is wet.

"It happened when you were about eight or nine," she proceeded to tell me. "I hired a woman who had excellent references. I was thrilled with the way she took care of you children. She was only with us for two weeks, but during that time all of you thought she was terrific. She had a sunny personality, loved to play games, and cooked great dinners when I had to stay late at work. Then one day she disappeared. Just like that. No note. No explanation. You children came home from school and no one was there. The door had been left open so you were able to get into the apartment. But the place was empty. You called me and I came home immediately. We looked in the baby-sitter's room and all her belongings were gone. Also missing was the bedspread from her bed and, we later discovered, a collapsible shopping cart. It was a few weeks before we noticed that there was one other thing missing: our safe. Apparently, our 'wonderful' baby-sitter had stolen the safe, put it in the shopping cart, covered it with the bedspread, and left.

"When we reported it to the police they weren't surprised. 'You've been hit by the Condado Bandit,' they told us. 'She has pulled this so many times we've given her a code name. She works long enough to find out where the family valuables are kept then steals them.' "

My mom concluded by saying that after all was said and done, she wasn't sure which made her sadder: the loss of the safe and its contents or the baby-sitter who had seemed so wonderful.

CHAPTER 1

The Nanny Solution: Yes or No?

For some families the decision to hire a nanny is effortless. Marie and Ross Dupont knew from the start that they would hire a nanny to care for James, their first child, when they both returned to their jobs. Marie is a flight attendant; Ross owns his own company. Ross explained, "For us there wasn't any option. We needed the flexibility of home child care due to the nature of Marie's job. The questions that plagued us were whether or not Marie should return to work and if so, when. We also worried about the loss of privacy inherent in bringing someone to live with us; our house is not very big, in fact we only have two bedrooms. I also was concerned about the cost. I thought that only rich people had nannies, and we aren't rich. But we decided up front that if we couldn't be home to care for our children ourselves, we would do the next best thing—hire someone else to be there in our place."

Marie had a different point of view. She told me, "I thought about the things Ross mentioned, but they were considerations after the fact. The real reason I decided to get a nanny was emotional. I just couldn't envision taking my baby to someone else's home or to day care every day. It didn't feel right. There is a very good day care center near our home, but every time I would pass it and see the children playing outside, I would feel sad. The children looked happy there, but it just wasn't for me. Besides, I had been raised from the age of three by a woman who lived with us. We didn't call her a nanny, but she functioned as one. I adored her. I wanted my children to have this experience too."

"We were quite sure the nanny road was the right one for us," Ross concluded. "The questions were logistical ones: How could we afford one? Where would she sleep? How could we arrange our lives so she didn't intrude?" The Duponts ended up renting a bedroom from a neighbor for their nanny. They also shared their nanny with another family who needed child care, which greatly reduced their cost of employing the nanny. Looking back at their decision to hire a nanny, the Duponts conclude that it was not only the best solution for them, it was also well within their budget.

Julie, a dress store manager and single mother of a five-month-old son, is equally certain that a nanny is *not* the best child care option for her. She elaborates, "My neighbor told me about a woman who lives a few blocks over who cares for children in her home. I went to see this person and instantly knew it was the place for Dane, my infant. I really didn't think, Do I want family day care or a nanny? I just fell into family day care.

"The day care provider is wonderful with children; she is a former nurse who just loves kids. Dane smiles when he sees her. And the cost is only $16 a day! She cares for six children, but Dane is the only infant. I work three days a week, but between commuting and working, I am sometimes gone twelve hours a day. I miss Dane and sometimes I worry he will think she is his mom, but overall I'm really happy with my choice."

For others, the decision about child care is not so straightforward. Max explains, "I am a single dad. My two children came to live with me when Andrew was five and Melissa was three. I didn't know what to do as far as child care. I had a lot of other decisions to make at the time and frankly this one overwhelmed me. Where would I find a good nanny? Didn't the children need other children? If I found a day care center or family home with an opening for Melissa how could I tell if it was a good one? And how would I arrange for Andrew to be picked up at kindergarten? The biggest single worry for me was quality. Their mother had been abusive and the last thing I wanted was another abusive woman in their lives.

"I listed with a nanny agency, called a child care center referral number, and asked everyone I knew about family day care. I leaned toward using a day care center because in this setting there is a multiple of caretakers and they would watch each other. I had interviewed some nannies, but I was afraid I didn't have what it takes to select one. I was still smarting from my divorce and also just not comfortable bringing a woman into my house even though it was an employment arrangement. Even so, I went back and forth: thinking day care center, then nanny; deciding nanny, then changing my decision to day care center.

"I finally decided: day care center. The problem was when I went to enroll there was only one available place in the best day care center in town and I needed two. Just as I was despairing, I lucked out and found a great family day care home. It wasn't as close to home as I would like, but I decided it was worth the drive."

What feels right for you? The final decision about where to place your children is ultimately an emotional one. Research has shown that children do well in a variety of care situations as long as two variables are met: the care is consistent and of high quality. In the chart on the next page I have listed some factors that may immediately disqualify the nanny option for those of you who don't have a clear emotional direction. If this simple list is insufficient, consult the more detailed pros and cons in the overviews of each option (child care center, family day care, nanny).

Every solution brings forth its own problems. Don't expect any child care option—even the decision to stay home and take care of your children yourself—to be perfect and pain free. Listen to your heart and make the selection that feels right for you. Then spend your energies on ensuring you find the very best of the option you've chosen.

As you ponder what avenue to travel, think about your children and their personalities. Do you have a child who is shy or insecure? One who needs a lot of stimulation? Consider how each of the options will cater to your individual child.

At this stage do not focus too much on financial considerations in selecting your child care. The costs vary according to where you live and how many of your children require child care. People automatically assume that employing a nanny is the most expensive child care option. That isn't necessarily true. In fact, if you have more than one child requiring care, or if you share with another family, or if you hire an au pair, this can be one of the least expensive options. We will cover costs later in this chapter. It is worth noting at this point, however, that the families I interviewed who employ nannies have household incomes of at least $35,000 annually.

Is Hiring a Nanny Right for Our Family?

YES, IF:	NO, IF:
1. You want individualized care	1. You can't handle another close relationship
2. You want to control your child's schedule	2. Privacy concerns are paramount
3. You want your child cared for in his/her own home	3. Concern about leaving child with unsupervised care is paramount
4. Your family income exceeds $35,000	4. Your family income is less than $35,000

This checklist is not comprehensive. I discuss each of the most popular child care options more thoroughly later in the chapter. This quick checklist does cover the most significant issues determining whether a nanny is the best child care option for you. Many parents focus on logistical issues such as where the nanny will sleep, or cost issues involving individualized care. I suggest that you leave these aside and think about the emotional component first. Ask yourself: Will I feel better knowing that someone is giving my child individualized care in his or her own setting, or will this arrangement cause me to feel anxious because it means I will have to bring another person into my life and entrust my child to this person?

DEVELOPMENTAL CONCERNS: MY PERSONAL BIAS

In choosing child care options, consider the ages of your children. Infants need a care giver who is attentive and consistent. They don't need other children or fancy toys. They don't necessarily need exclusivity. After all, only the eldest in any family gets that. But they do need to be cared for by someone who has enough time (and arms) to pay attention when the baby needs attention, whether it is feeding, changing, or physical closeness the baby requires. The same care giver or team of care givers should tend the infant. An infant needs continuity of care.

A nanny who is trained in infant care or who has had prior experience with infants is an excellent choice for the family who has an infant. A family day care provider can also offer an infant the consistent, loving care required if the provider has the right mix of ages and number of children. Many day care centers don't accept children under the age of two. Those that do should have enough staff and *assign a designated person* to each infant to be a good choice. They should also have low staff turnover rates.

Toddlers have different needs. In addition to an attentive adult, a toddler needs a stimulating environment. Toddlers don't need "friends" the way an older child might, but toddlers do thrive from having other people around part of the time. As your child matures, placing him or her in a group setting for a *short* period of time can teach social skills and be fun. Some children benefit from this at around age two, some need to wait a little longer. The best preschools and day care centers allow a parent or nanny to stay with the child until he or she feels comfortable in the setting and learns to rely on a teacher for comfort and help. Unfortunately not all programs welcome parents in the classroom. As the child grows, he or she can spend more time at the preschool or day care center. In my experience, most children aged four and older do very well for up to five hours in such a setting. If a good group care facility is available to you, you may decide to combine daily one-on-one nanny care with some time spent with peers. If not, a play group can accomplish the same thing.

As children reach school age, the amount of time a child feels comfortable spending away from home tends to increase. Many parents feel their children thrive by going straight from school to an after-school care program. Others choose to hire a nanny to care for the child after the school day is over. No current research indicates that either is best for children.

CHILD CARE CENTER

Description

A child care center is a licensed facility that cares for children in a group setting. State licensing requirements vary, but standards usually stipulate adult/child ratios and space requirements. Most states lowered standards in the late 1970s to increase the number of slots available.

Some day care centers are for-profit, others are nonprofit; some are on-site at companies; most are not.

History

The first United States publicly funded day care center opened in 1815. It watched over infants and very young children, primarily feeding, bathing, and keeping them safe. Most children over seven went to work (child labor laws did not exist until the 1900s) and it was not uncommon for children as young as three to do piecework such as sorting feathers or tobacco.

Many experts believe that the best child care facilities in the United States were opened during World War II. In Portland, Oregon, the Kaiser shipyards, for example, developed model care centers. Within two years of the war's end, the centers were closed.

Pros

- They are reliable.
- They usually have equipment and facilities superior to those at home.
- Other children provide play partners.
- Several care givers support each other and maintain standard of care.
- References are easy to check; other parents can describe their experiences.

Cons

- The best ones usually have long waiting lists.
- Many do not take children under age two.

- Many do not take sick children.
- Children in day care get ill much more frequently than those at home (pneumococcal infections—the leading cause of earaches, pneumonia, and meningitis—occur 36 times more frequently in children under two who attend day care centers than in stay-at-home children).[1]
- High employee turnover means children must get used to different care givers.
- Hours can be very rigid, with stiff penalties for noncompliance.
- Centers often do not have enough staff to cater to children with special needs; a shy child, for example, may be overwhelmed.
- You must provide transportation for your child.
- Child care centers can be expensive.

How to Distinguish the Best

- Inquire about the director's and teachers' credentials. Studies have shown a positive correlation between level of education and quality of care given.
- Spend a day and observe. Is the shy or tired child treated appropriately or is he or she required to participate in group activities? How are conflicts between children handled? Do the children seem happy?
- Talk to as many parents as you can who use the facility. Do they use it because they have no other options, or are they genuinely happy with their choice?
- Inquire about staff and teacher turnover rates. The best facilities have low turnovers.
- Ask to speak to parents who have left the center.
- Pay attention to whether children are involved in activities and with toys that are developmentally appropriate.

---

1. *The Journal of the American Medical Association,* in its March 14, 1995 issue, reported these findings from a Finnish study.

- Are parents allowed to drop in unannounced? They should be. If you decide to enroll your child, stop by unexpectedly and observe how well your child is doing.
- The center's status (nonprofit or for-profit) does not indicate quality, nor does the fact that it is licensed.

FAMILY DAY CARE

Description

The most used of all day care alternatives, this method involves a woman caring for several children in her own home. Some states require licensing; others do not. Some family day care centers are run on a drop-in basis. Others require that parents commit to a certain number of hours a week.

History

The practice of sending children to other families for care is very old. Until the discovery of pasteurization and the resulting increase in bottle feeding safety, infants were frequently sent to wet nurses. Sometimes this was because their mothers had died, but not always. Wealthy families often did it in order to "spare" the mother's breasts.

Among wealthy families in the Middle Ages it was customary to send children to another household to be raised and to accept in turn another household's children.

Pros

- This is the least expensive alternative, if care is for only one child.
- The setting is homelike.
- The situation may have some flexibility, depending on the care giver.
- In the best ones, children receive individual and personalized attention.

Cons

- Standard of care can be difficult to determine.
- Transporting a child is inconvenient.
- The demands of caring for several children simultaneously may mean your child doesn't get attention as promptly as needed.
- Safety standards vary widely.
- Licensing does not indicate quality.
- Care giver's child-rearing philosophy may differ from yours.
- When the care giver is sick, or one of the children comes down with a communicable disease, the whole facility may close down.
- Children under two who attend family day care are 4.4 times more likely to come down with pneumococcal infections than stay-at-home children.[2]

How to Distinguish the Best

- Spend a day or drop in unannounced several times. Be wary if you observe babies propped with bottles, crying babies who are unattended, children hurting each other without intervention, or children sitting in front of a TV for long periods of time (or adult programs on while children are there).
- Is the facility too neat (too much attention to housekeeping) or so messy it is dangerous? Is there enough indoor space for the number of children? Is there an appropriate outside space for the children to play in?
- Is there enough light? Are there developmentally appropriate toys within reach of the children? Are there multiples of some toys so children don't always have to take turns?
- Is the house safe? Does it have fire extinguishers, emergency phone numbers, covered electrical outlets? Are cribs, high chairs, and other equipment up to current safety standards? Is a first aid kit handy? What plan does the care giver have for an emergency evacuation?

---

2. *Journal of the American Medical Association.* March 14, 1995.

- What experience and training does the care giver have? Does she go down to the child's level often to talk or play? Is she warm and supportive? Does she seem to really enjoy children? Does she encourage and praise? Does she discipline calmly, addressing all the children's feelings if more than one child is involved? Is she safety conscious? Does she practice good health habits (washing hands after changing diapers, not letting children share utensils, etc.)?
- Check references of as many former users as you can. Also check your Chamber of Commerce to see if any complaints have been filed against the home.
- Inquire about the maximum enrollment she allows. Evaluate whether your child's needs will be met when the maximum number of children are present.

NANNY

Description

A nanny is a person who lives in or out who cares for a child in the child's home. The experience and qualifications of a nanny range from university or nanny school degrees to less than high school diplomas. According to the American Council of Nanny Schools, most nannies who go to nanny schools are between the ages of twenty-two and twenty-six, have a high school diploma and a driver's license, are nonsmoking, come from large families, and hold traditional views on male/female roles. The agencies I queried reported the average age of the nannies they place is thirty-five years old.

History

Hiring women to care for children in their home is quite ancient. The Chinese have used amahs for centuries, typically employing one amah per child. In England, girls normally started nanny training at the age of twelve or thirteen when they entered domestic service. They learned from other nannies, starting as a nursery maid and going up the ranks, eventually becoming First Nanny. In the 1920s the first formal training schools for nannies came into existence.

Pros

- Flexibility—you determine the schedule.
- Less disruption for children since care is in their own home.
- Personal attention for each child.
- More control over your child's world—you determine guidelines for food, sleep, and play, and you can set education standards.
- Dependability.
- Household help—you can include cleaning, cooking, laundry, errands, etc., as part of the nanny's job description.
- No child transportation needed to and from day care.
- No need to make other arrangements when your child is ill.
- Bonding—your child has one, consistent care giver.
- Specialized attention for children with special needs.

Cons

- Lack of back-up help if the nanny is sick or on vacation.
- Infringement on your privacy.
- Lack of supervision.
- Necessity of cultivating a personal relationship.
- Demands of being an employer, including the paperwork involved in paying taxes.
- Available space to accommodate another person as a live-in, or ability to pay the higher salary of a live-out.

How to Distinguish the Best

Read the rest of this book.

RESEARCH

The effects of group care on children has been studied for only the last two decades or so (with the exception of Israeli kibbutzim and custodial care in orphanages, neither of which has much relevance to modern group care) and the results are inconclusive. Proponents of group care such as Alison Clark-Stewart, point to studies revealing that children ages 3 and 4 in day care centers do better on scales of social development and cognitive skill than those left with baby-sitters.[3] However, they also agree that studies have demonstrated that children in day care are sometimes less polite, agreeable, and compliant, more irritable, louder, more rebellious and more likely to have behavior problems than children who are not.

Another study found that babies and toddlers were better off in their own homes or day care homes than in centers because the latter usually don't provide enough adult interaction for the really little ones.[4] Jay Belsky, professor of human development at Penn State University, analyzed the findings on child care from the viewpoint of attachment behavior between parent and child, generally regarded as the best indicator of emotional well-being, and found that the general quality of center care, particularly for infants, is poor.[5]

One finding does seem clear in the research: The child care worker's training and the number of children left in her or his care are the most critical indicators of care quality. However, the "training" found to be most significant is a B.A. degree, and the vast majority of child care workers either in the home or at a center don't possess one. Nanny schools have been sprouting up in the United States in the past few years as quickly as mushrooms after a rain, but most resemble technical schools more than colleges. None requires even close to the amount of time British nanny schools do (approximately two years). It is not unusual for a U.S. nanny school to offer three months' training and claim their graduates are "trained nannies."

After reviewing the literature, I've concluded that the research to date seems to indicate that given an equal playing field—comparing excellent family day care, an excellent day care center, and an excellent nanny—a child who is developmentally at age three will do equally well in all three settings as long as the hours in a group setting are not extensive. Children younger than this should not be in a group setting for more than a few hours at a time and infants should be cared for by one person, preferably in their own home.

---

3. Alison Clark Stewart, Christian R. Gruber and Linda May Fitzgerald, *Children at Home and in Day Care.* Lawrence Erlbaum Associates, Publishers. Hillsdale, New Jersey, 1994.
4. Pamela Schwartz, *Length of Day-Care Attendance and Attachment Behavior in 18 Month Infants,* "Child Development," August 1983.
5. Jay Belsky, "The 'Effects' of Infant Day Care Reconsidered," *Early Childhood Research Quarterly,* 3, 235-272 (1988).

The reality is that more research needs to be conducted. To complicate matters, the playing field is not equal. The quality of group care and individual child care varies enormously.

I have opted to use nannies for my child care needs because I feel it gives me the most control over the quality of care my children receive. I also have an emotional bias that young children should have plenty of time to play in their own homes, if at all possible. However, even with my strong preference for individualized care, I have sent my children to preschool for a few hours a week starting at age two and gradually increasing the time so that by age four the children were in school up to twenty hours a week.

I enrolled my children in preschools because they were very outgoing and enjoyed the stimulation of others *for limited periods of time*. Had this not been the case, I may have delayed introducing my children to a group setting until a later age.

Only you can decide what form of day care is best for your child. There is no magic formula to help you. For some families, financial considerations are of paramount importance, so let's look closely at the financial side of hiring a nanny.

FINANCES

At the end of the nineteenth century you were considered "barely middle class if you did not have a nursemaid for the children." Anne Talbot, born in 1899, said that her family was considered extremely poor; yet they had a cook, a nanny, two nursery-maids and a housemaid.[6]

Today, a nanny is generally believed to be the most expensive child care alternative. This is not necessarily factual. What is true is that if you compare the most expensive nanny salary with the most expensive day care center, the nanny salary will undoubtedly be higher. But you do not have to pay the highest nanny salary in your area to get a wonderful nanny. Furthermore, if you have more than one child, the nanny's salary does not go up proportionately. The cost of all other forms of child care do.

---

6. Jonathan Gathorne-Hardy, *The Unnatural History of the Nanny*. New York: The Dial Press, 1973, p. 180.

Among the families I interviewed, the nanny salaries ranged from $75 a week for an au pair who did not come through a government-sponsored agency to $612 a week for a professional nanny who was working for a Middle Eastern diplomat. The latter worked in a multiservant household, wore a uniform (although she had cautioned her employers it was best for her not to wear it in public because of the danger of kidnappers), and most approximated the Hollywood image of a nanny. She did child care exclusively and observed the life of the rich and famous from a front row seat.

By and large, most of the nannies I interviewed earn between $200 and $360 a week. They live primarily in coastal, metropolitan areas and care for up to six children. Listed below are all the costs associated with a live-in nanny. Nannies who live out generally earn larger salaries than those who live in.

1. Recruiting expenses
2. Salary
3. Taxes (approximately 10% but varies according to state)
4. Accounting help to do tax paperwork
5. Benefits such as health insurance
6. Increased utilities from having someone home all day
7. Food
8. Extra car, if needed
9. Extra car maintenance and fuel
10. Reduced rental proceeds if you would otherwise rent out the facilities the nanny is occupying
11. Cost of equipping the nanny's facilities
12. Gifts

One way families lower the expense of employing a nanny is to share her services with one or more other families. Even states that require licensing for family day care homes do not require licensing if only two families are involved.

Extra work is involved in setting up a nanny share since you must find another family to share with. It is essential that families who share a nanny have similar philosophies and expectations, which can make finding the right family to share with tricky. However, once an arrangement is established, both families can enjoy the advantages of a nanny with only a portion of the cost. The families I interviewed who share nannies seem for the most part to really like the arrangement. In some cases, the families used this approach to be able to afford to pay top wages for their care giver. Others paid standard wages, but lowered their individual child care cost to below that of other alternatives.

Another way to lower the cost of one-on-one care is to combine nanny care with some form of group care. One single mother I interviewed arranged for her child to be in a family day care center during the mornings. In the afternoons, a college student (majoring in early childhood development) took care of the child. The total cost of child care was extremely low because the college student exchanged child care for room, board, and a nominal salary.

One excellent arrangement was organized by the parents of a child who attended the area's top preschool. They hired one of the teachers who taught half days to bring the child home and care for him until the parents arrived. The family got a discount at the preschool and had one of its best teachers (a male named William) as their nanny. The parents' jobs are intellectually stimulating, but not very lucrative. When I asked them what advice they could give parents with financial considerations about affording a nanny, the mom told me with a wink in her eye, "Where there is a Will, there is a way."

SUMMARY

1. Given equal excellence, all forms of child care can be equally beneficial for children, depending on the children's ages.
2. Very young children, especially babies, do best with a single, consistent child care provider.
3. Deciding which child care option is best for you depends on the availability of high-quality centers, day care homes, or nannies in your area, the ages and needs of your children, and your emotional response to each of the options available.

4. Regardless of which option you choose, make sure that the care provided is excellent.

5. While financial considerations cannot be ignored, the cost of employing a nanny should not be a family's primary consideration in deciding which child care option to use. For those families who feel that nanny care is best for their children, creativity in the arrangements they make, such as sharing their nanny with another family, can lower the cost significantly, putting it on par with or even lower than the other alternatives.

CHAPTER 2

Visualizing a Nanny from Heaven

MYTH
Finding what you want is difficult.

TRUTH
Knowing what you need is the tough part.

A good friend once told me that lots of things are simple, but not all of them are easy. The first two steps in recruiting a Nanny from Heaven—developing a job description and an applicant profile— fall into the simple-but-not-easy category. The *job description* is a written synopsis of the position: duties, hours, salary, etc. The *applicant profile* is a list of personal traits, skills, and prior experience. I discuss both in detail in this chapter. However, before you can even begin a job description and an applicant profile, you will need to have realistic expectations. This part is both simple and easy because I'm going to tell you the answer.

REALISTIC EXPECTATIONS

The tricky part of realistic expectations is in the first word, "realistic." After all, how hard is it to visualize the perfect nanny? The perfect nanny is someone just like ourselves, perhaps more patient, more skillful at toilet training, more in love with cleaning and cooking. She will love our children just as if they were her own, but be sure they love us back more than they love her. She must have a life of her own, but always be available when we need her, and of course, she must promise to stay with us until we no longer need her. She must be presentable, but not too beautiful. Wonderful with the kids, but not too wonderful. In other words, we want someone better than ourselves who won't compete with us for the affections of our family. This is a nice daydream, but somewhat unrealistic.

So what can one realistically, reasonably, and fairly ask of a nanny? After more questioning than a youngster going through the "why?" stage, I finally arrived at an answer. Let me save you the delight (I use this word loosely) of learning by trial and error what is the "realistic" portion of realistic expectations. Here is what you can and should expect from your nanny:

1. She should keep your children safe and secure.
2. She should nurture and care for your children so that for most of the day they are happy and, in the long run, they thrive.
3. She should decrease rather than increase the stress in your family.

All else, my friends, is jackpot money.

THE JOB DESCRIPTION

Having realistic expectations is just the first step. You will need to fill in the details and be very clear about the specific job you want your nanny to perform. In business, when managers want to fill a position, they usually create a job description. This document is a written picture of the job; it lists the duties, hours, commitment period, salary, benefits, and expectations of a position.

You are the manager of your household and as such are in charge of developing the job description. It doesn't matter that as well as being chief honcho you are also the personnel director and theoretically shouldn't have to write down what you want in order to hire someone. Don't you already have enough to do? You've kept up with the baby book (if you have more than one child, don't expect me to believe this). You've filed all your children's artwork in separate folders, labeled with names and dates (Right!). Haven't you done enough to be the perfect parent? Besides, you don't need to write your expectations down. Knowing what you want in a care giver is easy. After all, you are a person who has birthed or adopted a child. In comparison this is a piece of cake.

Take it from me. Developing a job description for a caretaker involves one of the first in a lifetime of decisions about separation from your child. And nothing about this experience is easy. Sure, writing a job description is about as easy as eating a piece of cake— five-year-old fruitcake.

When my eldest child was born, I couldn't decide immediately whether I wanted someone to live in or live out or whether I wanted the person to be full-time and have housekeeping responsibilities or to be part-time and do child care exclusively. Or maybe I needed two people: a full-time child care worker and a full- or part-time housekeeper? How was I going to afford all of this?

I hadn't even decided whether to stay at home after my maternity leave was up or to return to work, and this uncertainty contributed to the difficulty of knowing what I needed. But an even greater problem was that I was unsure how much outside parenting help would feel right. Also, my first child woke up at least three times every night for what seemed like an eternity, so at the time I was struggling with developing a job description I was also sleep deprived.

In anticipating the nanny's duties most first-time parents err in their expectations of how much work a child care provider can reasonably be expected to do well. Usually, the more experienced the parent, the shorter is the list of duties. The accompanying "Sample Job Description" illustrates this idea.

To begin developing your job description, list all the responsibilities you would like your child care provider to perform. Be as complete and specific as you can be. More than one parent has cautioned that she and her nannies got into conflict over duties because they were not specified up front. Next, rank the duties and responsibilities in order of importance, putting the most important one first.

Review the list. Then draw a line separating the top twenty-five percent of the items from the rest. These are your "must haves" and are not negotiable. Consider all others "gravy"—delicious, but not necessary if the mashed potatoes underneath have enough butter and salt in them.

Only the most experienced employers know every single duty an employee can handle. And then, exactly at the point one has a sense of what is required, things change. No job description is totally accurate. Strive to make yours as honest and complete as possible, but warn your nanny that circumstances might change and you may need to add or subtract responsibilities. Somewhere on the description be sure to include a sentence or two stating this again. Job descriptions used in business regularly include some statement such as "and other duties as assigned." In spite of this disclaimer bear in mind that if you add duties later on without additional compensation, you may be asking for a disgruntled nanny. Many nannies are young and inexperienced employees. They won't remember that you warned them that their job description was an *approximate* outline of expectations and no more. However, even (especially) the most experienced nanny will not appreciate more and more duties being added to her job description once she has started work. One very experienced nanny, when pressed to describe a Family from Hell said, "I worked for one. They were extremely busy and as time went on, kept adding duties to my job description. Make breakfast. Make the beds. We're having a party, can you help out?"

Take heart! Once you have developed your first job description, subsequent ones will be easier. And if you've made a mistake on your first one, save it to work from later. Almost all nanny job descriptions change as the children grow older. My own have gone from being five-page masterpieces to one-page, doable plans as the number of children I have has increased and my ability to concentrate has gotten as loose as the skin on my upper arms.

The time you spend putting down on paper what you expect of your nanny is time well spent. A written job description will help you decide what is really important and what is not. It will also help you to communicate your needs to agencies, design an ad, decide on interview questions, and develop a work agreement (Appendix B). The job description doesn't need to be typed, and it doesn't need to be long or exhaustive. Its sole purpose is to define your expectations. Please do it.

Sample Job Description

Duties and Responsibilities

CHILDREN:

Total care for children including but not limited to getting them up in the morning and ready for school, taking them to school and after-school activities, cleaning their rooms and play areas and teaching them to do the same, preparing their meals, bathing them, and caring for their clothes and toys.

HOUSEHOLD:

Cleaning the kitchen area daily. Doing laundry for the family. Putting dishes in dishwasher in the evening. Unloading dishwasher in the morning. Doing driving errands such as grocery shopping, post office, etc.

OTHER:

Cleaning nanny automobile at least once a month. Organizing and cleaning children's closets every two months. Other duties as listed in the work agreement and as assigned periodically.

HOURS OF WORK:

7:00 A.M. to 6:00 P.M., with two hours off each morning. Work week is Monday to Friday. Saturdays and Sundays are off. Will baby-sit one evening a week, to be determined by mutual agreement, and at least one week in advance.

continued

SALARY AND BENEFITS:

$___ per week, paid weekly. $___ per hour for overtime hours. $___ per night for overnights. A review is offered after three months, and then six months after that. $___ bonus given after completion of one year.

　　Room, board, automobile, automobile expenses provided. $____ per month allowance for health insurance given. __ holidays per year honored. If nanny works on these, double pay is given. __ weeks of vacation time is given after one year's employment. Nanny will travel with family on their vacations.

This sample job description does not specify salary information because pay standards vary considerably in different parts of the country, depending on the area's affluence and the availability of nannies. There are also considerable differences between wages paid for live-in and for live-out help, and between au pairs' salaries and those of professional nannies.

There is no typical nanny work week. They tend to work anywhere from a few hours to sixty or more a week. And the variation among benefit packages is equally broad. Some families offer perks such as health club memberships and huge end-of-year bonuses; others offer nothing.

To determine a fair compensation for your position, call some local nanny agencies and ask for their guidance. They will usually give you top-of-the-range numbers; you can expect to pay less if you recruit using another source. Another way to determine the going rate for a job such as yours is to run an ad for your position and solicit prior salary information from all respondents.

Once you get a feel for what is reasonable, adjust your expectation of a fair salary to the level of difficulty of your job. Consider the number of children involved, the number of hours, and any special considerations. Think about the caliber and level of experience you expect of a nanny. Expect to pay more for someone with a relevant college degree or with nanny school training. Someone who has long-term relevant experience will also expect to earn more than someone who doesn't.

THE APPLICANT PROFILE

Although developing a job description has its challenges, it is nothing compared to developing an applicant profile, a description of the traits you require or hope for in the nanny you seek. After all, how can you describe the person who is best going to take your place in caring for what you value most in life—your family?

I'll share with you a trick I developed when I first faced the task of deciding what combination of personality, skills, and experience our new nanny should have. It's called the Nanny from Hell Method.

First, hire someone you don't like (I'll be glad to forward addresses of Nannies from Hell if you feel you're not up to finding your own). As your new hire proceeds to aggravate you with the way she treats your children, home, husband, and you, take notes. Does she watch TV all day and stuff the children's mouths full of popcorn so they won't make noise and interfere with her enjoyment of the program? Write this down, with a note next to the entry that reads something like: Must air out the children at least twenty minutes a day. Does she wear minuscule bikinis around the house and consistently ask your husband to come to her room at midnight to kill the fly that is scaring her? Jot down something like: Must be strong and fearless; must definitely like insects. See? It's really not difficult to develop a clear picture of what is important to you using the Nanny from Hell Method.

Listed below are some of the most common traits parents consider imperative; I've included some of the examples my interviewees offered for clarification.

Essential Qualities in a Child Care Provider

1. IS WARM, NURTURING, AND KIND TO CHILDREN.

The emphasis here is on *children*, as opposed to warm, nurturing, and kind to every male eighteen and older who comes into view.

2. HAS COMMON SENSE AND WILL COMPETENTLY MAKE THE MYRIAD DECISIONS REQUIRED DAILY IN CARING FOR CHILDREN.

In other words, it is not a good idea to teach toddlers to "hide somewhere near the swimming pool and I'll be right back after I take a short nap" and other games like that. We had one baby-sitter who taught our two-year-old to "pick the pretty flowers in Daddy's prize-winning garden." Another told our middle son that ghosts only come out at night.

3. IS DEPENDABLE, HONEST, AND WILL DO WHAT IS EXPECTED.

"You mean I was supposed to call if I was sick and couldn't come? But I was so sick, I couldn't get to the phone."

4. IS ABLE TO FOSTER THE CHILDREN'S INTELLECTUAL, SOCIAL AND EMOTIONAL GROWTH.

"When we caught our four-year-old explaining a "Sesame Street" program vignette to our au pair, we decided we might need someone a little bit more intelligent to care for her."

"We told her excursions to the video arcade were not what we had in mind when we said we wanted her to take him on field trips. She replied that libraries were for nerds. Did we want our child to grow up to be one?"

5. HAS AN APPROACH TO DISCIPLINE CONSISTENT WITH YOUR OWN.

"In our family we use 'time out' as a discipline tool. We never thought to mention to our nanny that we only used it for the older children until we found her giving our ten-month-old baby time out."

"Our baby-sitter told our six-year-old daughter to bite her three-year-old sister back to teach the younger child not to bite."

Every family's list will be different. As you develop yours, try to limit the traits you seek to twenty or so. Then you can rank them and eliminate all but the top five. You can change the items on the list every time you hire someone who is not great and you realize you've left out something vital or included something that really isn't that important.

When considering what would be relevant training or experience for your ideal caretaker, focus on your specific family needs and disregard the temptation to look for someone with a specific background just because it may be currently in vogue among your acquaintances. If you are the parent of an infant, do you really need someone with a degree in early childhood education or would a relatively uneducated, but nurturing person be better? If your job involves more housework than child care, do you think a graduate of a nanny school will be satisfied? Do you have teenagers who require a lot of limit setting at the moment? Be aware of the variation with which different cultures handle discipline and be sensitive to this difference when considering caretakers from other countries.

What about your own personal needs? Are you an at-home mom who doesn't need a take-charge, don't-tell-me-what-to-do nanny sharing child care responsibilities? Be sure to list as a prerequisite that you need someone who has had prior experience working for an at-home mom and likes this arrangement. Do you need someone to handle all aspects of your household, not just the children? Be sure to look for someone who thrives with this level of responsibility. Do the cats insist on sleeping in the nanny's room, no matter how often you have tried to prevent this? Better look for a cat aficionado.

The accompanying sample applicant profile is for a weekend nanny to care for three toddlers whose parents sometimes work on the weekends. It doesn't strive to be comprehensive. It just lists those qualities considered essential.

Weekend Nanny Profile

Our ideal nanny would be: warm, loving, and *fun*. She must
have a driver's license and be a good swimmer.

We want someone who is energetic and can handle several children at once. Also, on those weekends when the parents are at home, we would like someone who will pitch in
with household tasks such as laundry and toy pickup (even
though ninety percent of her time will be spent with the children even when the parents are not at work).

She needs to be an animal lover since we have several pets.

You will refine your concept of the ideal nanny as you accumulate experience. If you do have an experience with a Nanny from
Hell, or even a nanny who wasn't that bad but who had one prominent characteristic that drove you crazy, don't throw out your entire
list of desired traits. A common reaction when things don't work
out well with an employee is to attempt to hire someone who is totally opposite in one salient feature, while forgetting that other
qualities on this list should not be thrown out the window.

My term for this is "ping-pong" hiring. For example, several
families told me things like, "First we hired someone mature, because we thought we wanted a 'grandmother' type for the baby.
The older woman we hired didn't have the necessary stamina, so
we decided to find a younger woman who would have more energy.
When the younger one left, we decided it would be better to hire
an older person who was more stable and not so boy crazy. The
person we hired was very nice, but she had back problems and
couldn't do a bit of housework. So to replace her we decided to
find a younger person who would be healthier."

Get the picture? Ping-pong hiring is such an obvious mistake,
you wouldn't think *you* would ever do it, would you? As the accompanying story illustrates, ping-pong hiring is actually very common.
Do your best to resist its temptation when you need to hire a new

person immediately after you have just had an unpleasant child care experience.

You also should try to avoid the temptation to hire someone just because the person shares one trait with a Nanny from Heaven that you adored. This is "umbrella" hiring, the one trait being an umbrella under which you shove all other considerations. Just because you had a super nanny who was Irish (or a preschool teacher or who told good jokes or was a whiz at developing rainy-day projects, etc.), don't be swayed by someone new just because she also is Irish. Umbrella hiring is just as common as ping-pong hiring, and just as big a mistake.

We Hired "Quiet" Because the Last One Wasn't

THE SUTTONS' STORY

She was quiet, that was Caroline Sutton's first impression of Helen. And her aunt was with her; they had driven all the way down from Seattle to visit the aunt's daughter, who was a nanny. As the aunt and Caroline talked, Caroline reflected that Helen had two points in her favor. Her cousin was a nanny so she would know at least secondhand what the job was all about. And she did seem to come from a nice family; her aunt was delightful.

The Suttons' first nanny had been a professional baby nurse who they felt was too domineering. Maybe a young, inexperienced, but sweet and loving girl was what they really needed, Caroline decided.

She hired Helen on the spot. When she told her the job started in two weeks because the family was leaving on a ten-day vacation shortly, Helen's face fell. She was here. Where would she stay in the meantime?

Caroline recalls her decision: "I thought, So what's two weeks' extra salary and the risk of leaving a perfect stranger in your house while you're away? Perhaps it was the sleep deprivation, or the trust I somehow felt in the aunt, but I agreed. Helen

continued

---

could move in right away, and get the 'hang' of the area while we were away. After all, how much harm could she do? She was new to the area. And besides, she could substitute for our regular house sitter and feed the cats while we were away. We would even save the car fare to and from the airport. Helen could drive us.

"We called several times while we were on vacation. Once the phone was answered. Helen said all was well. There were no details, but then again, one of the reasons we had hired her was that she was quiet. We really didn't begin to panic until we arrived back and had been waiting at the airport curb for thirty minutes. No Helen. No answer when we called home. We were just entering a cab about half an hour later, when our car came screeching to the curb. It was Helen. Very apologetic. She had gotten lost. In Oakland. A city fifty miles away. And why had she been there? Well, the answer to that also answered why there was no child seat in the car. She had to remove the seat to fit her friends who needed a ride to Oakland. And she had gotten lost because she had not been able to figure out the lights in the car.

"Friends? That was fast. Lights? But it was daylight now. Well, that was last night. And since she didn't know how to work the lights she thought the prudent thing to do was not to drive in the dark. Then all we got was quiet. Well, that had been her strong point."

Was everything okay at home? the Suttons asked Helen not a little anxiously.

"Sure," Helen replied calmly. "Of course, there was a little trouble with the garage door, and I don't know what happened with the shelf in your closet, but I'm sure they'll be easy to fix. Diane is trying to fix it now."

"Diane?" the Suttons asked in escalating panic.

"Oh, you know about Diane, my cousin the nanny. She got fired just after you left, so I figured since the house was empty and all, you wouldn't mind if she stayed with me while she looked for a job. The people she worked for were very weird. They never let her have any friends over and when they

continued

found the baby asleep without a diaper on, they didn't believe her when she said she had put him in the crib fully dressed. She knows all about children. She'll be a big help teaching me and she won't charge you a cent."

By now it was the Suttons who were speechless. They didn't even comment when they drove into the driveway and saw the entire garage door off the hinges and hanging sideways. The cats raced to their sides as they opened the car and mewed in sheer delight. Maybe it was their imaginations but they thought the cats seemed to be saying they hadn't been fed in a week.

The Suttons never did figure out how the shelf in their closet collapsed. They do have an idea about how a man's wallet full of IDs but no cash got under the master bed, but since they have no proof and only theory, they wouldn't share their thoughts. The cousin was rushing around trying to clean up as they entered. She too was quiet and seemed sweet. But I guess by this point the Suttons decided quiet and sweet was not enough.

The cousin, Diane, coaxed, "Let me feed the baby," as they walked in. She placed him in his highchair and covered him with a bib. She then said "Boo" and shoved the food into his surprised, but open mouth. At that point, the Suttons decided they had had enough.

"Helen's parting words to us," Caroline finishes, "were, 'Well, it was only a summer job anyway. I'm going back to school in August. You said you wanted someone to stay at least a year, so I wasn't sure how to tell you. But you've made it easier for me. Thanks for letting me see the area. The shops are great and I found a cool restaurant that probably needs waitresses so I'll be fine.'"

Caroline and Louie Sutton both work in the retail clothing industry. They have one child, three cats, and two house rabbits.

SUMMARY

1. Being clear about your expectations is the first step in hiring the right nanny.
2. A written job description and applicant profile are important, even though they may not be fun to develop.
3. Be realistic about your general expectations.
4. Try to avoid ping-pong or umbrella hiring.

CHAPTER 3

Potential Sources

MYTH

The best nannies come from nanny agencies (or by advertising, or through referrals, or from abroad . . .).

TRUTH

Different nannies use different approaches to job hunting. The "best" nannies can be found any number of ways.

Once you are sure about the parameters of the job and have a clear mental picture of the perfect candidate, it's time to set off on the hunt. Where do you look for the perfect nanny for your family? The parents I queried all swear by their individual methods. Some stated without equivocation, "Nanny agencies: that's the only place to find a quality person." Just as many said, "I never use an agency. The best people come from newspaper ads, and they are so much cheaper." (Ads are cheaper than agency fees, too, I might add.)

I also heard vehement endorsements of the referral method. One mom insisted "I have hired seven au pairs using only the grapevine. I've had wonderful experiences with all but one person and I haven't spent a cent on recruiting." Which brings up another consideration. Do you want to hire locally, from out of state, or from other countries? Do you want to employ only someone who is legally allowed to work or is this not a consideration? Options, options, options.

My preference is a combination of all of the options—agencies, ads, and referrals—and to recruit both locally and out of state.

A broad-based search gives you the widest possible selection of candidates. However, sometimes circumstances dictate that you focus your resources and limit yourself to one or two sources. In this case, you will base your choice on the amount of time, energy, and money you have available, and how quickly you need to fill the job.

If you have more time than money, you could pass on using a nanny employment agency. Agencies can be expedient but expensive. Instead put out the call and ask others to help you look.

On the other hand, if you are snowed under with projects or going to be out of town during the time you should be recruiting or if time is worth more to you than money, use an agency.

Advertising for a nanny is the means most often used, and for good reason. It is less expensive than an agency and more efficient than asking your friends for referrals. Also, ads yield candidates with a broader range of salary expectations than agency referrals have.

In this chapter I evaluate the different methods of finding home child care and rate them from one star (least) to four stars (most) based on the time, energy, and cost they typically require.

AGENCIES

Time and energy required**
Cost****
Number of applicants you are likely to interview before selecting one: 6–10

I hired my first nanny more than a decade ago. I found her through a nanny placement agency. I don't remember exactly why I chose this avenue to find child care help; I had lots of business experience hiring personnel without the use of agencies. I think I had the notion the agency would have access to the "best" nannies, nannies that were unavailable from any other source. I also felt I was inexperienced in respect to child care and that the agency would be a better judge of a good nanny than I. The choice of which agency to use was easy. There was only one in my area.

The woman I hired and for whom I paid an agency fee of over $1,000 was a nanny school graduate. After she started working for us, I discovered that the school where she had trained ran its own placement service and charged $50 for the service. She had also answered several ads in our local newspaper. Had I advertised, she probably would have responded. Our paths could have crossed in another, even less expensive path. She was friendly with a nanny who worked for a neighbor. Had I asked my friends and acquaintances for referrals, I might have heard about her. Instead I unknowingly traveled the most expensive route to meeting our first nanny. When I terminated her three months later, the agency was understanding and helped her get another job quickly. They got another fee for placing her. I was minus a hunk of change and left with no nanny.

The agency's method for helping me hire my original nanny was to give my telephone number to the nannies they thought I should interview: everyone in their files, I suspect. I did all the screening myself. In addition, I discovered that their reference checking was not sterling. Therefore when I began researching agencies as part of my search for a good nanny I had some skepticism. What could an agency do that any parent couldn't do for him- or herself, better, cheaper, and with more control?

The first thing that struck me in beginning my research was the increase in the number of nanny agencies since my original experience. I was later to find that this is both good and bad news for parents: good because the competition has resulted in better and more comprehensive service from the better agencies; bad because now parents have to separate high-quality agencies from ones that are not.

I first met with the owner of Mothers in Deed, Monica Frei, an energetic young woman who had once been a nanny herself. I told her about my one agency experience and my doubts about the industry in general. She laughed and assured me that many things had changed since my initial experience.

"This is a new industry," she explained. "We've grown up a lot in the last ten years. We now do a much better job of screening, we never give out employer telephone numbers, we do a very thorough job of reference checking, and we offer a number of services for clients that would be difficult for them to get by themselves.

"We can arrange for group health insurance for nannies, we help nannies network with each other, we access nannies from other parts of the country, and we can direct you to services such as ones that set up payroll deductions for you. We check motor vehicle records and do police checks within forty-eight hours on all nannies. We only work with people who are legally able to work in the United States. And after you've hired someone, if you have problems, we can act as intermediaries."

What Monica told me was validated over and over again as I talked to the owners of agencies, questioned their clients, and met some of the nannies they had placed. As in any business, some agencies are better than others while some are downright terrible. How do you determine which is which? You can check several things:

1. Ask to be introduced to satisfied customers. The agency should let you speak to at least three.
2. Does the agency require an up-front fee just to look? The best agencies in our area ask for payment only if you hire one of their applicants. Although fee structures differ, a typical fee is an amount equal to one month's salary paid to your nanny. Most agencies charge a fee only to the employer. The nanny shouldn't have to pay anything.
3. Before you hire anyone, ask to see the agency's records on the person, including the original notes from its reference checking. One mom reported learning from one candidate's application form that she refused to do laundry and was allergic to dogs. The agency had not mentioned these restrictions. She hired the nanny anyway, but avoided a potential misunderstanding by reviewing the nanny's original application form herself.

   Ask to personally review the agency's reference check forms too. Don't accept the agency's assurance that references were checked. You need to see how many people were contacted and who they were. An assurance from a nanny's neighbor that she is great is not as good as that same assurance from a former employer. Ask the agency to allow you to recontact these people on your own.

Information from references is the most important data regarding a person's potential to be a Nanny from Heaven or a Nanny from Hell. Agencies have a vested interest in getting good references on individuals they wish to place (most agencies have a shortage of nannies, not of job openings). They often reference check with an ear to hearing good things about an applicant and don't delve beneath the surface to uncover problems. You need to doublecheck the reference information they have given you.

4. Does the agency actually interview its applicants in person? One agency in our area got many rave reviews from parents, but it also got the most complaints. It turns out that the agency found its applicants by using a computer network and sometimes it failed to interview them in person before referring them to job openings. The families who reported dissatisfaction with the nannies they had hired through this agency had usually hired women the agency staff had not personally met first.

5. Does the agency check references by phone (good) or in writing (not so good)? Reference checks by phone are more revealing and accurate. An astute reference checker can tell a lot from a person's tone of voice.

6. Does the agency belong to any nanny associations? There is at least one national organization and many states have local ones. Although the national organization does not monitor its member agencies, it does have a code of standards to which members are supposed to adhere. The members of local nanny organizations often monitor themselves.

7. What is the agency's guarantee policy? Will it give it to you in writing? Will it allow you to alter it? You should be able to stipulate that if you find out that any of the information given to you by the nanny or agency is false and results in the nanny's termination, your fee will be returned or the agency will replace your nanny with no charge.

I no longer think that using an employment agency to hire a nanny should be only an avenue of last resort. Nor do I feel it is the most expensive way to get help. The most expensive way is to hire the wrong person, regardless of how you found that person. It can be costly without measure in a number of ways, not the least of which is the trauma it inflicts on you and your children. If an agency supplies you with a Nanny from Heaven who stays for a long time, the money you spent on a fee was well worth it.

However, don't be misguided to believe that just because you pay a large fee to an agency, you are guaranteed a Nanny from Heaven or you cannot get the same nanny by using other methods of recruitment. Agencies do not have magical ways of finding nannies that are not available to you or me. Their nannies are neither better nor worse than the ones who will answer your ad or who your friends will refer, and in fact, they may even be the same people. Savvy nannies, like savvy parents, do not rely on just one avenue to find a job. They answer ads and ask their friends if they know of jobs. Also, agencies cannot place anyone from abroad who does not have a "green card" (permanent immigrant status), so if you rely exclusively on agency referrals you will be locked out of this excellent (but illegal) source of child care.

If you don't have the time to do a good job of prescreening, interviewing, and reference checking all by yourself and you don't mind paying a four-figure fee, then by all means utilize an agency to do this for you. But choose a good agency. Be smart in your dealings with them. Go to their office. Give them a detailed job description and nanny profile. Call them regularly to remind them to send the wonderful nanny they just found to you instead of to another, more vocal client. *And remember, recheck the agency's references.*

Make sure you agree with the agency's guarantee and other follow-up practices. Finally, remember to listen to your own intuition, and do not allow yourself to be sold on an individual the agency wants you to hire. Their staff may be experts, but what they excel in is selling people, not necessarily choosing the right person for your family. You are the only expert on this. And remember, if you hire someone through an agency you are making it easy for this person to leave you if she is dissatisfied. She will merely call the agency and ask to be placed elsewhere, an action that sometimes involves less effort on her part than working out whatever problems you might have with each other.

The following story illustrates what can happen if you use an agency you haven't checked out thoroughly, and you then allow the agency to handle all aspects of selection and hiring.

If You Can't Trust a Child Care Agency . . .

THE ATASSIS' STORY

"We have seven requests for every available nanny," the nanny agency representative confided solicitously, "but I'll see what I can do." This was the third local agency Eleanor Atassi had called. She was six months pregnant and her first child, a daughter, was in the midst of a record breaking case of the "terrible twos."

"How will I manage alone with a new baby? I can barely manage now," she wondered.

"Small towns in the South," a fellow patient asserted to her as they both waited for their obstetrician. "The most wonderful nannies come from there. They are unspoiled, hardworking, and don't expect a huge starting salary. There's one agency in particular that I've heard about that finds these girls. The agent flies out to your home to meet you and then personally hunts for the perfect nanny for you."

One week and several phone calls later, the Atassis had tracked down this wonder nanny finder and invited her to their house. As luck would have it, the woman had already planned a trip to their area to visit two other families, so the Atassis would only have to pay a third of the cost of her air travel. The charge for hiring the nanny was on par with agencies in their area, but they would have to pay the nanny's airfare, give her a paid vacation, and offer her a salary that matched that recommended by the agency. It all sounded reasonable. They didn't ask about refund policies or ask for a list of satisfied customers.

continued

On the appointed day, the agent entered the house. She was a fashionably dressed, middle-aged woman with pearl earrings and a poodle brooch. She seemed to take it all in with one glance: the house, the two dogs, the little girl looking angelic in pj's and pink bunny slippers. Forty minutes later, the Atassis had completed a long verbal questionnaire covering topics as diverse as their eating habits and who were their most admired people. After the questioning there was a brief silence and then the woman handed them a contract and asked for an advance so she could start the search right away. The couple signed the contract, glancing just briefly at the sentence that noted a month's guarantee on placements, and handed over a check.

They felt proud of themselves. If they had been smart enough to answer her questions satisfactorily, they must have been smart enough to hire the right agency. She had seemed to try her best to get to know them and they had done a good job of communicating their needs. They wanted someone who could stay at least one year and therefore needed to be free of commitments. They preferred a nonsmoker/nondrinker and insisted on experience with newborns and toddlers. And they needed someone who loved animals since they had several underfoot.

The nanny she referred stayed thirty-two days, which is one or two days more than a month, depending on the month. In this case it was the agency's definition of a month, so it really didn't matter. No refund. Zero. Arguments that they had called within a week of the nanny arriving to say she was unsuitable fell on deaf ears. They reminded the nanny finder of the numerous phone calls they had made complaining the nanny spent too much time on the phone, defined anything except playing with their daughter as "housework" and therefore not in her job description, and in general was treating the experience as if she were an exchange student and not an employee. The agency had given a lot of advice about adjustment periods and counseled the Atassis to be patient. Didn't that entitle them to some refund or at least a replacement? Against company policy was the answer.

continued

They pointed out that the nanny had returned to her home twice during the month (coming back so jet lagged and exhausted she couldn't work the next day). So what was wrong with that? Some girls have a hard time leaving home. But the reason she had traveled home was to talk to her boyfriend who wanted her to marry him; wasn't she presented as someone free of commitments? The agency promised to find out about this.

The boyfriend was easy to explain, they were later told. The week this nanny had completed the agency questionnaire she had no boyfriend because they had broken up. So how was the agency to know otherwise? They also got no sympathy when they complained that she was not well matched to them because she was allergic to animals (allergic or afraid, they never really could find out) and would not enter a room if one of them was there. "Did you hire her to take care of your animals or your children?" the nanny finder asked accusingly.

The Atassis asked the nanny to repay at least part of her airfare since in the midst of the time they had given her to work things out she decided to give notice. She said they could deduct $35 from her last week's pay and that when she was settled she would send them $35 a month until half the fare was repaid. They agreed.

They never did see the $35 a month. In fact, they never saw the nanny again. When she did not leave her room the next morning, they went to investigate and found a note pinned to her door. She said the agency had advised her to leave immediately because it was irresponsible of the Atassis to suggest she pay them anything back. She said that she thought they were very nice people and she "loved" their daughter, but it simply hadn't "clicked" the way the agency had promised.

The Atassis called the nanny's mother. She informed them that her daughter had been very disappointed in them. Unlike the other nannies she had met in California (the family had introduced her to two others in the hopes that new friends would ease the adjustment to a new place) the Atassis

continued

did not have a swimming pool or separate nanny bungalow. Now that her daughter had seen what was available she didn't want to settle for anything but the best. And apparently she had made the right decision because the agency had immediately been able to find her a job with exactly the right facilities and in addition, a Porsche to use as her personal car.

The nanny's mother's final words to the Atassis were, "Taking care of your children is the most wonderful experience you can have. Why are you hiring a nanny anyway? Why don't you just raise your children yourself?"

The Atassi family lives in Los Angeles. They have two daughters and are expecting a third child. Eleanor is a real estate agent and her husband, Ethan, is a juvenile probation officer.

ADVERTISING

Time and energy required***
Cost**
Number of applicants you are likely to interview before selecting one: 5–50

Advertising your job in the newspaper is the most cost-effective way to reach a broad spectrum of candidates. For the most part, the people you reach will tend to expect less compensation than those who are registered with agencies and it is possible to find individuals who are every bit as qualified.

So why do some parents cringe at the thought of placing an ad in a newspaper in order to find a caretaker? Three reasons are common:

- They worry that some of the individuals answering the ad will be untrustworthy and have bad motives.
- They are concerned that it will be a lot of work.

• They fear that a current caretaker will see the ad and know she is going to be replaced.

These are all legitimate concerns, but none should disqualify the idea. Advertising is an excellent way to find a Nanny from Heaven. This section will give you pointers on how to do it effectively. But first we will discuss these perceived barriers to advertising.

SAFETY AND SCREENING CONCERNS

Do undesirables answer advertisements? Is it too risky to advertise your child care position to the general public? The answers to these questions are "yes" and "no." There is a chance that the person you hire will turn out to be a Nanny from Hell, no matter what the source you used to find this person.

Testimonials from former employers and others who know the person is the single best guarantee you can have that the person you plan to hire is a decent person. Check references on anyone who answers your ad and you will be just as safe as hiring from any other source.

In my interviews with parents, an equal number of Nannies from Hell came from newspaper ads as from employment agencies and referrals. Yet, the single most successful source of a Nanny from Heaven was advertising. I don't know the exact reason for this, but I suspect that advertising gives one the most applicants to choose from.

TIME REQUIREMENTS

Advertising does take more interviewing time than hiring from an agency, but less time than referrals (see next section). After you place an ad, you will be tied to a phone for a few days answering the ad response. This is the single most annoying aspect to advertising. If you follow my advice on constructing your ad, you can cut down on the number of unqualified individuals who respond to your advertisement, but having many phone conversations will be unavoidable.

You will not, however, have to interview face-to-face more individuals than you would ordinarily through agencies or referrals. As with each of these, the only individuals you will invite into your home will be those you have prescreened and reference checked.

DISCRETION CONCERNING A CURRENT EMPLOYEE

One of the nightmares of every employment manager is that an employee will first find out he or she is losing a job by seeing the job advertised. This is a cruel experience for the individual and a major faux pas on the part of the person placing the ad. I've seen both sides of this. Once, when I was an employment manager, one of my recruiters placed an ad to run in three weeks. The newspaper made a mistake and ran the ad immediately. The person whose job was being advertised saw the ad. It caused a lot of misery for everyone involved.

Fresh in my mind as well is a story told to me by one of the nannies I interviewed. She had worked for a family with seven children for a year. She then saw her job being advertised in a local paper—the tip-off was the mention of seven children. When she confronted them, the family acknowledged having placed the ad, saying they weren't dissatisfied with her performance, they just wanted to test the waters to see if there was anyone better. My subsequent checking with the family verified this story. They lost their nanny before they were ready to do so and her feelings were understandably hurt. It was a lose-lose situation for everyone.

So, what do you do if you want to advertise an opening to replace a current nanny? You invest in a screening device that keeps your identity hidden until you want it revealed.

Screening devices take several forms. At a minimum they involve a different telephone number from your ordinary one. You can "rent" a friend's number, hook a temporary new phone line into your home, hire an answering service, or ask your employer to let you use a business number.

Next, except for the answering service alternative, you will need someone else to answer your phone. The most obvious choice is an answering machine, with someone else's voice on it. Also possible is the use of the telephone company's answering service. For a small monthly fee, you are saved from having to purchase your own answering machine. You simply use the service for as long as you need and then cancel it.

I know of at least two families who hired someone to answer and prescreen their phone calls. In one case it was the daughter of the husband's secretary. The daughter was a recent new mom and looking for a way to make some extra money while at home. The other family used a student from a nearby college. In both cases even though the families paid someone to assist them, the overall cost of hiring someone through an ad was significantly lower than through an agency.

Advertising Guidelines

WHERE TO ADVERTISE

The single most important mistake parents make in advertising child care is in where they place their advertisement. Often, they automatically place ads in the newspapers they themselves read.

The trick is to advertise in the periodicals that nannies read. Nanny agencies regularly advertise in economically distressed areas, areas where people are likely to be looking for work. They also place ads in towns that have community colleges and nanny training schools.

Choose at least one mass circulation newspaper most commonly read in the geographic area from which you wish to recruit. In addition, consider advertising in other sources. Do you live in a city and want someone with small town or rural values? Advertise in an appropriate geographical location. Would a person with a certain religious orientation fit in best with your family's values? Many churches and synagogues have their own newsletters and can be a source of recruitment. Do you want someone who speaks a different language? Try an ethnic newspaper in your own city or advertise abroad. Are you looking for someone with early childhood development training? Advertise in the periodicals put out by local colleges and in journals aimed at teachers. Do you want an au pair? Preschools and grade schools often have their own newsletters and accept advertisements that typically are very inexpensive. Often the au pairs who currently care for children in these schools have friends they can refer to your opening. Are parenting newspapers and magazines distributed free in your area? Nannies as well as parents read these periodicals. And there is a high percentage of professional nannies in this group.

WHAT TO SAY IN THE AD

Every ad needs to impart several pieces of information: highlights of the job, the most salient applicant features, and how you can be reached.

Contact information comes last and need only be an area code and telephone number. Some people also put in their town so that applicants who live too far away to commute easily for a live-out job will be discouraged. Job and applicant requirements require a little more consideration.

Job and Applicant Requirements

Deciding how specific and comprehensive to make your communication about job requirements and applicant profile can be bothersome. Review your written job and applicant descriptions. (Aren't you glad you developed these?) Circle the top few items on each document. This will help you decide what to put in your ad. You need to put enough information so that unqualified individuals will select themselves out and not call you, yet not so many requirements that you screen out a potentially great person who might not have one hundred percent of what you need. One family almost screened out their Nanny from Heaven because they advertised they were seeking a teacher or nurse. Why? Because the previous two au pairs they had hired and loved were respectively a nurse and a teacher (remember umbrella hiring?). Luckily the woman who saw their ad had the confidence to answer it in spite of the fact she had only a high school education. She had worked as an au pair previously and felt qualified. She turned out not only to be a wonderful nanny, but also to stay with the family for many years. The nurse and the teacher had left after their year's commitment in order to resume their previous careers.

You do not, however, want to make an ad so general it attracts hordes of people you really wouldn't consider. Every applicant means at least one phone conversation, which is time consuming. And you will need to tell every unqualified applicant you aren't interested, which isn't exactly the most pleasant task in the world. Therefore, it is smart to include any job requirement that is absolutely necessary for the job.

In one family's case, the need to have transportation to work was high on their list because they lived far away from public transportation. They also needed someone who spoke English well because one of their children had a speech impediment and needed correct modeling. Another family felt that they could only hire someone who had handled multiple children simultaneously. Still another needed someone with strong swimming skills.

Some common nonnegotiable requirements include: availability during specific working hours and days, excellent child care references, experience with children of certain ages, an unblemished driving record, willingness to do tasks other than child care, being a nonsmoker, having his or her own vehicle to use at work. The list can be long so choose only your top six or seven requirements to put in your ad. Save the others to use when you prescreen candidates—a procedure we discuss in the next chapter, "Selecting a Nanny from Heaven."

The United States has very strict laws against employment discrimination. You are not allowed to specify in an ad that you seek candidates of a specific age, nationality, religious orientation, race, or other factors that might discriminate against certain protected groups of people.

These restrictions do not apply in all countries. In fact, almost all nanny ads in England state a preferred age range and most Asian and European ads specify both gender and desired age range.

Job Attractiveness

There are two ways to make your ad stand out so a Nanny from Heaven will call you instead of some other family. The first is to make your ad larger than others. This is expensive.

Just as effective—in fact, I think more so—is to be creative with the content of the ad. *You need to communicate what makes your job an attractive one.*

What is unique about your position? Your family? The setting? You should have at least one adjective in your ad that gives a flavor of what a nanny can expect when she works for you. Here are some examples:

Describing your family:
- Young, hardworking couple seeking warm, caring nanny to . . .
- Parent who travels extensively looking for . . .
- Overworked mother starting new business seeking . . .
- Three adorable children and snugly St. Bernard need fun-loving au pair . . .
- Bright, lovable, but sometimes difficult child needs firm but loving . . .

Describing the setting:[1]
- Family living in high-rise penthouse seeking nanny who likes city living . . .
- Family who lives in horse country seeking . . .
- Empty cottage needs wonderful nanny to live in it while caring for . . .

I learned the value of making an ad unique through a mix-up when running an ad several years ago. The ad was supposed to end with the sentence "Must love children, like animals." The printer left out the comma and the ad read, "Must love children like animals." I got the biggest response I ever got to an ad. The first question many respondents asked was "Are your children *really* like animals?" The newspaper offered to run a corrected ad free the following week, but I didn't need it. I found the person I was seeking, even though I had inadvertently advertised the wrong message.

---

1. British ads describe such wonderful settings! More than once I was tempted by some appealing description. One that caught my eye read, "Live in idyllic country manor during the week and travel with the family to the seaside on the weekends."

A frequent question parents ask when planning to place their first ad is whether to include the salary offered. The answer is yes only if either you have a salary in mind that you don't want to exceed (this salary is then a job requirement) or you are offering a salary higher than that typically paid in the geographical area in which you are recruiting (the salary then becomes part of job attractiveness). Otherwise, don't include the salary or a salary range (everyone who responds will ask for the maximum number).

A word of caution: don't make your ad *too* enticing. You want to attract someone who is interested in filling your needs, not just her own.

REFERRALS

Time and energy required****
Cost*
Number of applicants you are likely to interview before selecting one: 3–10

Word of mouth is how executive recruiters fill most of their jobs. It's a good way to find a nanny. It takes more time and effort than any of the other methods, but it certainly is inexpensive. At the most it will cost you a dinner or a gift for the person who introduced you to your new nanny.

Here's how this technique works. Ask all the nannies you meet and all the families you know who use child care to help you fill your position. You can do this in person or by phone or letter or a combination. The important thing to keep in mind is that it may take two or three months for you to find your person using this method, but the nannies referred tend to be good. Why? Because by and large they have been referred by someone who knows them and people are generally reluctant to refer somebody they have misgivings about.

The section on nanny agencies explained that you could use the same sources the agencies use to find their nannies. The primary source they use is advertising, followed closely by referrals.

Agencies regularly ask the nannies they place if they have any friends who would also like to be nannies. This is the same as you asking your friends to ask their nannies to help you fill your job.

Using referrals is an especially effective way to find an au pair, a subject we discuss later in this chapter. Generally, au pairs from a specific country form social networks with others from their country. Tap into this network by meeting just one and you can have a seemingly endless source of other women from the country in question. Typically, if the person you first approach doesn't know of someone who needs a job offhand, she will know someone else who might. And if no one knows anyone locally, someone is bound to know someone who is still in her country and would love to come to the United States.

I interviewed several families who rely exclusively on referrals. They swear by this approach. It works best if you are well established in a neighborhood and have a lot of contacts. If you have just moved into an area, it may be more difficult. But it just might help you make some new friends. Approach other moms and dads you see at school or the park or at kids' activities and explain your predicament. Ask your children's teachers (preschool teachers and aides often like to moonlight after work and you may be surprised at the referrals you get; the teachers themselves might be interested).

It is also acceptable to approach women you don't know who look like baby-sitters or au pairs and enlist their aid. A word of caution, however. Savvy executive recruiters always make a point of beginning a request for referrals with some statement indicating they are not attempting to recruit the person being approached. For example, if you want to approach a baby-sitter who regularly picks up children at your child's school, make it very clear that you are not asking if she is interested. Explain that you just were wondering if she had any friends or relatives who had child care experience and needed employment. Otherwise you will appear to be trying to steal someone else's employee, an act that will not endear you to that person or help you make friends.

The main advantage of using referrals is that the cost is nominal. Also, anyone you find through this method will probably be well connected with a network of friends. Problems? You may have to make a number of phone calls while you search. And, don't forget, the same network of friends who lead your nanny to you will lead her away to another job if she is at all unhappy.

Although referral by a friend is a great way to find a Nanny from Heaven, it's always possible to get a Nanny from Hell, so don't let down your guard just because someone else says this person is great. Interview thoroughly and check each and every reference.

BULLETIN BOARD NOTICES

Time and energy:**
Cost:*
Number of applicants you are likely to interview before selecting one: 5–10

This method works for me. In fact, it works very well. Unfortunately, I forget to use it sometimes. When my fourth child was born my husband and I decided we needed extra help on the weekends. I advertised in two papers, forgetting I should have tried bulletin board notices first. Admittedly it was a forgivable mistake, but I should have known better. During this time, I also went one whole day without noticing I was wearing two different shoes. It was one of those "best of times; worst of times" periods. At least I didn't lose any of the children or leave the baby on a car seat on the roof of my car.

The person I ended up hiring worked at the preschool that two of our children were attending. At the school entrance was a bulletin board with notices posted from nannies looking for work and families needing nannies. Instead of simply posting a three-by-five-inch card up there on my way to deliver our children to school, I spent money on an ad and time responding to the phone calls it generated. The end result was the same. I just took a more complicated and expensive route.

Signs and notices on bulletin boards can be very effective if they are placed in appropriate locations. Schools, colleges, and religious institutions are all great. You can be creative and place it in a special location not usually used for this purpose, such as a bulletin board in a college dorm, at the college's department of education or in the foreign student lounge. It's probably not wise to plaster a poster looking for child care on a pole on the sidewalk or at a supermarket. One professional nanny I interviewed said, "It makes me so mad when I see posters on walls near a sidewalk asking for child care. Don't these parents know how dangerous this is? I called up one and blasted the parents for doing this. If they cared about their children, they would be more careful."

In every method of recruiting, a parent needs to interview and reference check well, as well as do a trial work day or days. That is the best safeguard. It doesn't matter how a person found out about your opening. What does matter is your thoroughness in establishing the person's reputation. I do agree with the nanny, however, that notices should not be placed on a building on a public street. Be more targeted and selective where you place your notices. And remove them when the position is filled.

If you decide to post your notice on a busy bulletin board, one way to attract attention to it is to have it be an interesting shape. One innovative parent wrote her requirements on a white paper plate. Another attached it to a child's drawing. Many of us temporarily lose our imaginations in the labor and delivery rooms (I found mine in hiding with my memory, which still refuses to come home). If this is true for you, peruse any crowded bulletin board and observe which notices stand out. Copy the ideas. When your children have left home you can then repay society by coming up with an original idea for a bulletin board notice and tacking it up for a tired parent with young children to copy.

RECRUITING ABROAD

The time and energy required, the cost, and the number of applicants you are likely to interview before selecting one are all dependent on whether you use advertising, agencies, or referrals to find your person.

Au pairs (pronounced "ow pears") is French for "on par," meaning even exchange. Merriam Webster's Collegiate Dictionary defines au pair as "usually a young foreign person who does domestic work for a family in exchange for room, board, and the opportunity to learn the family's language." I define most of them as Nannies from Heaven.

Au pairs come in two flavors: legal and illegal. The illegal ones are the source of most of the Nannies from Heaven. If you are an IRS or Immigration agent, please read only the first part of this chapter, the one that discusses legal au pairs. This advice is also for anyone who intends to get a presidential appointment. All others read both sections and make your own decisions about what to do about this volatile issue.

Legal Au Pairs

The U.S. government runs an au pair service that supplies full time, tax-exempt baby-sitters to families who request them. The U.S. Information Agency (USIA) runs this program. There are some restrictions: the au pairs must be between the ages of eighteen and twenty-five and can only stay for twelve months. She or he can work up to forty-five hours per week and is paid $100 a week plus room and board. In addition the family must allow the au pair to attend educational classes and cultural events at least two evenings a week and promise to treat the au pair as a household member and not as a servant.

The USIA processes almost three thousand au pairs each year under this program. Eight "sponsor" organizations, certified by the USIA, have affiliate offices throughout Europe, the only place the program exists. They screen au pair candidates overseas and the U.S. sponsor tries to match them with the right family. The process takes approximately three months, and employing the au pair costs about $8,000 a year (including an up-front fee for using the program plus the $100 weekly stipend and some reimbursement for educational classes), plus round-trip airfare.

Au pairs in this program enter with J-visas. These were established in the Mutual Educational and Cultural Exchange Act of

1961 to enable nonimmigrant "bona fide students to study and in-crease mutual understanding between countries." An immigrant does not require certification from the Department of Labor to work under a J-visa, nor do employers need to pay Social Security taxes or fill out IRS W-2 forms.

So what's the catch? Sounds like a pretty great set-up. You get a full-time child care provider at a sale price, you don't pay taxes on this person . . . and the government gives you its blessing.

The problem with this whole program is the choice of child care provider, or rather the lack of choice. Families submit applica-tions that detail their interests, activities, number of children, and so on and the agency matches them with an au pair. The family must take the person referred. If they don't like the individual, they have little recourse. A replacement can be found but it takes at least three months and once again the family must accept the match.

Some families luck out and are happy with the au pair selected for them. Others aren't. Either way, they are commited for a year. As one parent who used this program told us, "My au pair is okay; she's just not excellent. I found out I was pregnant with triplets the month she arrived. I already had two toddlers. Needless to say, the extra three children were not in the original bargain when we hired her, but once they came she was definitely the wrong person for us. Five o'clock would come, her normal quitting time, and she would walk out the door, even if I had five hungry kids to handle at once. I wanted to change her hours or to pay her more for extra hours but she was inflexible. I hired extra help of course when the triplets were born, but it all had to be live-out since our au pair was living in our only extra bedroom. The program gave me less flexi-bility than I needed at the time."

I strongly advocate insisting upon quality child care no matter how difficult it may be to find, so I don't feel comfortable recom-mending this program as a good way to find a Nanny from Heaven. It just doesn't give parents enough control in hiring or flexibility after the person starts work. If you'd like to try it anyway, you can find the names of some of the sponsors advertised in any parenting magazines.

By the time this book goes to print, this program may be canceled. At the time of this writing, the Justice Department is investigating the possibility.

Illegal Au Pairs

I would never admit in writing to hiring an illegal au pair. My attorney also asked me to include a disclaimer telling you I do not advise you to hire one either. So for the record, let me say I do not advise you to hire an illegal au pair either.

Not surprisingly, it is estimated that at least 200,000 households employ illegal immigrants or au pairs as child care workers. Although the Immigration and Naturalization Service (INS) does not distinguish between au pairs and all other illegal immigrants, I believe that a distinction should be made. Illegal immigrants are individuals who intend to stay and work in the United States even though they do not have a visa that allows them to do so legally. They come from a variety of backgrounds and have diverse skills. You should know that many seek work as child care providers because it is a field usually open to them, not necessarily because they love children or have special training. This is not to say they aren't good. Many are very good.

Au pairs are usually young women and (a few) men who come to this country to experience the culture during a "working" holiday and then return to their own countries after one year. They come with the intention of working with children and you can prescreen them for experience, skill, and aptitude for this kind of work. Some are college students, others have already completed degrees and want to travel before settling down to a career. Others are professionals who want a change. Most come with the idea of only being here one year, although it's not uncommon for some to fall in love with the United States and stay on for several years. All enter the country with a visitor's visa, which typically is good for three months to a year, depending on what INS grants them when they enter.

Au pairs become illegal as soon as they start to work and earn an income. It is highly unlikely that an immigration official would find out that a person who entered on a tourist visa is now earning an income in the United States, as long as the person is paid in cash and the earnings are not reported. So for all practical intent, once a person clears Immigration, she is in the country, free and clear of government intervention.

A complication arises when a person's visa expires, which almost always occurs before the employment period is over. She has two options: to attempt to renew the visa or to ignore the problem. If the au pair attempts to renew her visa, she runs the risk of having this request denied. Furthermore, the Immigration Service now knows where to contact her. So, many au pairs simply allow their visitor's visas to expire. At the time of this writing, the Immigration Service is not in the habit of reviewing visas as visitors exit the country, so an expired visa does not at present pose a problem. But this could change. Some au pairs do elect to go to the Immigration Service or apply by mail to get their visas renewed. They make no mention of employment, stating instead a desire to see other parts of the United States. We have heard of several who have had their renewals granted.

According to my interviews, most families who employ au pairs or other illegal immigrants hate breaking the law. So why do it? Because securing high-quality child care is more important than playing by the rules. And au pairs and illegal immigrants, if carefully chosen, can be wonderful child care providers.

Why do people hire au pairs? My husband and I disagree on this. He feels that families hire au pairs mainly for financial reasons. Most au pairs expect to be paid much less than domestic child care workers. My feeling is that families use au pairs because they cannot find domestic workers who are as good. The truth is probably a mixture of both. And lest I overstate how wonderful au pairs can be, it is only fair to report that several families I spoke to had had Nanny from Hell experiences with au pairs. The au pairs had been party girls, a few had crashed cars, and more than a few had left large phone bills when they left. By and large though, the Nanny from Heaven stories prevailed.

Without even asking, most of the families who employ au pairs discussed the legalities of it with me. The parents told me time and again that if they could find a great nanny at a salary they could afford who was legal, they would jump at the chance to hire her. As one mother said, "I hate breaking the law. But I tried several American baby-sitters and no one was willing to treat my job seriously. What became most important to me, more important than the legalities, was finding someone who would be there every day at 6:30 or 7:00 A.M. so I could go to work—and someone who isn't sick all the time so I don't have to call in sick."

A father who is an executive said, "We make good salaries, and would rather pay taxes and do the whole thing legally. It is nerve-wracking to annually coach our new au pair how to slip past Immigration on a tourist visa. But the au pairs we have had are terrific, head and shoulders better than the nannies we've been able to find locally. We've had to choose between the welfare of our children and the relatively low risk of being caught. What would you do in our place?"

The best way to begin your search for an au pair is to try tapping into an au pair network. Meet just one Swedish au pair at the park and you are likely to be introduced to a Volvo station wagon full of them if you request it. Tell just one nanny from Fiji that you have a job opening and ask if she has friends available to fill it and you may find her volunteering to put up a notice at the church she attends. Chances are that if you rely on referrals to find an au pair you may be able to find one who is already in this country. That is a large emotional savings, since you'll skip the hassle of getting someone into the country.

Some families I interviewed use nanny agencies as a source of personnel. England, Ireland, South Africa, Australia, and Germany all have nanny agencies; other countries probably do as well. Write to the country's Department of Commerce or Tourist Bureau or go to an international newspaper stand and buy a newspaper from the country of your choice. Many international newspapers carry ads from nanny placement services, typically on the weekends.

If you can't tap into an au pair network and don't want to pay an agency fee, then the best way to find an au pair is to advertise in the country you have selected. Find out the name of a major newspaper in the city of your choice. There are a number of ways to do this. Libraries can be helpful; you can call the country's embassy or you can even call the country's telephone directory assistance and ask an operator. Next, contact the newspaper in writing (which works best if you are recruiting in a non-English-speaking country) or by phone or both. Ask to run an ad on the days most likely to generate results and ask the newspapers to place the ad in the appropriate section. Many newspapers will accept credit card charges for payment. The following is a sample letter sent to place an ad abroad.

Sample Au Pair Advertising Correspondence

July 2, 1996

To whom it may concern:

Please place the following advertisement in your paper for two consecutive Saturdays following receipt of this letter. Please charge it to my American Express #_____, expiration date _____. The name on my card is _____ .

Please send a copy of the bill as well as the advertisement that ran in the paper to: *[your address]*

_____

_____

AU PAIR needed for warm Chicago family with 3 boys. Female, non-smoker, minimum age 20, driver's license, with child care experience. US$100 per week. Write about qualifications to [your address], *include picture and phone number.*

As part of any ad placed abroad, be sure to include "U.S.A." as part of your address. It is legal in most countries, except the United States, to specify desired sex and age range and to request photos of applicants. As long as you bear in mind that it can be expensive to return these (courtesy dictates you do so), having a picture of the applicant is helpful. One parent explained, "I couldn't decide between two applicants; they both seemed great. I showed the photos to my kids and they overwhelming chose one of the girls. I looked at the picture and realized why. She was wearing Mickey

Mouse pants in the photo. Sure enough, she's turned out to be a playful and fun-loving nanny, something that was important to us."

Responses from an ad abroad can take anywhere from three to six weeks to reach you. Be prepared for an onslaught. And also be prepared for pretty amazing people to reply. Some may be unexpected: whole families, retired individuals, artists, secretaries, athletes, single men. Others will be intriguing: cordon bleu chefs, midwives, preschool teachers, nurses, professional nannies.

Rules about interviewing, selecting, and reference checking, covered in chapter 4, apply doubly to au pairs. It may be harder to do all of this long distance, but don't skip any of the steps—with the exception, of course, of having the person do a trial work day. The decision of which au pair to hire is an important one for both the applicant and your family. Have many conversations over the phone getting to know one another. Send a detailed description of the job, your area, your family. (However, caution her not to bring this written information with her on the airplane. If it is uncovered during an Immigration search it is sufficient evidence she is planning to work and reason for immediate deportation.)

Once you have selected your au pair it is better to have her make plane reservations in her own country. If she is under the age of twenty-five or a student, she will probably be able to get a student fare, which is cheaper than you can arrange for her here. It also will be cheaper for her to get health insurance through her parents, her college if she is a student, or special traveler's insurance through her travel agency. It is prudent for you to require that she furnish you with written proof of this, along with a copy of her driver's license, if her duties will include driving. Ask her to get a TB test and send you the results.

Who pays for your au pair's airline ticket is a matter of negotiation. Some families only hire individuals who pay their own way. Some lend the money. Still others are willing to pay the whole thing. Considering typical au pair compensation—$100 to $150 a week—even the payment of the person's airfare is a bargain if she turns out to be good and to stay the typical commitment period of one year.

Counsel your au pair to buy a book on U.S. youth hostels and other U.S. travel books so she can have a set travel plan in mind if questioned by Immigration. Some families say they tell their au pairs to dress like students on vacation, to wear jeans and carry backpacks. Others say it is better to look well dressed. In either case she should have enough cash with her to make plausible her story that she intends to travel for several months in our country. She should also have a return ticket (which can later be turned in for cash or extended). It is helpful if she has some evidence of a need to return to her own country in a short period of time, such as a letter from a school or an employment letter stating a return date. *The Au Pair and Nanny Guide to Working Abroad*[2] states that some au pairs go so far as to bring wrapped wedding gifts to corroborate the story they are coming to attend a relative's wedding. Under no circumstances is the au pair to mention anything about working or even visiting a family with children.

Once your au pair is in the United States do not let her leave the country until she is prepared to return home. If she even crosses the border to Mexico or Canada, she is subject to scrutiny when she attempts to reenter. We know of at least one case where a young woman was denied reentry after spending a holiday visiting relatives in Europe even though her visa was current. She did not have her story down pat as to why she wished to return to the United States after having spent nine months there. She also was not carrying much money. An Immigration official questioned her aggressively about her specific travel plans and after about twenty minutes, the young woman admitted to living with a family. Before long she was cornered into admitting she helped with the kids and got paid for this. She was denied entry and deported. Her clothes, belongings, and a family who loved and needed her were left behind without notice. She was left with no job.

Considering the pitfalls of hiring abroad—the difficulty in hiring long distance, the tension while waiting for your au pair to be

2. Susan Griffith and Sharon Legg, *The Au Pair and Nanny Guide to Working Abroad.* 9 Park St., Oxford: Vacation Work, 1993. The authors also caution potential au pairs that American children tend to be "noisy and rambunctious with a proclivity to interrupt adult conversation more often than would be tolerated in Europe. They are energetic, self-confident and fearless. Their wishes tend to be indulged to an excessive degree which makes the task of imposing a workable routine difficult in some cases."

allowed to enter the country, and the reluctance most of us have to participate in breaking the law—why hire an au pair at all? Because some can be so wonderful. Many come because they are adventurous young women who love children. They don't view child care work as a long-term career—to my mind this is the major drawback—but they do give their all to doing a great job caring for your kids. The fact that you have to arrange for this quality care annually is balanced by the fact that you will pay much, much less in salary than if you hire someone locally.

Abuses of the au pairing arrangement may arise from both ends. Some families treat au pairs unfairly by asking them to work too many hours for too little money. Some au pairs forget the "working" portion of the "working vacation" concept. But by and large these are the exceptions, and normally it is a win-win situation for all involved. The au pair gets a chance to see and experience a new country and the family gets affordable, quality child care.

What happens if your au pair is a Nanny from Heaven and you both want her to stay in the United States? Is there a way to do this? The many hours I have spent on the phone with the INS (mostly on hold) and conversations with two immigration attorneys have convinced me this is nearly impossible. The following story illustrates this sad truth.

Can I Adopt Her?

THE CAROLS' STORY

The Carols had a run of awful baby-sitter luck. One sitter crashed the car. Another got pregnant. Another was the niece of a friend and she refused to follow directions. It was a nightmare.

Every time Ann Carol had another bad experience, her manicurist, a Filipino woman, would say to her, "Let me find someone from my country." But the Carols were very conservative and cautious. They didn't cheat on their taxes. Nick Carol worked for a bank. They went to church. They kept to

continued

the speed limit. They themselves admit that they were really square. They had always paid the taxes and filed the necessary paperwork for employing a nanny and knew they wouldn't be able to do this if they hired someone who wasn't a citizen or didn't have a green card.

On the other hand, they simply couldn't stand to go through any more of the hell they were experiencing with child care. They had gone to an out-of-state nanny school and interviewed young women for a week but that hadn't worked. They had networked, advertised, and used an agency; they simply couldn't find someone who was warm, dependable, mature, affordable, and trustworthy. So they finally gave in. Ann Carol asked her manicurist, "Do you know of anyone I can hire?", knowing full well that the person she would recommend would not have working papers.

The manicurist suggested her sister-in-law, a middle-aged woman who had raised her own children in the Philippines and had now come to the United States. She had entered on a visitor's visa, which had expired. Ann agreed to meet the sister-in-law.

The sister-in-law and her whole family came to check out the Carols. The couple had the feeling that they were making sure this was not some white slavery arrangement.

Apparently, the Carols passed the test. The woman, Cecilia, came to work for them and she was terrific. She was kind, gentle, yet maintained discipline. She loved the kids and they loved her back. And what a hard worker! She would take breakfast orders the night before and then get up at 6:00 A.M. to have everything ready when the kids got up. The Carols told her she didn't have to do this, and that her day started at 7:00 A.M., but she continued to do it anyway. It was her pleasure, she said.

At first, Ann paid her half what she had paid her previous nanny. Cecilia thought this was terrific because it was much more than she would have earned back in her country. When the family saw how good she was, they raised her salary every

continued

couple of months so it wasn't long before they were paying her the same amount they usually paid. "Boy, was she worth it!" Ann exclaimed. "She did all the housework, laundry . . . The house ran like a charm. She had a good sense of what it takes to raise children. We were all happy."

Except about breaking the law. Even though the Carols knew they would probably never be found out, they were bothered by the illegality of the arrangement.

They talked to Cecilia's brother and asked him to sponsor Cecilia for permanent residency. They said they would pay lawyer's costs, and promise to guarantee her salary for two years. But when they checked into it, they found it would take between fourteen and seventeen years for Cecilia to get to the head of the line. And in the meantime, she couldn't work.

Mrs. Carol called the Immigration Service. She spent one whole day getting lost in the voice mail system. She just couldn't reach a real, live person. She would give up for a while and go have a meal or go to the bathroom, and then would have to start all over again, just trying to get the phone answered.

Finally, she got through to an immigration officer. She explained the predicament and then listened to him tell her about an alphabet soup of visas that would enable Cecilia to legally stay and work in the United States, none of which she was eligible for because she would be working in the home. He said that a first step would be to certify that no one in the United States could fill the job. The Carols would have to prove this by advertising in the paper and having the responses go to the Unemployment Department. But they probably wouldn't even be able to get this far. As soon as they filed for a working visa, notice would be sent to the Immigration Department and Cecilia would be deported. It was a real catch-22. If you file to be legal, chances are the person will be deported. In desperation, Mrs. Carol finally cried out, "Can I adopt her? Why don't I adopt her?" The officer laughed, but

continued

she was serious. When he realized she wasn't just joking, he told her there was a legal cutoff age for adoption.

They gave up. Cecilia stayed with them for four years. Then she met a really nice man at a Christmas party. Unfortunately he lived in another state. They dated long distance for a few months and then got married and she moved away.

Ann Carol concluded by saying, "You try to find someone with a good work ethic who will do a good job. If this person turns out to be someone foreign who doesn't have a lobby group in Congress and isn't a person protected by the current immigration rules, then you have to make a choice. It was a painful choice for us, but we would make the same one again."

The Carols have twin daughters and a son. They live in the Midwest. Mrs. Carol is a home economics teacher.

SUMMARY

1. Which recruiting source you decide to use depends on how much time, energy, and money you can spend on the process.
2. There is no "best" source of Nannies from Heaven.
3. Employment agencies are the most expensive method, both because of their fees and because their referrals tend to expect higher salaries. However, employment agencies can be the fastest and easiest route to finding a nanny.
4. Advertising, done properly, is an excellent source of Nannies from Heaven. The best way to advertise effectively is to communicate what makes your job attractive.
5. Using referrals is the most cost-effective, but time-consuming, of the recruitment methods. It is the best way to find an au pair.
6. Bulletin board notices can be effective if they are posted in appropriate places.
7. Au pairs often are wonderful nannies.

CHAPTER 4

Selecting a Nanny from Heaven

MYTH
Competent parents hire competent child care.

TRUTH
*Finding great child care is almost always a function of luck—
and the harder you work at it, the luckier you will get.*

I have had three experiences I wish never to repeat: I rode the Cyclone roller coaster at Coney Island, my car engine caught fire miles from a repair station, and I've had to interview and select a nanny. These situations all cause the same reaction in me. My heart races, my mind slows down, and all thoughts are drowned out by a persistent one screaming, "Let this please end!"

Needless to say, my wish to be spared nanny selection has already been denied by the Great Wish Fulfiller in the Sky. I've gotten the signal, loud and clear, this is one task I can't avoid.

The ironic twist to this nightmare is that if anyone should be adept at hiring personnel, it should be me. I was a professional in the field. Starting as a recruiter, I hired salesmen, assembly workers, engineers, administrators, just about every imaginable employee. I was so good at it I became an employment manager, overseeing a department that often hired more than a thousand people annually. In this job, I trained other people to recruit and hire. I ultimately became a vice president of human resources, charged with hiring the most senior personnel in the company. I hired presidents, vice presidents, and senior managers. All because I was an ace at finding, interviewing, selecting, and attracting the best people.

Then I had children. I expected everything about mothering would be new and difficult. Except, of course, finding quality child care. Because of my business experience I was confident that would be a snap. Ha!

It wasn't easy to hire as many Nannies from Hell as I did in the beginning. It required a real bang-up job at getting the basics wrong in all areas, not the least of which was selection. So, I submit the following hiring guidelines to you with a heavy dose of humility. They come not from professional knowledge, but from my experience as a mother, and from the advice of other parents who have learned by making mistakes.

It is very hard to hire someone to replace you, Mom or Dad, even if it is only for part of each day. You are selecting someone with whom to share your home and your children (but hopefully, not your spouse). This is no small task.

THE HIRING PROCESS

The process of hiring a home child care provider is different from hiring personnel in a business setting. The procedure itself should be professional, and it is important to use business documents such as an application form, written job and applicant descriptions, and an employment agreement.[1] But selecting someone to work in your home with your children requires that you observe the person's skills and not rely solely on the information you gather through interviews and resumes, as often occurs in business. You have certain safety considerations in bringing a person into your home that one does not have in a business setting. So, the hiring steps I suggest you follow in your home occur in a different order than people typically follow in business.

---

1. See Appendix B for a worksheet and sample work agreement.

Consider this scenario: You have run a newspaper ad and now need to talk to the respondents. They have left phone messages on your telephone answering machine. As part of your answering machine message, you may have left instructions such as, "Please tell me briefly about your child care experience" or "Leave your telephone number with area code twice." Whether or not a person has followed the instructions is a first clue to whether she is the person for you. Call back those individuals who sound the most promising first.

STEP 1: PRESCREENING

Arrange to have your children in another room. (Actually, in our house that means they will be at the door knocking, crying, or yelling something tantalizing like, "Mom, the baby has swallowed something and looks funny.")

On second thought, arrange to have your children at the park, asleep, or in another country. Then start calling prospective nannies and, after you identify yourself, ask some preliminary questions. I usually start with maintenance-type questions, those that are straightforward and can be answered with a yes or no. Some maintenance questions might be "The hours I need someone are between twelve and seven. Is this all right with you?" "Are you able to commit to working for at least one year?" "We collect poisonous reptiles; are animals a problem?"

Next, you should ask the person to tell you about her previous experience. Sample prescreening questions and a form to fill out for each person you talk to are provided on the following page. The more information you can get over the phone, the more time you will save yourself later on by not scheduling home interviews with anyone who is unsuitable.

Be sure to ask for a mailing address and for all previous job references. Ask permission to check the references. If the answers to your questions are satisfactory, go to step 2. If not, tell the person then and there that you have other individuals who are more qualified for the job. Thank her for her time, but be clear you have no interest.

Prescreening Hints

- Cut off the conversation as soon as possible if you find out something about the person that makes her unsuitable. Don't be rude, but you don't need to waste your time with someone who is clearly not a candidate.
- Don't give out salary information (you want to keep this data secret now for later negotiation purposes) or your address (for security reasons) until you have checked references.
- It is better to spend an extra ten minutes on the phone finding out essential information than to conduct an on-site interview, which will take at least forty-five minutes, and find out then the person is unsuitable.
- Do tell a person right away that you are not interested. It's not kind to leave a person with false hopes, even if it seems easier to do so at the moment. I try not to tell the candidate she isn't good. Rather I say something to the effect that I've already found someone who is closer to our perfect profile. I often say, "I'm afraid I've already gotten a response from someone who is more qualified for our job. Good luck in your job search and thank you for calling."
- If you are an especially organized individual, you may want to use a worksheet to record the results of your telephone interviews.

Sample Prescreening Questions

Hi. You responded to my ad in the _____ newspaper. I'd like to ask you some preliminary questions. Is this all right?

We need someone to work _____ days during the hours of _____ to _____. This is a _____ (live in or live out) and requires that you have your own transportation. How does this sound?

continued

Now, why don't you tell me a little about your child care experience, starting with your first job? I'd like to know the ages of the children and the extent of your responsibilities.

Why did you leave these jobs?

What salary are you looking for?

(Providing you like the answers so far:)
You sound as though you might be someone who matches our needs. Can you give me the names and telephone numbers of your previous employers? I'd like to call them before we set up an interview. *Is this O.K.?* Also, why don't you give me your address so I can send you an application form to fill out.

(If you don't like the answers or are undecided:)
Thank you very much for the information you've given me. I am just doing some preliminary screening now. If I am interested in talking to you further, I will call you back again. If you don't hear from me by _____, you can assume we've hired someone else.

Telephone Prescreening Interview Worksheet

Applicant name_____ Date _____Tel#_____
Current location _____Live in? _____
Live out? _____ Own trans.? _____
Hours avail._____
Salary requirements? _____ Has own children? Ages? _____
Can travel with family? _____ Baby-sit one or two
evenings a week? _____
Available? _____ Swim? _____ Restrictions? _____

continued

Previous Experience

Dates   Family name   # & ages of child   Responsibilities.
Reason Left?   Salary?

1._____

_____

2._____

_____

3._____

_____

4._____

_____

References: Name   Telephone number   Relationship

1._____
2._____
3._____

Personality?

Comments?

STEP 2: REFERENCE CHECKING

Check the references you've gotten from your preliminary phone conversation. Call *all* references and ask detailed questions. You should not invite anyone to your home before you have checked at least one and preferably more references, for both practical and safety reasons. I will not hire a person, no matter how presentable she looks and sounds, without information from people who have employed her in the past. So why waste the time to interview anyone without sterling references? It also helps to know areas of strengths and weaknesses before a formal interview; it lets you know what areas to probe in depth.

Because reference checking is so important, the next section discusses it in more detail. For now we will continue running through the hiring process steps.

STEP 3: THE APPLICATION FORM

Call the candidate back and schedule a preliminary interview. Tell her you will mail her an application form and ask her to fill it out and mail it back to you or bring it to an interview. We cover this form in detail later in the chapter.

STEP 4: THE ON-SITE INTERVIEW

Invite the person to your home during the busiest, most chaotic time. Although your candidate probably thinks the purpose of the visit is to answer more questions, it isn't really. The real purpose of the first on-site visit is to observe the candidate's attitude and behavior toward your children. You want to see if she or he is the kind of person who will pitch in if the baby's diaper smells like something died in it or your toddler starts to throw his teenage brother's rock collection. Does she smile sweetly and continue to focus on you (a good sign during an interview in a normal workplace; not optimal behavior in a home while one child is trying to strangle another much smaller one who is grasping rocks in each hand)? If the dog jumps on her lap as she is describing her views on early childhood education, does she absentmindedly stroke him, or does she yell "Yuck, get off of me!"?

The second reason to schedule the interview at a terrible time is to show the candidate a real glimpse of the job. It never has discouraged anyone I've hired, but it does give you the chance to say after she's moved in and the dog vomits in her favorite shoes, "Well, I did let you see . . ."

Before the applicant leaves, ask her to provide proof of driver's license (if needed for the job or for a background check), and tell her you will need proof of a negative TB test (some families also require proof of a negative AIDS test) to be supplied during step 5.

STEP 5: TRIAL PERIODS

Schedule a second interview and conduct it at a time when you both can sit down and calmly discuss such issues as discipline and routines. It is amazing how different some individuals look during a second visit and how your opinion might change after discussion of nitty-gritty subjects such as the best way to encourage children to share toys.

The second meeting is a good time to ask your potential nanny questions that for a job in a normal work setting might be considered overly personal, but is relevant for a child care job in the home. Some of the delicate questions parents (and the more thorough nanny placement agencies) ask are:

1. Have you or anyone in your family had a problem with alcohol or drug abuse? Emotional illness? Eating disorders? If yes, who? How was this resolved? How did this affect you?
2. Have any of your friends or family been convicted of a crime?
3. As a child, did you ever suffer abuse, either physically or emotionally? How was this resolved?

You need not disqualify a candidate if she answers "Yes" to any of the questions. What you will need to do is probe further and gain an understanding of whether or not the experience will have an impact on her ability to perform her job. Does she have an emotionally mature attitude about what has happened in her past or does it cripple her? Do you feel comfortable with the way in which the problem was resolved? People often don't have control over what is done to them, but they do on how they handle the situation. If she or someone else in her family was a substance abuser, has she resolved this? Sometimes victims of abuse repeat the pattern. Is there potential for this happening? If a friend or relative has a criminal record, this is a good time to find it out. How close is she to this person? Does she anticipate this person visiting? Many of the families I interviewed whose nannies had stolen from them felt the nannies had been influenced by unsavory personal associations.

Questions like the ones above are difficult to ask and for many people difficult to answer. Keep any information you acquire strictly confidential.

If you still like the candidate after this second meeting, invite her to work for you for one or two days. Pay her for this time worked. Go in and out during the day, being available to observe how things go, but also leave the children alone with her. Later you can ask them for input as to whether or not they liked her. Even very young children can give feedback by their behavior if they are still preverbal.

I used to think it was unfair to judge a person the first day on the job, which is what you will be doing if you make a decision based on the applicant's performance during this trial. After all, the children don't know her, she doesn't know the routines . . . Too bad! Wonderful child care givers show their stuff immediately in the way they talk to the children, hold the baby, and assure your teenager she doesn't need to change clothes a sixth time. She may not demonstrate the same level of directness she might later on, or get the same level of cooperation from the children that she would if they knew her better, but you can certainly glean glimpses of the real person from the way she handles the first day on the job.

If you hire the individual, be sure to say the first month is a trial period. If at all possible, train your new nanny yourself. It will give you the opportunity to get to know her better, to see if you and she really agree on child-rearing philosophy. Also you will avoid the temptation for the leaving nanny to pass along her own perceptions of you and your family and prejudice your new nanny. Even if your parting with the old nanny was friendly, it is better to start fresh with your new nanny and let her form her own opinions of you.

Use the first trial month wisely. After you have finished training your nanny and gone back to your own job or schedule, drop in unannounced as often as you can. I have no personal experience with leaving tape recorders or video cameras on to observe what really goes on, however a few parents admitted to doing this. At the same time, I understood why a mother secretly followed her new baby-sitter to the park in another car in order to observe her driving ability and to see how she treated the children. However, if I did it, I'm sure one of the kids would see me and yell, "Hi, Mom! What are you doing in the bushes?" Perhaps you can handle the surveillance with more finesse.

REFERENCE CHECKING

References are the single most valuable part of the interview process. Require that every applicant give you the names and telephone numbers of all previous employers. Check *every* reference! To illustrate how vital reference checking is, I will share a story. I tell it with personal embarrassment, because in it I did a poor job.

Several years ago, when we just had one child, we considered hiring a young woman from another country whom I'll call Sandra. We exchanged letters. She seemed extremely nice, but was only nineteen. At the point where we had to decide whether or not to extend an offer, my husband and I got cold feet. We decided it was too risky to hire a teenager, sight unseen, from abroad. So we declined. But we did invite her to visit us when she arrived in the United States, which she did.

Sandra was lovely. We realized we should have hired her. However, it was not a total loss. She expressed interest in doing occasional baby-sitting in the evenings. We agreed and arranged a few baby-sitting dates.

When Sandra showed up to baby-sit for us she brought along a friend, Jean, a thirty-two-year-old woman from the same country. Every subsequent time Sandra baby-sat for us, Jean accompanied her. It turned out that Jean had been a teacher before she came to the United States and Sandra had been one of her students. Over the course of almost a year, we watched the two women care for our son on several occasions. We didn't actually spend a lot of time with the women because we would normally leave ten minutes after they arrived, but because it was over an extended period of time, we felt we "knew" them.

When it came time for Sandra to return to her country, both women came over to say good-bye. Jean mentioned that her nanny job was coming to an end and did we know of any other position? I was due to have another baby and needed full-time help. She might well have asked a shark if he wanted a snack. What timing! What luck! What a jerk I was!

The list of questions I should have, but didn't, ask is longer than I care to admit. I didn't ask her why she had accompanied a woman thirteen years her junior every time the younger woman sat for us. I didn't ask to speak to her present employer. I didn't try to contact previous employers. I told myself it was too difficult to reference check someone who had worked abroad. Besides, this woman was a teacher, she had already baby-sat my child . . . she was a known entity. Why bother reference checking? What could I learn?

The only question I asked was when she could start. *Big* mistake!

It turned out that Jean had spent time in a mental institution just before coming to the United States. After she worked for us for a few days, we knew something was wrong. For one thing, she couldn't bear to be alone. Ever. Day or night. Which is one of the reasons she had tagged along on Sandra's baby-sitting jobs. She especially couldn't bear to sleep alone. During the thankfully short time she was with us, the bed in her room got a lot of exercise and we were repeatedly awakened before dawn by our dog barking at the men (who were not supposed to be there and whose existences were vehemently denied) leaving the house before dawn. On the bright side, she did supply more than her fair share of material for this book. But given the choice, I would have preferred to have done a better job of selection and been spared the wisdom. Had I checked references I might not have found out about her mental health problems directly, but at a minimum I would have known that there was a gap in her employment history requiring explanation.

Thank heavens she wasn't an ax murderer. ("Oh good. I've found another family who doesn't reference check. Where do they keep their chopping block?")

Lest my message so far is too subtle, let me reiterate: Do reference checks on *anybody* you consider hiring. Friend of the family, recommendation of your best buddy, distant relative? Reference check. Following are some tips and sample questions that will give you an idea of how to make the call.

Reference Checking Hints

- Start off with factual and easy-to-answer questions such as confirmation of working dates. Save the judgmental questions for when you have already established a rapport with the other person.

continued

- If a person seems hesitant to give you any negative information but you sense there is some, give some encouragement such as, "Every one has weaknesses. By telling me some of _____ (applicant's name) you will help me create an environment to help her succeed in spite of these."
- Appeal to the person's sense of identification with you as a parent. Say, "I'm a mom and I need to be really careful about whom I bring into my household. I'm sure you as a mom (or dad) can understand this. It really is important that we hire someone who fits in well with my family. Please tell me what weaknesses I need to be aware of with _____(applicant's name)."
- Listen to the person's tone of voice and whether he or she hesitates before answering a question. The manner in which a person tells you something reveals a lot.
- _The most important question you must ask is "Would you rehire this person?"_ Once again, listen not only to the answer, but to the tone of voice and how quickly the person responds. You are looking for an immediate, enthusiastic "Yes!" Anything less than this means you need to ask some more probing questions.

Reference Check Dialog and Questions

Hi. My name is _____ (your name). I'm considering hiring _____ (applicant's name) for a nanny position to take care of my children ages ____ and _____. Is this a convenient time for you to talk? Everything you tell me will be kept confidential.

_____ (applicant's name) said she worked for you from _____ to _____ (dates). Is this correct?

Can you describe her job responsibilities?

How many children did she watch? What were their ages? Did they like her?

continued

How would you describe her personality? Up? Moody? Other?

Is she a take-charge type of person or does she need a lot of direction? Were you at home supervising or did she work independently?

Does she use good judgment? Is she safety conscious? Can she handle an emergency?

Was she reliable? Was she sick a lot? Was she timely?

Does she have any annoying habits?

Did her outside social life interfere with her job?

Is she a good communicator with adults? How did she resolve problems when they occurred? Did she discuss them with you or keep them bottled up?

What motivates her?

Why did she leave?

Would you rehire her?

Is there anything you can tell me about potential problems? Is she emotionally and mentally stable? Any drug, alcohol, or driving problems? Any eating disorders?

Additional comments?

Okay. Now that I've repeated it (reference check) and said it loudly *(reference check!)*, let's talk about who you should call for references.

The best strategy in reference checking is to contact everyone who can give you information on the person. Start with all former employers. Leave friends, relatives, teachers, clergymen, and neighbors for last ("She lived next door to me and always smiled when I walked by with my children; she is such a nice girl, I'm sure she would do a great job caring for your triplets.").

You are told that all former bosses have mysteriously died, moved or gotten unlisted numbers? Hmmm. This is called the "Everyone I have worked for has vanished" syndrome. No matter how good this person may appear on the surface, do not hire her. Nannies from Hell frequently suffer this illness; don't take a chance.

What do you do about the person who looks like a reasonable candidate but who leaves out some information in her past? For example, there may be an unexplained gap in employment, or she may tell you how to contact some former bosses, but not all. This is not a clear-cut case. I have to admit that when I sense information is missing from a person's past, especially something as important as a previous job, this taps something primeval and suspicious in me. This sounds farfetched, but I suspect one of my ancestors was part bloodhound and part fox.

Ridiculous, I can hear you saying. That would be impossible. Everyone knows that bloodhounds and foxes are mortal enemies; they would never interbreed. I realize it is a little hard to believe, but at the first whiff of something hidden, the bloodhound in me sniffs the air and becomes very, very attentive. Meanwhile, my fox ancestor's voice whispers, "Appear casual. Don't show you're interested." With these two battling for position, I go into sleuth mode and try to coax out the hidden information.

First the fox, with bland face and nonchalant voice, says something like this: "I am very reluctant to hire anyone without talking to *all* former employers. This really is too bad because up until now I really liked what I was hearing from you. I don't care if one or two references are negative (right!) because I realize sometimes things go wrong in a job situation and it is the employer's, not the employee's fault (my former Nannies from Hell swear this is true). So, it's okay to let me talk to an employer who you might not have gotten along with. I understand." (Understand, yes; accept, not readily.

You'd better believe I'm going to pay close attention to a negative reference.)

By now the bloodhound, nose to the ground in grand bloodhound tracking mode, is thinking, "We're on to something. Which way will the chase lead us?"

The fox meanwhile, cool and casual, slyly looking for nonverbal cues, watches the applicant preparing her answer.

If the person persists in saying the contact information is not available (as indeed it sometimes is not), the fox will try another tack.

"Well, if we were to find that person who employed you and who now has moved to Beirut without a forwarding address, what do you think that person would say about you?" The fox listens closely to what is said and, I have to admit, has sometimes been amazed at the answers received. One young woman answered, "She would say I left without notice and she was quite angry about this."

"Well, did you?"

"Yes, but she deserved it. She went into my room and touched my stuff."

"Why did she do this?"

"She was selling her house and some buyers were coming over; she said she needed to clean things up and I was away for the weekend, but she should never have touched my things."

As soon as the missing information surfaces, my fox and bloodhound instincts go underground, and my mature, more honorable self resurfaces. I award the applicant one point for honesty (albeit delayed) and deduct four points for attitude, maturity, courtesy in giving notice, and probably neatness. Final score: no hire.

Over the years I've had the opportunity to do a lot of reference checking. On several occasions I've been very appreciative of the willingness of strangers to give me honest appraisals of care givers who had worked for them. I remind myself of this when I am at the information-giving end and do my best to return the favor. Most of the conversations I've had weren't particularly memorable; however, a few did stand out. The following references are some of the ones I haven't forgotten.

References I've Gotten (HONEST!)

THE CLEANER

"I can't believe she gave us as a reference. I just can't believe it! Where is she? Can you give me her number? Yes, she worked for us. Her strong point? I'd have to say cleaning. She cleaned us out of our Baccarat crystal, our wedding silver, even the baby clothes. Some things she cleaned out totally. As far as others, she was selective. We still have half a service of stainless steel."

"THE KIDS SLEPT WELL WHILE SHE WAS HERE"

"My friend heard you were interviewing a nanny who used to work for us. Even though we don't know each other, I thought in good conscience I should call you. She worked for us for one month. I came home from work unexpectedly one afternoon and found all the children asleep. Deep asleep. When I commented on how unusual this was, she showed me her secret to getting a quiet afternoon. She had given them cough syrup that contained a narcotic. The bottle was almost empty and she told me she needed a refill."

THE WALKER

"She is the daughter of a business associate. She comes from a good family and is fairly well educated. One day, our next-door neighbor heard our burglar alarm go off. She came over to investigate. It turned out our three-year-old had been left alone in the house, while our nanny went for a walk with the infant. Our three-year-old had gotten bored and pushed all the buttons on the burglar alarm, triggering it."

THE SAVIOR

"She was terrific. Let me tell you just one story about her.
    "My wife was unloading groceries from the car and left the

continued

driver's car door open. Our two-year-old was on the hood of the car, and our nanny was inside the house, drying her hands so she could come out and give my wife a hand. Fortunately, there is a window above our kitchen sink that looks out on the driveway. Our nanny noticed our Labrador retriever, Sam, jump into the driver's seat. When he jumped in, he disengaged the emergency brake, which allowed the car to start rolling. Our son was still on the hood of the car and Sam was in the driver's seat. Our nanny raced outside and grabbed our son off the car by his belt loop just as the car began to pick up speed.

"Our car rolled down the driveway, across the street, and crashed into our neighbor's truck. Sam was fine. The truck had a large dent in the side. Our car needed quite a bit of work. When I talked to our insurance company, I wasn't sure what to say when they asked me who was driving. After all, Sam was not only uninsured, but also unlicensed. Luckily, they laughed when they found out Sam's identity and agreed to pay."

THE BIG IMPRESSION

"She said she worked at our school for three years? Gee, I don't remember her."

THE ICE CREAM ADDICT

"She was okay. Our two sons loved her; she's athletic and roughhoused with them, which they enjoyed.

"Any problems? Well, she's not a great communicator with adults. We never could tell what was on her mind.

"Oh, if you hire her, make sure you buy a lot of ice cream. We never could keep ice cream in the house while she was here. Entire gallons would disappear in a day. I told her I would buy her her own ice cream, any flavor and as much as she wanted, if she would leave some ice cream for the rest of the family to eat. It didn't work. She would eat it all."

continued

THE BABY-FOOD LOVER

"When I asked her if she wanted me to buy any special food for her when I went grocery shopping, she always asked for baby food. She said she liked to spread it on toast. It took a few weeks and a lot of baby food before I discovered she had a couple and their baby living in our cottage with her."

THE SHORT-TERMER

"She has taken care of our children off and on for several years. She's great for the first two months. She'll volunteer to work extra hours, decorate your house with flowers, and bubble with enthusiasm about everything. Then she tends to get depressed and lethargic. But you don't have to worry about this; she's planning to go to fashion school at the end of the summer. She told you this, didn't she?"

YOU'RE HIRED

"She's back in town? I wonder why she didn't call me? I'd like to hire her back. Please tell me how to reach her."

THE APPLICATION FORM

I am a real advocate for using an application form for any hire, especially for a home child care provider. I don't like paperwork any more than the next person, but there is real benefit in having information about a person organized in a single format especially designed for your needs. It makes comparing different people easier, it ensures that you have collected complete information, and it is a convenient way to collect information that might be useful later on, after the person is working for you. Besides, an application form lends an air of professionalism to the hiring process and communicates from the beginning that you are hiring someone for a "real" job.

The application form I use (see next page) is based on one developed by a mother, Robin Katzaros. I've made some changes, as should you, to apply to my family situation.

The first page of the form asks for basic information. This is important for several reasons, not the least of which is that it provides information you might need should your child care worker get ill. It also asks questions that many of us forget or are embarrassed to mention in an interview: whether the person has an illness that might interfere with job performance or whether she or he has been convicted of a crime. In addition it covers health insurance data and driving record.

Robin Katzaros insists that all out-of-state applicants send copies of their driver's license and health insurance. In her words, "I want to know how long a person has been driving because I don't want a new driver driving my kids. Also our insurance company will want to know this information when we put our nanny on our policy, so it's helpful to have it up front.

"I also insist that she have health insurance before she starts to work for us. Most of the women we hire are young and can still be covered under their parents' policies.

"Health insurance is very important for us even though we've never had a serious illness or injury with any of our nannies. But you never know. And if our nanny were to become ill without coverage, what would we say? You can't have treatment? Of course not. We would pay for it. I'd rather know up front that a person has or does not have coverage. If I found someone excellent who didn't, I'd want to be able to arrange for her to have coverage."

About medical insurance: Is the gamble one takes by hiring someone without health insurance a real or imagined risk? Only you can answer that. The results of my discussions with families convinced me that even though most of the nannies they employ were young and in good health, accidents and illnesses that required expensive hospitalization did happen. One family's nanny developed terminal ovarian cancer. Another died from heart disease while on the job. Still another was discovered to have tuberculosis. One had complications from a miscarriage. Another broke her leg.

Child Care Provider Application Form

Your name: _____ Today's date: _____

Your address: _____

_____

_____

Your parent or some other relative's address and phone number: _____

_____

_____

Your telephone number (if outside the U.S., please include country and city codes):

_____

The address and phone number of someone we could contact in case of an emergency:

_____

_____

_____

_____

Driver's license number: _____ Date obtained: _____

Driving history (accidents, tickets, etc.): _____

_____

_____

Health insurance company: _____

Describe any health problems:

_____

_____

Date and results of last TB test: _____

Medications you currently use:

_____

Have you ever been convicted of a felony or been in jail? ____

Do you have any relationships or involvements that would interfere with your making at least a one-year work commitment? _____

continued

A. Tell us about your background. You might want to include where you were born, your parents' occupations, names and ages of your brothers and sisters, what schools you attended and for how long, what subjects you studied, and your hobbies. In summary, include any information that gives us a picture of you. You may use additional pieces of paper for any questions on this form if needed.

_____
_____
_____
_____
_____
_____
_____
_____
_____
_____
_____

B. The following is a list of personality traits. Please rate yourself on a scale from 1 to 10, with 1 being the *least* amount and 10 being the *most* amount. Circle the numeral.

Outgoing	1	2	3	4	5	6	7	8	9	10
Patient	1	2	3	4	5	6	7	8	9	10
Neat	1	2	3	4	5	6	7	8	9	10
Organized	1	2	3	4	5	6	7	8	9	10
Analytical	1	2	3	4	5	6	7	8	9	10
Independent	1	2	3	4	5	6	7	8	9	10
Friendly	1	2	3	4	5	6	7	8	9	10
Private	1	2	3	4	5	6	7	8	9	10
Flexible	1	2	3	4	5	6	7	8	9	10
Self-confident	1	2	3	4	5	6	7	8	9	10

continued

C. Please list all jobs, dates of employment, and reasons for leaving:

Start date (month/year)	End date (month/year)	Employer	Reason for leaving
1.			
2.			
3.			
4.			

D. What did your previous employers like most about you? What did they like least about you?

_____

_____

_____

_____

_____

E. When did you decide you wanted to work with children? Why? Please describe your past experiences taking care of children. Describe your responsibilities and the children's ages and sexes. What did you like most and least about the jobs?

_____

_____

_____

_____

_____

F. The following is a list of questions about child care skills. Imagine you are in the situation described and tell us what you would do.

continued

1. One of the children that you are watching is doing something wrong. You have already asked him/her three times not to do it. What would you do now?

_____

_____

_____

2. It's a rainy day. The children, who are two and six years old, want to play outside but it is too cold and wet. You must keep them inside for the entire day. What would you do to keep them busy? Please be as specific as possible.

_____

_____

_____

3. You need to go grocery shopping. You get the children in the car. The youngest has been ill and didn't sleep very well the previous night. On the way to the store, he falls asleep in the car. You really don't want to wake him. What do you do?

_____

_____

_____

4. The parents go out for the evening and you are babysitting. The children are asleep and it is late. You are watching TV. You hear a frantic knock at the front door. By the time you get to the door, the person is pounding on the door saying, "I've been hurt in an auto accident. I'm hurt and bleeding. Please let me in and help me." What do you do?

_____

_____

_____

5. One of your responsibilities will be to cook the children's meals. Describe three meals you have learned to cook that you think would be nutritious and balanced for young children.

_____

_____

_____

_____

continued

6. The mother and father go away for a few days. You are in charge. They have made arrangements for another baby-sitter to relieve you two of the three nights they are away. One of those nights you have made plans to go to a concert with your friends. The tickets were expensive. You will be driving your friends to and from the concert. The baby-sitter scheduled to baby-sit cancels because she is sick. What do you do?

_____

_____

_____

_____

7. You are baby-sitting and expect the parents to call and give you the telephone number where they can be reached. You are bathing the children, ages one and three. The phone rings. It is in the next room. What do you do?

_____

_____

_____

_____

G. Please describe the perfect family to work for. What would the parents and the children be like?

_____

_____

_____

H. Please tell us what special needs you have. For example, do you have any dietary restrictions, are there religious holidays you want to observe, do you have vacation or travel plans? Is there anything else we should know in advance to make sure your needs are met?

_____

_____

_____

_____

continued

I. Do you like animals? Elaborate.

_____

_____

J. Do you swim? _____ K. Do you know CPR? _____

There are several approaches to providing health insurance. Some families share the cost with their nannies. A few I talked to, for example, gave a monthly stipend that covered part but not all of the cost of medical insurance. Other families include paid health coverage as part of their benefit package. The cost and type of coverage available varies state by state and almost always is an individual policy. In California, the monthly cost at the time of this writing is between $68 and $93. If you hire your nanny from an agency, the agency will sometimes assist in securing health insurance.

Some families consider it the responsibility of the nanny to arrange and pay for health insurance herself. Nannies who are also students can usually get health insurance through their schools. Those twenty-five years old or younger can sometimes be covered under their parents' insurance. Nannies from abroad can often get special traveler's insurance arranged through their travel agencies.

Questions A and B on the application form ask the applicant to describe her family background and her own personality. It is a good cross-reference to use when you interview the person. Has she circled all 10s? You might want to probe her self-perception. Does she indicate she is disorganized? How would this fit into your lifestyle? Does she circle 9 for friendly, yet appear withdrawn? There really aren't right or wrong answers in this section. It is included to give you a broad picture of the person you are interviewing and an indication as to whether her style will blend with yours. Does her self-perception track with your impression and with what she has done in the past? In other words, does the self-portrait she presents to you appear to be consistent and realistic? And if so, do you feel it is one that will thrive in your environment?

Questions C, D, and E are all very important to me. I have found that even when an applicant has already submitted this information in a letter format, it is extremely useful for me to have it on a form. A recent hiring experience highlighted this.

A few months ago, I used the application form to help a relative hire a nanny. We advertised out of state and got many appealing letters and resumes. We liked several and sent their senders application forms. When the completed application forms were returned, one of the applicants who had initially seemed the strongest because of her style of writing and unique experience dropped out of consideration. She had originally impressed me in her letter by stating she had worked as a clown at children's parties during weekends. That shows a real love of children, I thought to myself. But when I saw on the application form that the experience had only been for three months and was several years ago, I realized it was inadequate. Her main job experience had been as a clerk for several different retailers over the past few years, and that just wasn't appropriate experience for a child care job.

Question F sets this application form apart from all others I have seen. Please change the scenarios to fit your family, but do ask questions that reveal how a person would react in an unlikely, but possible situation.

Question F is designed to give insight into an applicant's common sense and judgment. This is called "experience-based questioning." While it is not a foolproof method for determining how well someone will actually do while on the job, it is a step in the right direction. There are no really wrong or right answers to most of these questions. However, most parents have preferred methods for handling each of the situations presented. Hopefully the answers to the questions will reveal whether the parents and applicant agree on the best way to handle a potential situation. They also give an opportunity for dialogue when the approaches differ and provide subject matter to discuss during an interview.

The application form is long. Therefore I only ask those candidates I am really interested in to complete it. Tell them they can use extra paper or the back of the form to answer the questions if needed. You could also ask the questions on the form during a verbal interview and jot down the answers yourself.

BACKGROUND CHECKS

Some parents do background checks routinely; many have never even considered them. If the laws in your state allow you to get criminal and civil information about a potential hire, I recommend the investment. You don't need to hire a personal investigator. All you need to do is to ask your local police department how to get criminal and civil background reports on your potential hire. You will need at minimum the person's social security number.

Do obtain a copy of the nanny's Department of Motor Vehicle record even if she will not be driving during her job. It will show whether or not she has any convictions for driving while under the influence of drugs or alcohol. One parent looking for infant care told me about almost hiring a nanny whose work experience looked ideal. Luckily, the nanny's DMV record arrived before the first day of work and it showed several DWI convictions. Upon being confronted, the nanny admitted having lied during the interview and hidden an alcohol problem. Furthermore, she had not listed several short term jobs on the application form because she had been fired from them.

Several parents called all schools that applicants had said they attended in order to verify the dates of attendance. One couple I interviewed also told me that they had any final nanny candidate give them a signed medical release form enabling them to request health information from the candidate's doctor. They wanted to make sure the candidate did not have any physical or mental problems which would interfere with her performing their job.

Invest as much time and money in verifying information about your nanny as you would if you were going to put your life savings into a piece of property or business venture. What you have at stake is much more valuable.

THE INTERVIEW

The application form and prescreening interview should give you enough factual data to decide if the applicant has appropriate and sufficient experience for your job. A face-to-face interview should then follow. It is the best way to gather the intuitive information that is so vital in making the right hiring decision. For out-of-state applicants you may have no recourse other than phone interviews, but if so, conduct several. However, if you can arrange it, try to meet even out-of-state applicants in person before you make a final decision to hire.

The interview is the time to understand a person's motives, approach to problem solving, attitude, and style: in other words, her personality. In all but a few jobs, personality plays a role in an individual's ability to get a job done. In the position of home child care provider, the person's personality can be a determining factor separating a Nanny from Hell from a Nanny from Heaven. It is vital that the nanny's personality mesh well with yours and your family's, especially if she is going to be a live-in.

Interview all applicants—even those who will be live-out—as though you were interviewing for a roommate, business associate, teacher and role-model for your children, and employee all wrapped up in one. If you do not feel comfortable with an applicant on all levels, you are asking for trouble down the road. A significant portion of the Nanny from Hell stories I heard ended with a statement like, "The kids liked her; she just drove *us* crazy."

Trust your instincts. One parent commented that when her interview with a male au pair from Italy had finished, he said good-bye to her and then kissed the children on the tops of their heads. She said, "He did it so automatically, as if it would be unthinkable to leave a child without showing affection, that I felt comfortable he was a warm person. I hired him and even though he didn't stay as long as I would have liked, he was very nice to my children while he was here."

Be positive about the person you select. If you have any doubts at all, keep looking. It is much easier not to hire someone in the first place than to fire the person later.

The following tips will help prepare you to conduct your face-to-face interviews effectively. While you are talking with your nanny candidate, you will be gathering a wealth of information simply by sitting in a room with her or him. To make it easier to sift through and interpret both the verbal and nonverbal data you'll gather at your face-to-face, at-home interviews, I have developed composites of nannies who seemed to recur time and again in the stories parents told me. These portraits may make it easier for you to cross the bridge between gathering information about a person and being able to predict whether you and the applicant can work together smoothly as a team. The following chapter describes these composite nannies.

INTERVIEWS TIPS

- How does the candidate relate to your children during the interview? Does she smile when they interrupt the conversation? Does she remember their names when she is leaving? Does she take the time to say good-bye to them? If they are young, does she stoop down to their level to say good-bye? And if so, do these actions seem automatic and almost unconscious? Yes? These are good signs.
- Start off with questions that are easy to answer and nonthreatening. This will help the interviewee feel comfortable.
- Ask questions that get the person talking. In other words, do not ask questions that can be answered "yes" or "no," but rather, begin your questions with words such as "why," "how," "explain," "tell me more about. . . ."
- A silence (in professional recruiter lingo called a "pregnant pause") is a good way to elicit more information about a subject. People usually don't like silences. If you remain quiet after the person has finished talking, he or she will fill in the silence with more information. Often you will get information that is unrehearsed and revealing. This technique is best used when you suspect that the person is not totally straightforward or forthcoming about a subject.
- Ask for information about any gaps in employment. People sometimes leave out information about jobs that ended poorly. You will want to talk to all former employers, especially those who did not like the applicant, so be sure to find out who they are.

continued

- Probe the reason that former experiences did not work out. We all have failures; it is the way people deal with these that differentiates them. I look for individuals who admit their mistakes and have learned from them.
- Pay attention to the *way* in which questions are answered. Does the person hesitate, seem awkward or reluctant? What is her tone? Does she respond to clues you give her, such as when to talk or when to listen?
- Is the applicant's description of herself consistent with her experience and behavior? If she describes herself as a person looking for a long-term commitment, has she had jobs where she demonstrated this? If she says she loves animals, does she appear affectionate to the ones you have? Does her history indicate involvement with children, not just in paid activities, but through hobbies, volunteer work, or schooling?

SUMMARY

1. The hiring process for a nanny is different than for a typical business employee. Prescreening and reference checking come before the applicant fills out an application form and is interviewed.
2. A trial period before you commit to the hire is very important.
3. Reference checking is perhaps the most important part of the selection process. Always check multiple job references! Also, check the person's civil and criminal background, driving record and medical history.
4. Conduct a minimum of three interviews with a candidate before you hire. The first is to gather factual data and takes place on the phone, the second is to watch the person interact with your children, and the third is to ensure that you and the nanny have similar child care philosophies and can work together.
5. Trust your instincts and only hire someone you are absolutely sure about. It is better to take a little longer in hiring than to make a compromise hire and regret it later.

CHAPTER 5

A Gallery of Nannies: From Heaven to Hell

MYTH

*Young nannies are energetic and older ones are
more responsible.*

TRUTH

*No generalizations are true for everyone, however categorizing
nannies can be a useful technique to ensure a good match with
your family's needs.*

Generalizations about any group are inaccurate and unfair. However, it helps to have a sense of humor and a broad perspective when dealing with child care issues. In this context, I have taken the liberty of categorizing nannies. Undoubtedly, most individuals will not exactly match the pictures painted here or will cross over categories. However, more than a hundred interviews with parents and nannies indicated consistent patterns of behavior among child care providers. This wealth of experiences cried out to be shared. If you are the current or past employer of a nanny whose behavior is or was a mystery to you, these portraits not only will help you understand what is going on, but may also give you the comfort of knowing you are not alone in dealing with an extremely thorny problem. I cannot be with you when you interview for your next nanny, but I can give you the benefit of a hundred other families' experience to guide you.

A final word of caution: there aren't "bad" or "good" types—pure Nannies from Heaven or Nannies from Hell are few. There are only good and bad fits to the needs of a family. So, as you read about other people's nannies, think about your own family and how it would interact with the different personalities. After you have read about the different types, you can refer to the Table of Red Flags at the end of the chapter to refresh your memory the next time you are interviewing.

THE PRINCESS

She arrives at your house doe-eyed and excited about finally being in the Big Time. She may sniff the air and comment on how wonderful and different from her home it smells. She can be from a smaller town, another country, or maybe just from a less affluent section of your own community. However, it is clear from the start that she thinks being your nanny is going to change her life.

Her background usually consists of lots of baby-sitting for friends and neighbors. She may have been active in a church and taught Sunday school. She may have aspired to be a cheerleader or flag bearer in high school. More often than not she went to modeling, beautician, or travel agent school afterward and now feels like life has finally dealt her a lucky hand. Being your nanny means she will see the world, meet Mr. Rich and Famous, and live happily ever after. During her interview she told you she is very healthy. She forgot to mention, however, that she is allergic to housework.

While the Princess is delighting in her new surroundings, you begin to have a suspicion the future will not be as rosy as it appears to her. She wants glamour. Being a nanny has a lot of rewards, but glamour is not one of them. You expect her to take your children to parks, museums, libraries, and their (as opposed to her) friends' houses. She'd rather be at the mall. You expect Raffi, Linda Arnold, or some other children's musician to be playing on the tape recorder. She can't understand why this is better than the heavy metal or country/western music she plays instead. She is genuinely surprised that you are surprised she spent the afternoon painting your daughter's toe- and fingernails and French braiding her hair. Didn't you give her instructions to do art together? And why can't she talk on the phone most of the afternoon or have the TV on in the background, as long as she simultaneously watches the children?

If you ask her to do housework—any housework—even if it is clearly child-related, she will be resentful. Housework is not the reason she came to work for you. Reminders that the issue was discussed beforehand and that she had assured you she had done plenty of housework at her own home fall on deaf ears. She has become your nanny because she wants a step up in life, and being required to do any household maintenance is a reminder she hasn't gotten very far.

The first few days after the Princess has arrived, she will be full of enthusiasm and gushing over everything because it is new and, by definition, better. She will pay a lot of attention to her dress (one Princess arrived from Italy sporting an entire wardrobe of designer clothes), hair, and makeup. Her enthusiasm quickly turns to disappointment and resentment. Her original self-view as Cinderella being blessed by her fairy godmother shifts to one of Cinderella as miserable slave. No matter how minimal your expectations or how carefully worded your instructions, you will be viewed as the wicked stepmother, intent on overworking, criticizing, demeaning, and in general making life miserable for poor Cinderella.

It will not be hard to tell when things have begun to sour for the Princess. She may start to pay less attention to her appearance; she may sigh or lower her eyes every time you speak to her. She may be happily playing with one of the children and when you enter the room suddenly look solemn or sad. You will start to get a funny feeling that something is wrong although you will not be able to fathom why because the situation is as described in your letters and phone calls and she did seem happy when she first arrived. Nothing has changed. Why is she unhappy? The Princess may never tell you directly, but she will make sure you get the message sooner rather than later that she is not suited for the role she finds herself in. As one mom recollected, "I looked outside and she was sitting on the porch eating a banana and looking miserable. A piece of banana fell on the ground and she mashed it in with her foot. I knew the end was near even though she had only been with us for a few weeks."

The Princess spurns anything unglamorous, but not because she feels too important. (Although there is a small subset of au pairs who come from privileged backgrounds, have been accustomed to servants, and may scorn the domestic side of caring for children, as often as not, this is because they don't know how to clean up rather than because they feel "above" it.) Rather, the Princess has low self-esteem and feels trapped and unhappy in her life. She wants desperately to be a different person. Unrealistically she thought your job would accomplish this for her. When she discovers it won't, she blames you rather than her expectations.

The Princess defines her job in very narrow terms, usually limited to playing with the children and sometimes even to only observing them while they play. Even if at previous jobs such as waitressing or retail clerking she had to work hard, she will not now jump in and help wherever the need may be.

The Princess is not all negative. In fact, she can be very warm and loving toward your children—a Nanny from Heaven trait. She may have come from a large, traditional family and exhibit some of the more positive qualities one associates with such an upbringing. She can teach your children to be polite, to share, and to be nice to each other—no small feat. Also, when her interests coincide with yours, as when she accompanies you on a family vacation trip, her enthusiasm can be heartwarming and infectious.

Princesses rarely give adequate notice. Some do not give any at all and disappear Cinderella-like at the stroke of midnight. Don't expect to find a glass slipper. Far more likely are a messy room and lots of undone chores or unpaid bills. They justify their actions on some inadequacy of the job or employers (you). As you seethe at the inconvenience her sudden departure has caused you and the pain it may have caused your children, who for the most part like Princesses, try to temper your anger with understanding. She is acting like a Nanny from Hell, but her behavior is in some ways out of her control and fundamentally has nothing to do with you. She is unlikely to be happy in any job. And now that you have had exposure to a Princess it will be easier to sniff out another. As the Newtons' story about a nanny named Chelsea illustrates, a person's background may hold clear signs that she is a Princess.

Modeling School Is a Warning Sign

THE NEWTONS' STORY

The Newtons were desperate. The nanny who had been with them for sixteen months had left unexpectedly. Her replacement, whom they found through an ad in the newspaper, lasted only three weeks. They had to find someone fast. Mrs. Newton couldn't face another round of answering phone calls responding to a new newspaper ad. The family had been very specific about their requirements in their last ad, but most of the people who called weren't qualified. It really was a nightmare. They invited way too many people over for interviews and became exhausted from the process. After all of that they chose the wrong person! They had already asked most of the people they knew with children to pass along any referrals they had. They finally decided to use an agency.

The agency they called was out of state. A friend had had good luck with them. The woman who answered the phone seemed nice. Mrs. Newton explained the situation (they needed someone fast), the job (care for two active toddlers, five days a week, ten hours a day), and their requirements (English speaking, experienced with young children, and able to drive). Salary was negotiable. The agency representative seemed to think that "under normal circumstances" (her words) the job would not be too tough to fill. Unfortunately, she had just filled several vacancies and was temporarily out of candidates.

"Oh no," Mrs. Newton gasped. "Don't you have *anyone?*"

"Well, there is one possibility. I'm interviewing a young woman tomorrow who comes highly recommended by one of our best nannies. Shall I call you after the interview and tell you what I think?"

continued

"Absolutely," was the response. Mrs. Newton gave her phone number, and mentally she hired this unknown, soon-to-be-interviewed young woman.

The call from the agency came as promised the next day. Mrs. Newton was as nervous as a person just contacted by Publishers Clearing House to be told how many millions of dollars she had won. At least, she hoped she was this lucky. In looking back upon this experience, she considered that hysteria and desperation had overcome her good judgment. Anyway, the agency woman called and said, "Your new nanny just left and she seems perfect for the job." Bingo! They had won their fortune! Now to settle back, breathe easily and find out just how rich they had become.

"Tell me about her," Mrs. Newton said. "Tell me first about her experience with children."

"I spent a lot of time talking to her mother," the agency person responded, "and she has raised six children. She has a lot of experience and is a really fine person."

"My nanny or her mother?"

"Oh, her mother."

"Well, how about my nanny? Was she the eldest of the six children? Is that how she got her experience? Did she help raise her brothers and sisters?"

"No, not exactly. In fact, she's the youngest. Her mom is a little unsure about her going so far from home, but I assured her that her daughter would be fine."

"So, how did she get her experience? Has she been a nanny before?"

"Well, not exactly. But she does have a lot of experience. She has taken care of her nieces and nephews. Her mom assured me that they all adore her."

"Has she worked at all?"

"Yes. She worked in a dress shop. And now she is working at a 7-Eleven. She doesn't have to give them any notice because it's such a terrible job. Isn't that great? She's available right away."

continued

By this point Mrs. Newton was getting a little bit uneasy. Several of the people who had called in response to her ad had only had family baby-sitting experience and she had discounted them as being too inexperienced. This woman did not appear to be a strong candidate. And she didn't like her not giving notice to her present employer.

"How about schooling," Mrs. Newton asked hopefully. Maybe there was something relevant there.

"Modeling school," was the response. "She wanted to be a model, but now she's not sure. She didn't like the teachers at the modeling school."

"I don't think this is the person for us," Mrs. Newton answered. "Taking care of my children is not going to satisfy someone with modeling ambitions."

"I already talked to her about this and she understands. She's willing to make a one-year commitment no matter what. There really is nothing for her where she lives. It's a small town. Some of these women go to modeling school to improve their lives. It actually shows she has some initiative and drive. Why don't you just talk to her? She is very sweet and, as I said, her mother swears she is wonderful with children."

"Give me her number," Mrs. Newton agreed reluctantly. "But I don't think we will hire her."

To make a long story short, they did. That night Mr. and Mrs. Newton called Chelsea on the speaker phone and talked to her. She was giggly and sweet. They excused themselves to talk over their impression of her and left the speaker phone on by mistake. They heard her say to someone else who was with her, "Oh, I hope they hire me. They sound great! I really, really hope this happens!" Her enthusiasm swayed them.

"Hooray!" Chelsea shouted when they told her she had the job. "I'll be there in a week and send you a picture right away so you can recognize me at the airport."

The picture she sent showed a pretty girl, with shoulder length blond hair and a vivacious smile. She was no extraordi-

continued

nary beauty, but the picture was small and perhaps not that flattering. The agency application form which accompanied the picture listed her height as 5'4" and her weight as 138 pounds—hardly a model's measurements, thought Mrs. Newton.

Chelsea arrived a few days later. Mrs. Newton spotted her as she was emerging with the rest of the passengers. At twenty feet she looked very much like her picture, young and pretty. As she came closer her face began to take on an overdone, flamboyant, too colorful look. The amount of makeup she used was incredible. Her false eyelashes jutted out almost half an inch, her emerald-green eye shadow was liberally applied, her eyebrows extended too far down her face, and her lipstick was bright red with small heaped-up mounds at the corners. They said hello to one another and collected her bags and went home.

Everyone was asleep when they got home. Mrs. Newton said good night and told Chelsea she would see her the next morning at 8:30.

The next morning the family was at breakfast and Chelsea had not come out of the second bathroom for forty-five minutes. It was 9:00 and Mrs. Newton was worried that something might be wrong. She knocked and was assured all was well. Chelsea emerged ten minutes later. She was dressed in a floral print party dress. Her eye shadow was orange, her lipstick peach, and each of her cheeks had large circles of red rouge on them. By then Mr. Newton had gone to work and Mrs. Newton had fed and dressed the children. She was to stay home to train Chelsea.

The day went all right. Chelsea listened politely, played with the children when requested to do so, took them outside to the swings, and many times during the day expressed her delight at being there. She refused to get into something more casual when Mrs. Newton suggested that she do so, and was somewhat perturbed when her dress got muddied from the children's shoes. Repeated suggestions that she wear

continued

something more appropriate were finally accepted and she changed into jeans. However, half an hour before Mr. Newton was due to return from work, she excused herself and went into the bathroom.

Harvey Newton arrived home, asked about Chelsea, and then, as if on cue, she emerged from the bathroom wearing purple eyeliner, short thick eyelashes, flamingo pink lipstick, and so much facial powder that she left a trail. And she had on the same print floral dress she had worn that morning.

After dinner, Chelsea pitched in and washed the dishes, but she was very upset when she discovered one of the yellow gloves she was wearing had a small rip in the side. She asked where the grocery list was kept, and wrote down THREE PAIRS OF RUBBER GLOVES FOR CHELSEA. After everyone was in bed Mrs. Newton explained the request to her husband. Chelsea hadn't wanted to change dirty diapers without yellow gloves on because she thought it would ruin her nail polish (lavender). She felt the same way about doing the dishes.

Mrs. Newton postponed her return to work because it became rapidly apparent that Chelsea had no clue as to what being a nanny entailed. She began to refuse to do daily household chores and any child care job that might mar her appearance or dirty her clothes. When Mrs. Newton complained to Harvey, he told her she needed to do a better job of explaining to Chelsea she didn't need to dress up for the family. Mrs. Newton suggested he give it a try.

"Well, Chelsea," he said the next morning, "how's everything going so far?"

"I'm beginning to get the hang of things," she said. "I am really looking forward to getting out and meeting some people in the fashion and entertainment industry. Eventually, I would like to get a job in this area. It's what I studied, you know."

"That's fine for the future," Harvey responded, "but you don't have to dress up in nice clothes and makeup for us.

continued

Being a nanny can be a messy job and you will probably wreck your good clothes if you wear them during the day."

Chelsea smiled and said, "Gee, I believe it is important to always look your best. I would never want to work for someone or go out to shop or do other errands and not look my best. Actually, I don't mind if something hurts my clothes. My mother owns a dress shop and I can always get more. Everything is okay. Really!"

The next week Chelsea returned after spending a weekend with some new friends. She was in seventh heaven and bursting with enthusiasm. "I stayed with a rock band promoter's family and rock stars came visiting until four o'clock in the morning. It was really exciting. One or two of the musicians said they would like to see me again," she said.

Mr. and Mrs. Newton were worried about Chelsea since she seemed to be rather naive about some of the interests of her new friends. They had a talk with her and warned her about potential problems: broken promises, drug addiction, sexually transmitted diseases, and pregnancy. Chelsea thanked them very much but said she was a mature person, and knew all about these things. She continued to gush and carry on about the rock stars she met.

One morning several days after their discussion, Chelsea failed to appear. Mrs. Newton checked the bathroom. No Chelsea. There was a note taped to the mirror that read:

Dear Mr. and Mrs. Newton,
　　Thank you so much for bringing me out here. I have enjoyed my time with you but I really must get on with my life. As you know, I have been to modeling school and I don't think that being a nanny suits me. I have found another great job helping to take care of a rock promoter's home, so I'll be fine. Thanks for your support and I wish you well. I am sorry to leave like this, but I hate emotional scenes.

Your friend,
Chelsea

Harvey and Judith Newton say they now are suspicious of any nanny applicant who has been to modeling school, participated in beauty contests, or has any acting aspirations. Glamour just isn't a strong point of the job, they explained. Although they were laughing as they told me this, I got the impression they were quite serious.

THE BOSS

She can be young and just out of nanny school or she may have just earned her B.A. in childhood education. On the other hand, she may be more mature and have raised children of her own. Regardless of age, the Boss will enter your household and take over. She likes to be in charge. Some Bosses want control only over the children. If you are an at-home mom who has hired a Boss, you may find yourself excluded from activities you enjoy, such as putting the children to bed or giving healing kisses when your child gets hurt. The Boss is not happy unless "her" children turn to her for help or affection. Other Bosses take over everything, from deciding what's for dinner to independently calling service people when something needs fixing. This trait isn't bad if you and your spouse are busy professionals and want someone to run your personal life for you. If this is the case, you will think of your Boss as a Nanny from Heaven.

On the other hand, there is a down side to having a Boss in your life even if she handles your household and children competently. As one couple, both physicians, said about the Boss who had run their household for several years, "We were never alone with our children. She expected to come on every vacation, be with us every holiday." The mother continued, "When I went to the children's school for special events everyone assumed I was the new au pair."

Having a Boss in your life can be wonderful or terrible depending on whether or not you want to share your children's affections and exchange control of your household for freedom to pursue other interests or needs. If you are grateful to have someone who takes initiative and acts like Mom or Dad in your absence, then you'll probably like having a Boss work for you. Children thrive under the care of Bosses, because Bosses take such good care of them. On the other hand, if you like to retain control and have strong ideas about how things should be done, fireworks will fly and you will find yourself thinking about her as a Nanny from Hell. The Boss secretly and sometimes not so secretly considers herself a better parent than you and will resent any direction you give her, no matter how innocuous. She may follow your instructions, but will resent the intrusion. And don't be surprised if her friends and yours are treated to discourses on the things you do wrong and, coincidentally, she does right. Usually Bosses are quite vocal with everyone about what goes on in your home. Frequently, they also are gossips.

One thing most Bosses seem to have in common is a dysfunctional family background. Not surprisingly, many come from substance-abusing households where as children they had to function as adults prematurely. Being in control is a role that feels comfortable and safe. They also tend to be perfectionist, have strong opinions about everything, especially drugs, alcohol, religion, and child rearing. They can be incredibly loving toward children, wanting to provide the nurturing they themselves never had. On the other hand, they may be very rigid. Bosses do not like change.

If you should come to a parting of ways with a Boss, initiate it as gently as possible. Underneath the self-confidence and self-assurance lies a vulnerable, insecure little girl with a lot of unhealed wounds. At first she will be very, very hurt that you don't need her any longer. The hurt will quickly disappear as soon as she swings into job search mode. She will find another position quickly because Bosses are so competent, and all will be forgiven. She may even come back to visit the children and act as though it had been her idea in the first place to find another job.

The Godbouts' story about a Boss took place in a family where the mother expected to return to work shortly after the birth of her first child. She hired a Boss with the hopes the nanny would take her place in the child's life while she was at work. She got what she wanted: someone very competent, in fact more competent than she. As with many answered prayers, this turned out to create its own complications. The mom felt displaced and alienated from the child. Her solution was to terminate the Boss and become a stay-at-home mom.

The "Perfect" Nanny

THE GODBOUTS' STORY

Hiring a nanny can be like finding someone to marry. Sometimes the strengths that attracted you in the first place turn out to be the ones that drive you crazy later on. In Roseanna and Ken Godbout's case, they wanted someone who could exercise independent judgment, who would know what to do in their absence, a take-charge kind of person who knew a lot about childhood development and could enrich their child's life. They wanted a mother substitute who would care for their child as if he were her own. They got all this and were miserable.

The Godbouts hired Nancy, a young woman who had recently graduated from a nanny's college. The school offered a whole range of appropriate courses including child rearing, dramatic reading for young children, and healthy menu planning. It even offered a course titled "children and their emotions." She had never actually worked as a nanny, but Roseanna and Ken had never been parents before. In spite of the couple's advanced college degrees, this woman seemed a whole lot better prepared than they were. Besides, as part of her training she had spent three weeks as an "intern" taking care of twin newborns. This gave her three weeks more hands-on experience than they had.

The couple looked at Nancy's school record. It contained almost all "excellents." Then they called the family with whom she had interned. When they asked for a reference the family was noncommittal. They basically said she had no bad habits and had done an okay job while working for them. The Godbouts didn't think to ask why they had ended up hiring someone else as a permanent nanny.

continued

Although she was only nineteen, it seemed as though Nancy was unusually mature. The Godbouts decided they had found someone who had relevant training and experience, was young and energetic, and who wanted to be a professional nanny for a long time. In short, she seemed perfect. They hired her after just one interview.

The baby, Luke, was born a few weeks later. When the family arrived home with the baby they were met by a young woman who was, to say the least, bubbling over with excitement. It would be a little unfair to say she ripped the baby out of the father's arms, but Ken hadn't taken more than two steps with him before Luke was taken away to be dressed in something "more comfy."

They didn't know it at the time, but this was the beginning of an undeclared "wholly" war. Nancy wanted the baby wholly for herself. The Godbouts were merely the parents, forces of darkness, from whom the baby needed to be protected.

They did, in fact, end up seeing Luke mainly in the dark. During daylight hours Nancy guarded him unceasingly, even when he slept. They told her, "It's really not necessary to stay in his room watching him while he sleeps. Why don't you take some time off." She responded: "Crib death. You've heard about that haven't you? I would never forgive myself if something happened to him while he slept." Admittedly, they probably resented all the late-night feedings less than most parents because at least they got to be alone with him. But the couple was disappointed at having to alter their prenatal visions of standing arm in arm, staring at their firstborn as he slept peacefully in his crib. Instead they watched over the head of a nanny who was watching *them* to make sure they didn't steal her little darling.

They began to feel more and more uncomfortable with the situation, but didn't know why. Their nanny really tried to do her job well. When Luke was a couple of weeks old Nancy started his education. And, like everything else she did, this was conducted according to schedule. Not only did every activity have its appointed time, but it was also written down in a diary.

continued

Roseanna explained to me, "Believe it or not, we were so inexperienced as parents, we never once questioned the necessity or even the wisdom of having classes for a baby. Instead we tried to look on the bright side: our son was being given every advantage in life. He not only had two parents who adored him, he also had a nanny who spent her off-hours reading child development books and her days implementing what she had learned. Our son got music development, visual stimulation, tactile exploration, he even got baby massage. Whereas we didn't even know what 'board books' were until our nanny asked for a supply of them, she had him sitting on her lap, looking at the pictures as she read to him. She varied her voice as she read (after all, she had taken "reading" in nanny college). We watched our son's rapt attention as our nanny tended to him and told ourselves we should be happy. We had someone who knew what she was doing to make up for our inadequacies.

"We were parents who were too old to remember most nursery rhymes and not young enough to have the energy to invent new ones. Our nanny knew every English verse to every rhyme ever composed for a child. She could even sing some of them in different languages. In fact, her skills were unequaled (by us anyway) in all aspects of child care. That is, in all aspects except breast-feeding. Not that she probably didn't try."

Ken picked up the narrative. "We felt strongly that Luke should be breast-fed. We decided to give him an occasional bottle to prepare him for when my wife returned to work, but planned even then to give him breast milk. Before Luke was born, Nancy was enthusiastic about the plan. Although once he was on solids, she assured us, she would make all her own baby food from organic produce. Once he was born, however, her feelings changed. It was as though each feeding was an affront to her competence.

"'But he was starting to get grumpy and needed something to eat,' was a common explanation when Roseanna

continued

would return home, less than an hour after having breast-fed the baby, to find our nanny giving him a bottle. Other times we were told, 'You don't want the poor darling to go hungry, do you?' 'But it's his massage time now; it's not good to give him a massage right after he's eaten.'

"We put reminders on the refrigerator: '*No* bottle feeding unless in an *emergency*.' Yet any time Roseanna left the house she would return to find he had either been fed or was being fed. No explanation or direction to the contrary was able to change this behavior. Finally we just put our foot down. We told her she could give the baby one and only one bottle a day if she felt he absolutely needed it, but it could only contain water.

"We realize now that winning the food battle was the beginning of learning the importance of limit setting, a lesson that came in handy when Luke turned two. Later, a friend told us that if we didn't learn to win battles when our son went through the terrible twos we would be sunk when he was a teenager. In our case we learned how to deal with limit setting by practicing first on a teenager, Nancy."

One evening when Ken returned home from work, Roseanna met him at the door and said, "Let's go for a walk. Now!" He recognized the tone immediately and out the door they went.

"I want to fire our nanny," Roseanna insisted as soon as they were out of earshot of the house. "She's driving me crazy."

"But she's so good with the baby. You'll never find anyone else as good," was Ken's sensitive reply.

"That's just it," Roseanna snarled. "She's wonderful. And I can never get near him. He's going to grow up thinking she's his mom and I'm some stranger. I go to pick him up and she tells me I'm interrupting some lesson. This morning I walked into the nursery. She was lying on the floor with him on her chest listening to country/western music. I wasn't sure if this was music appreciation or tactile stimulation, but I took him anyway. She scolded me and told me she couldn't do her job well if I kept interrupting them. She has to go! I can't take it."

continued

"Now honey," Ken answered in his most men-do-eat-quiche voice, "you know you need a lot of sleep and you haven't been getting much of it lately. Are you sure you aren't overreacting a little?" Roseanna then demonstrated what over-reacting was really like.

Ken later recalled, "That night I convinced Roseanna not to take any action until we both had a chance to think things through. Then, I got a chance to spend a couple of days with Nancy."

"Get me the washcloth from the bathroom," Nancy in-structed as Ken came in to see the baby during a diaper change. "Oh, and please close the window; it's getting a bit cold in here." Those were reasonable requests, but Ken admit-ted he was a bit aggravated by the imperious tone of voice.

"Get the phone, will you?" Nancy ordered, as she walked past the ringing phone to close the door to the kitchen. "And don't leave this door open; the baby could get a chill." Ken an-swered the phone, clenching the receiver a bit tightly. The phone call was for Nancy. "I'll take it in the study," she said. "Watch the baby." With that she walked into the study, put her feet on Ken's desk, and talked to her caller for about fifteen minutes. Ken fumed. "In my own house, a nineteen-year-old was telling me what to do and acting as though it were the most natural thing in the world," he said.

The couple told Nancy she could stay as long as she needed until she found another job, but that they no longer needed her. They felt guilty and sad for her. She found a new job almost immediately.

The Godbouts now comment, "We imperfect parents man-aged to survive without a perfect nanny. We even developed a degree of competence in child rearing. Luke thrived despite being denied enrichment lessons we couldn't provide."

This was the Godbouts' first experience in hiring a nanny. They now chuckle when they remember certain Nancy incidents.

SUPER NANNY

You walk in the house and hear sounds of laughter. The kids and your nanny are in the kitchen telling funny stories. Everyone is having a great time. You enter the kitchen and say hello. You find out that homework has been done, dinner is almost ready, and everyone is glad you're home because now your five-year-old can finally push out the baby tooth that's been hanging by a thread. It is the first tooth he's lost and your nanny encouraged him to wait until you were home so you could share the experience.

Fantasy? Fairy tale? No, it's the work of Super Nanny!

You notice the toilet roll holder is empty, but are too busy to fill it. You go back later and find it already filled. The children's clothes are mended without prompting. Their fingernails never seem to need cutting. Your toddler puts his dirty clothes in the hamper. The kindergartner sets the table. Your teenager leaves a detailed note stating where he'll be and what time he'll be home.

Magic? Delusion? No, it's Super Nanny!

She dispenses kisses and uses ice and Band-Aids liberally for the minor physical scrapes. She always has an ear and soothing advice for the emotional ones. She knows when it's important to be tough about a rule and when it is better not to be. *Her judgment is remarkably similar to yours.* She rejoices in the day's triumphs—a friend made or a math test passed—and has real empathy for the disappointments.

She's Super Nanny!

Although Super Nanny shares some characteristics with the Boss—they both take initiative and define their roles broadly—she's very different. Rather than view herself as pseudo mom or dad, she acts more like nurturing aunt. She cares for your children like a loving relative and she doesn't want to take your place. She fosters *your* relationship with your children. She often nurtures you. She's confident enough to know that when your children turn to *you* for comfort, approval, or soothing, it is not a rejection of *her*.

Super Nanny demonstrates an "I'm here to help you attitude" rather than an "I'm here to help myself" one. She continues to call or send the children cards on their birthdays long after she's left your employment. As one mom said, "Jan was with us for four years and she still is an adopted member of our family even though she doesn't work for us now. She is an aunt and her son is a cousin. She was recently at my son's birthday, which we held at a bowling alley. We had twenty kids and I lost it. I just couldn't manage. Jan took over. She organized a game with a jump rope and within a few minutes had at least sixteen of the kids under control. She is so in tune with children, it doesn't matter if she knows them or not." Super Nanny is truly a Nanny from Heaven.

She's glad when you're home. She doesn't view you as competitor—a perception that many Bosses hold—but rather as the other member of the team. Now that you are here, she can go off and do her "own thing." She worked hard in your absence and welcomes the opportunity to be relieved. Yet even on her days off, she would never lock a child out of her room or fail to stop on her way out of the house to admire a child's newly painted picture.

There is no foolproof way to know the person you are hiring is a Super Nanny short of only hiring someone who has lots of experience and references that reflect excellence. The problem is, Super Nannies with lots of experience rarely come on the market. Families who employ them hang on to them as long as possible, sometimes arranging other jobs when they don't need them full-time because the children are spending more and more time at school. We heard about Super Nannies becoming teacher's assistants, lab technicians, chefs, and office assistants, jobs tied to the profession of one of the parents, in order to keep the nanny part of the family.

The most likely place to find an unengaged Super Nanny is in a novice nanny. She may be the eldest in a large family, who has taken care of siblings and baby-sat since she was young, but an equal number of Super Nannies were middle or youngest children. Regardless of family background, however, a Super Nanny is eager to please, hardworking, and willing to learn. And most of all she has a nurturing personality. These traits can be exhibited in many settings, such as care for the elderly or animals, not just in child care. So, if your potential hire does not have a lot of child care experience, explore the other jobs she has had by talking to as many people as you can who know her and listen carefully to see if several people mention these traits.

Super Nannies are not perfect. Ours was grumpy in the morning and sometimes lost her patience toward the end of the day.
Super Nannies are super because they genuinely care. Their caring
means that they put the children's needs first. As one Super Nanny
put it, "I can't say that I've loved the children I've cared for like a
parent because I've never been a parent. But I do know that if a
truck were coming at us, I would jump in front of it to save these
kids." This woman, who had been a nanny for twelve years, also said
that the reason she was a nanny was that "you get so much from it. I
feel like I am a real influence in the children's lives. I get not only
affection and love from them, I also get the satisfaction of knowing
I've helped them become confident, caring people. There aren't
many jobs where you can feel this way—that what you are doing is
important and makes a difference."

The nurturing side to Super Nannies can be dangerous for the
nanny. Since she gives her all to the job, to the kids, and to you, she
sometimes will burn out physically or emotionally. Super Nannies
who work for families who are undergoing periods of stress because
of divorce, work problems, or financial or health difficulties are in
particular danger of overload and burnout. If this describes your
family situation and you have a Super Nanny working for you, protect her well-being as best you can by arranging for her to have
plenty of downtime. If she cares too much or works too hard, she
will eventually fizzle and not be able to work at all.

A Super Nanny is a rare gem, valuable beyond remuneration.
If you are unfortunate enough to lose one, you will discover the difficulty of finding a replacement.

The Super Nanny in the following story did not appear initially
to be good nanny material. As Elaine Kildare told it, she was at first
hesitant to hire Jill because she was so young and she smoked. In
retrospect, the decision to hire was an excellent one. Jill, the Super
Nanny, made a positive contribution not only to Elaine's child, but
to Elaine herself.

She Is Wonderful, Drives a Jaguar, and Earns Ten Times More Than I Do

ELAINE KILDARE'S STORY

Elaine hired a young woman who was no more than a child herself to care for her daughter, Lizzy. She was all of seventeen or eighteen and on the surface was not the world's most desirable nanny. She chain-smoked, drove a truck, and came from a broken home. Her dad called her a few times, but during the three years she lived with Elaine, she didn't speak to her mother at all.

This woman's name was Jill. She was about five feet, two inches tall and had long brown hair, which she always wore in a ponytail. She was not only a fantastic nanny, she was one of the most inspirational people Elaine ever met. She was one of those people who had risen from the depths and become a stellar person. You could not help but love and admire her.

Jill believed anything was possible if you tried hard enough. Her whole attitude was "We can do this! Oh yes, we can do this. No problem." She was almost always "up." And she genuinely loved Elaine's daughter. Photography was her hobby and the walls of her room were covered with pictures of Lizzy. What more could a parent ask for?

Elaine would come home and find them both laughing while they played some game on the floor. Jill was always excited about what they had done together during the day. She would find great, inexpensive places to take Lizzy. One of Elaine's strongest memories is of Jill asking her, "Please, please can I pick Lizzy up early at day care so I can take her to a neat park I've found? Do you mind if we go out for pizza afterward? There's a wonderful mechanical pony to ride at this pizza parlor near the park."

She was enthusiastic, fun-loving, and full of energy. She had a heart of gold. As a single mother, struggling to handle a

continued

lot of conflicting responsibilities, Elaine found her life being influenced a great deal by the person who took care of her child. It was a joy to come home to someone as optimistic and energized as Jill. She provided companionship to Elaine as well as to her child.

Elaine explained, "At the time, I couldn't afford to pay very much for child care so I gave Jill a very small salary in addition to room and board. We lived in a modest rented house. One day, the landlord sent me a notice saying that my rent would soon be raised a significant amount. It made me really depressed; I was just managing to get by. I was already working an extra job. I didn't know how I was going to handle a larger rent bill.

"Jill refused to accept the situation. 'Why don't you find a nice cheap house to buy?' she asked me. 'Then you won't have to worry about rent increases again.'

"Here was this kid suggesting I take a leap I would never even dream of by myself. I mean, I had never done anything so financially incredible in my life."

" 'No,' I told her. 'I wouldn't know how to go about finding a house. First of all, I can't afford very much. And then, when would I get the time to look?'

"Jill was her same old, 'Don't worry, we can do it!'

"Do you know what happened? In her off-hours, Jill went real estate shopping. In the beginning, she didn't even tell me she was doing this. After several weeks of house hunting, when she had found two houses she thought I might like, she told me what she had done. I couldn't believe it! One evening Jill said she had a surprise for me. She hid the real estate fliers behind her back, and then like a showman she whipped them out, saying 'Ta-dum!' I loved both places. They were both affordable and really cute. The one I chose was quite far away in the hills, which is why it was priced so low. It had a wonderful view and even had a children's playground built in the backyard. With some help from my parents, I was able to make the down payment. That house, a cottage really, turned out to be

continued

the best investment I've ever made. I wouldn't be able to afford the house I'm now living in if Jill hadn't taken the initiative and convinced me to take a chance.

"Jill left after three years to follow a boyfriend who was moving away. We talked to each other a few years ago. The boyfriend had not worked out, but Jill's work life was going well. She had gone into real estate sales. She loves her profession and now makes at least ten times more than I do!

"I knew her as a little girl who drove a truck. Now she handles million-dollar real estate deals and drives a Jaguar."

At the time this story took place, Elaine Kildare was a medical resident earning a modest income. She was also the single mother of a young daughter. A resident works long hours, and often must work during weekends and evenings. Thus, Elaine was faced with the necessity of finding affordable child care that was also flexible. She ended up putting her daughter in day care for part of each weekday. She hired a live-in nanny to assist the remaining time.

THE QUEEN BEE

In body type the Queen Bee can be anything from thin and lanky to heavy. She tends to have a lot of energy; most likely she has a bubbling personality and often a big smile. The most distinguishing feature of the Queen Bee, however, is people. She likes to be surrounded by lots of them; men or women or both. She has a large circle of friends and you can find her at the center of this circle. She's the one who knows everything about everyone. Her friends use her as a shoulder to cry on, rely on her to arrange the weekend outings, and spend as much time at your house as at their own. She is the Queen Bee. So if you decide to hire her, know up front that there will always be a lot of activity buzzing around her.

Queen Bees can make very good nannies and are often viewed by their employers as Nannies from Heaven. They tend to play actively with younger children of both sexes and get along well with teenage girls. They are slightly less well suited to taking care of older boys since they act like teenagers themselves in some ways and may be too flirtatious to make a good caretaker of a preteen or teenage boy. But they make good listeners for children of all ages, can be inventive in developing interesting activities, and are always willing to go on excursions.

Queen Bees like action. Don't hire one if you have a baby that you would prefer to stay at home or not be exposed to other kids. This is too boring for a Queen Bee. She will want to be surrounded by her friends—nannies with children (and their illnesses) of their own to look after. However, if your children are older and want the stimulation of other children, the Queen Bee can usually organize a play group from her circle of acquaintances.

Make sure if you hire a Queen Bee that she gets her own phone and is financially responsible for it. Otherwise, her phone bills will make her look like a Nanny from Hell. The telephone is a vital component of a Queen Bee's existence. If she can't be near her friends physically, she will be on the phone talking to them at every possible minute. It is her command central. Even if you insist that she have her own phone, expect her to be on yours during working hours. After all, she'll explain patiently, she needs to be near the children, and she can't hear the phone in her room ring while she is doing her job.

The family who employs a Queen Bee will get to know a lot of the nannies in the area, all of their problems, and a good many of the problems of the families who employ them. As one parent said, "I felt like we were running a safe house for nannies. On three occasions we even had nannies who were between jobs living with us.

"Her friends were always over. We got to know some of them pretty well. While she would sleep in on Saturday morning, one or two of them would be up, joining our family. I heard about their problems, their love lives, and I even heard from one of them that our nanny was leaving."

As the employer of a Queen Bee you'll be privy to information about fights other nannies have with their employers, family secrets, and all sorts of titillating gossip. A famous professional football player lives about ten miles away from us. We knew long before the local newspapers did that he was not going to be playing for his team in the coming season. We also knew that his injured arm, totally healed and functioning well according to press reports, had not in fact recovered. How did we know all this? Our Queen Bee knew a nanny who knew his nanny. While being impressed by this insider knowledge, we forgot to question what the football player knew about *our* family. Somehow, it is easy to forget that Queen Bees, in order to stay at the center of the hive of activity, give out information as well as gather it.

So, before you get too smug about the insider position you have as a result of being the employer of a Queen Bee, remind yourself regularly that nothing that goes on in your household will be kept confidential no matter what assurances to the contrary your Queen Bee gives you. Trouble with your boss? The families in your neighborhood will know the details. Had a miscarriage? People you don't even know will give you their condolences as you drop the kids off at school. No amount of direction or instruction to keep your family business private will prevent the Queen Bee from broadcasting it on nanny airwaves, so don't waste your breath in trying.

Should you and your Queen Bee come to a parting of ways, expect the scene to be emotional and for you to be cast as the villains all over town. Don't worry, however. The many nannies you have met through your former Queen Bee will empathize with her, but still remain friendly with you. You will have gotten to know many of them because they will have stayed with you in between jobs, hung around your kitchen moping about love lives gone wrong, and generally been around a lot more than you probably anticipated when you first hired your Queen Bee. Another positive is that despite the inconvenience or annoyance having to find a new nanny causes, the departure of a Queen Bee almost always brings sighs of relief because, unless you hire another Queen Bee, the house will be peaceful and feel wonderfully quiet.

There Is a Free Lunch

THE MICKELYS' STORY

Jake and Megan Mickely interviewed a Scandinavian au pair, recommended by a friend of theirs. They had never hired an au pair before, but since she was already in this country and could be interviewed, they were tempted. Megan Mickely explained, "I have to admit, the fact that she was asking for a much smaller salary than we had been accustomed to paying was also an enticement. I asked her what she was currently making, and when she told me, I realized I could give her a raise of several hundred dollars a month and still pay a great deal less than I had paid our previous nanny. When I excitedly told Jake about the hire, and how much we would be saving in child care costs, he warned me that 'there is no free lunch.' But he was wrong. We both know now that there are plenty of free lunches. We know because we provided them.

"In the beginning, things went very well with Tussie, our au pair. She was friendly, sort of chatty. I needed her to work an hour in the morning and then to work the afternoon. She always showed up for work on time, which I appreciated. She did seem to like to be out of the house a lot, but I didn't mind.

"Then things changed. I don't know if it was because she felt more comfortable with us or because one of her friends left to return to Scandinavia and that person's house had been the one where her friends congregated. Or it could have been because we asked her not to take our daughter Allison to any house that had a swimming pool—a feature of several of her friends' houses—because she didn't swim, yet loved to jump in water. All I know is, suddenly our house became the club house for all the Scandinavian au pairs in the area.

"Again, at first I didn't mind. I liked the fact that Allison was home more, even if the trade-off was that the house seemed to always have strange children and caretakers in it. I didn't object to feeding several 'guests' every day for lunch.

continued

Even when Tussie had gone out in the mornings, she had usually taken a gourmet picnic lunch for 'just a few.' As she herself pointed out, our compensation included board. And since she didn't eat very much—she was slender and rarely ate—why should I complain if she gave food to some of her friends? I didn't question her actions because I didn't want to seem petty. After all, despite my much bigger food bills since she had arrived, I was still ahead of the game financially when I compared her salary with the cost of live-out help I had had previously. So I overlooked the food issue. I also didn't complain when one or two of her friends seemed always to be at the dinner table. It was breakfast that was the turning point."

"Can I have the newspaper?" Jake asked Tussie's friend at the breakfast table. It is true he was a tiny bit rude. He could have said "please"—a point Tussie later pointed out. But, actually, Megan said she was glad he didn't. They both had just realized that the person reading Jake's newspaper had been breakfasting with them for five days straight. She was not someone who was just dropping by to play with Allison, the explanation they had been given for her presence. She was living with them.

"It took us five days to figure this out because our house was always being visited by one or more of our au pair's friends. Sometimes they came with their children. More often than not, they were alone. Actually, a better word is 'unaccompanied,' because no one was alone in our household during the time Tussie worked for us."

Jake's "attitude" made Tussie's friend feel unwelcome, which in turn upset Tussie. She talked to the Mickelys about it, saying that her friends were the most important thing in her life and if they didn't feel welcome, neither did she. They tried to compromise. Tussie had many good points, not the least of which was that Allison liked her. They suggested Tussie limit her visits to friends who had children the same age as Allison. Tussie didn't like the limitation. She argued that the reason

continued

everyone came to the Mickelys' was their restrictions on where she was permitted to take Allison. If she were allowed to take Allison out all afternoon, Tussie and her friends could meet elsewhere. The Mickelys couldn't agree to this. So they ended up agreeing to end the relationship. Tussie found a job almost immediately; her friends saw to that.

Megan explained, "I dreaded having to look for child care again, but felt almost elated by the prospect of having the house to myself again. On her last day one of the several friends who had come to help Tussie pack called out from the pantry, 'Gee, I'm glad you're getting out of here. These people don't have anything good to eat.' "

Megan said she smiled when she overheard the remark. They had finally gotten the message.

The Mickleys have continued to hire other au pairs from Scandinavia since their first experience with this one. They say they are very satisfied.

THE PERPETUAL TEENAGER

The Perpetual Teenager—a person of any age—hates to follow rules. She views you as her parents against whom she is rebelling. Perpetual Teenagers are often also Queen Bees or Party Girls. They can also show up as Princesses.

The Perpetual Teenager is often passive-aggressive. She will agree with you on the surface, but is really angry deep down at what she perceives as interference. She will follow your directions incompletely, incorrectly, or she will just plain "forget" them. She does more than her fair share of breaking things. Usually, however, she does her job adequately but rarely contributes anything beyond what is spelled out precisely. She may take good care of the kids—she probably sympathizes with them for having to endure parents—but will stiffen up when you enter the room. Or she may just get out of the way when you appear. What seems like passivity, however, is really a deep-seated resentment of authority. Over time this will become clear.

The Perpetual Teenager may seem like a Nanny from Heaven at first. It takes time to identify her as the Nanny from Hell, whom she often turns out to be really because she can be very good at hiding her feelings. She rarely expresses resentment directly and can seem cooperative in the beginning. And since she can be very playful with children, you will like her.

When the Perpetual Teenager unleashes her anger, which will inevitably occur, you will be surprised at the depth and extent of it. You might not have even suspected it was there. Thinking back over the situation, you will realize in retrospect that she had been resentful all along. The signs or clues she has left—broken rules, banged-up autos, lack of punctuality, and reluctance to reveal anything about her personal life—were more than just accidents or mistakes. As one parent said, "My first impression when she flew off the handle was that she had flipped out and become crazy. She started raving about needing the day off. I reminded her that I had discussed working this particular day several weeks in advance. I had put it on the calendar. It was the day we were having our family portraits done and I needed her help. All the time I was explaining this it felt like I was talking to a monster. Her face was contorted in fury. Frankly, I was in shock. I always thought of her as being calm. I realized now she wasn't calm, just controlled. Thinking back over the time she spent with us, every time I gave her instructions, which wasn't very often because I'm usually not home when she is here, she tightened up. She must have been angry for a long time. I just didn't realize it."

The Perpetual Teenager just doesn't have what it takes to do a good job caring for children, especially in a home setting. She's usually not a pure Nanny from Hell. (One Perpetual Teenager we know about, though, was definitely a Nanny from Hell—she was observed hurting a child. After she was fired she filed child abuse charges against the parents!) She can relate well to children. However, all of her skill with children is not enough to offset her powerful need to be an adversary toward you, the person she misperceives to be her parent thwarting her independence. This adversarial relationship is bound to have a detrimental effect on your children sooner or later.

The important thing to remember when dealing with a Perpetual Teenager or when analyzing what went wrong when she either furiously storms out the door or you terminate her because her attitude infuriates you, is that she isn't really rebelling against *you*. Problems in her relationship with her own parents remain unresolved. Your family will receive the brunt of this.

A clue that you are dealing with a Perpetual Teenager is the discrepancy between the situation and her response to it. When her reaction to instruction is too extreme—she sulks all day in response to your request that she keep a screen door closed—chances are you are dealing with a Perpetual Teenager. No amount of discussion or counseling will change this. If you are desperate for child care, you may decide to live with the situation for awhile. But Perpetual Teenagers rarely stay in jobs very long, so even if you try not to behave parentally toward her, she will eventually find something to justify getting upset and leaving.

The "Secret Sauce Nanny"

THE WALKERS' STORY

Erin and Isaac Walker told me this story about a thirty-six-year-old teenager they once employed. Erin did most of the narrating.

"We hired a nanny named Lucy. One of my first memories is asking her to put the lids on the outside trash barrels and she blurted out, 'I wasn't the one who left them off!'

"Lucy came from South America and brought with her a very secret sauce recipe she had developed. She had the ambition of selling it to an American food company and making millions. In her interview she was very emphatic that she loved to cook and would consider it a positive if I let her prepare most of the meals. It did not take much convincing to get me to agree.

"Eight days later, after every dinner made in the meantime had been smothered with this special and very secret sauce, I decided I needed to intervene. At first we just swallowed bravely. Then, we allowed the kids to eat yogurt and

continued

fruit for dinner (after "just one taste of dinner so you'll know what you are missing"), but by now it was clear no matter how much menu planning, coaching, hints, or suggestions that we didn't need sauce every night, no matter what she cooked, the meal would taste the same. So I decided on the direct approach. Well, not exactly the direct approach. Because after all, she was new, and I didn't want to undermine her initiative or self-esteem.

" 'I think you shouldn't make any sauce tonight,' I suggested, diplomatically I thought. One look at the devastation on her face and I knew I was in trouble.

" 'Don't you like it?' she asked, crestfallen and with just a hint of suggestion that perhaps I was a jealous chef who did not like to be outclassed in the kitchen.

" 'It's just that my husband'—husbands are great as excuses—'has a weak stomach,' I continued, 'and chutney and chili aren't good for him.'

" 'You know my secret ingredients!' she cried in outrage. 'I just knew someone would steal my recipe. How did you guess?' she accused as she stormed out of the kitchen. 'Did you spy on me?'

"I looked at her shopping list hanging innocently on the refrigerator door and sighed. It was headed by a request for eight jars of ginger chutney and two cans of chili."

The Walkers have two children who now love spicy food.

THE PROFESSIONAL

You will be excited when she answers your ad or the agency recommends her. She has had lots and lots of child care experience, some of it long-term. She will tell you about the twins she cared for since birth or the little girl she helped raise from ages three to ten. She is competent, she's trustworthy, she commands a high salary. She's a professional nanny. She can be a Nanny from Heaven, or at least she appears to be from her credentials and experience.

Families who hire professional nannies speak highly of them and with good reason. With a professional nanny you can rest assured your child is safe, will be fed properly, and will have his or her hair combed. The Professional will be very clear about her expectations, how many children she likes to care for at once, her favorite ages. You will also know up front her needs in terms of benefit package and salary. As one professional nanny I interviewed said, "I start off in the beginning of the interview stating my salary needs, that I expect eight sick days, eight holidays, two weeks' vacation, and medical insurance. I then explain that I expect to be paid whether or not they go on vacation or don't need me for some reason. I have bills to pay and being a nanny is my occupation. I promise to work the hours agreed; my employer needs to assure me I will be paid for these hours even if I am not needed to work. I also stipulate that I will be on time reporting to work, and I appreciate the parent being on time to relieve me." Lest her remarks be taken out of context, let me explain that she is a wonderful nanny, considered by her employer, who suggested I speak with her, a Nanny from Heaven. Her insistence on discussing her own requirements before those of the family comes from her view that being a nanny is a profession that she takes more seriously than some families do.

Professionals who care for infants will have them napping on a regular schedule, take them for walks in a stroller, and sometimes sing to them. Those who care for toddlers will read to them, teach them to dress themselves, and engage in lots of imaginative play. The Professional will supervise older children's schoolwork and make sure rules are followed.

What more could any parent want?

Enjoyment. Excitement at a task newly learned. Energy. Some, though by all means not all, Professionals are just that—professional. They don't often engage in that personal "you really mean something to me" way that is so much a component of Super Nanny and other Nannies from Heaven.

This doesn't mean that professional nannies don't grow fond of the children in their care. They do, but in a detached way. Caring for your children is a job, a highly personal one, but a job nonetheless. The paycheck is a prime motivator. The Professional is not to be faulted for this attitude. She is less likely to burn out than Super Nanny. And she does have motivators other than monetary compensation. Pride in a job well done is one. A sense of competence is another. The affection that children display toward her is another. Money comes first, however; these other compensations are definitely secondary.

You could certainly do a whole lot worse than having a Professional care for your children. Many, many parents expressed gratitude that one had worked for them. These nannies are stable, predictable, and will be long-timers as long you treat them with respect and compensate well. Children grow accustomed to relying on them. Their even-tempered, unruffled personalities can be a real asset in a household that has experienced upheaval or too much nanny turnover. Missing from most Professionals, however, is that spark of excitement, the genuine joy at seeing a youngster accomplish something for the first time. Like many experts who have spent a great deal of time at their jobs, the Professional no longer is moved by some of the magic of watching a child develop. Children realize this, whether overtly or subconsciously. Since much of what a child thinks about herself or himself is a mirror of what the important adults in his or her life see in the child, a child raised by a Professional may not experience the feeling of being special or uniquely wonderful. It is subtle, but a loss nevertheless.

Most Professionals refuse to work for an at-home parent. A Professional who will, though, can be a big asset to an inexperienced at-home parent. Unlike the Boss, she will not be competitive. However, for families in which both parents are gone all day, she is probably better suited to care for older children whose needs are more centered on transportation and homework supervision than on genuine emotional involvement. On the other hand, even for families with small children, the Professional is a much better choice than a Princess, Party Girl, or Perpetual Teenager, who may not be trustworthy in ensuring the basics such as safety, quality nutrition, and consistent boundaries—things at which the Professional excels.

The Professional Job Hunts

CULLEN McGEE'S STORY

Cullen, a professional nanny for several years, needed a new job. Her position with the Knight family was coming to an end because the two boys were going to be in school full-time and the family had concluded they could not afford to continue paying the top wages Cullen commanded for the few hours of child care they would now need. Following are excerpts from the diary Cullen kept during her job search, an extension of the diary she had kept about the activities of the children in her care.

Monday: I register with the most well known agency in this area. I am somewhat disappointed. They aren't very thorough. All they really want is paperwork; the interview doesn't cover many of the questions I was asked when I was placed with the Knights [by another agency, now defunct]. They refused to put down my requested salary and instead put down a lower figure. I felt less than secure as I left their offices.

The head of the agency leaves a message on my telephone answering machine and says that eleven families are interested in me. I begin fielding calls almost immediately.

The first family lives an hour away. They have a little boy and are expecting a second child, sex unknown. I much prefer boys and although I don't mind infants prefer toddlers and school-age kids. They request that I come right away for an interview but I refuse. I've had a tough weekend and I need some time to unwind. I agree to come tomorrow night.

Tuesday: The woman sounded so normal over the phone.

She's a schizophrenic who needs a "little selfish time" for herself and sometimes the two-year-old is more than she can handle. Eye contact is not her strong suit. Cute kid, but that mother needs some help.

Wednesday: I tell the agency there is no way I will work for that family. I want to care for children, not adults, and that

continued

woman is a high-maintenance basket case. The owner tells me they loved me and she told them I would get back to them after a few more interviews.

I hook up with another agency. I like the fact that they don't balk when I tell them how much salary I want. Also, they do a thorough background check on me. I have no intention of working for a family who would trust their children to a stranger, so that is reassuring.

The agency requires notarized proof of my car insurance even though I told them I owned an old, tiny car and would not work for a family who expected me to tote their kids around in my own car. Might as well let them Roller blade down the highway, for Christ's sake. The woman from the agency said, "You have very high expectations of these families." You're damn right, I thought. And I suspect the right family will have equally high expectations of me.

Thursday: I interview with a family who has two boys. The mom gets upset that the five-year-old gets chocolate on her white pants. Anyone lacking the sense to wear kid-proof clothing while letting a kid eat dessert on her lap is not getting me for a nanny.

I get home feeling very discouraged. The phone rings. It's an out-of-state woman who offers to fly me out for an interview. She has a private nanny quarters, but when the subject of salary comes up and she isn't willing to meet my expectations, I decline.

Friday: I get a call from a family with three boys. I normally will only work with two children at a time, but the call comes before I am fully awake and I agree. Later in the day I interview with another family. It's not the perfect setting, but they live in a cool place. The biggest problem is instead of paying overtime, they have this goofy idea about a day bank. They want to randomly give me time off during the week and then I owe them the same number of days in overtime when they need me. It's not for me.

continued

A family in Texas gives me an offer. The job sounds good: two boys in school full-time, private apartment, decent overtime pay. They say that instead of health insurance they will treat me for free because they are both doctors. Sayonara.

I get another call. The family has one child, is expecting a baby in six months, and then the mom will cut back at work. I will get full pay but only have to work four days a week. The hours are short too. I'm interested.

Saturday: I go for the interview and the parents are nice, but I have some misgivings which are hard to verbalize. The nanny's room is minute, but that isn't it. Also, although they describe themselves as being laid-back, when I see their pantry . . . Every can and label is in perfect alignment. Laid-back? I doubt it. The clincher comes when we discuss job duties. They expect me to do "light housekeeping." No way, Jose. I look after children, period. That's the only way I can do a good job; my full attention needs to be on the kids.

Sunday: I interview with the family that has three children. They don't blink when I tell them my salary and job expectations. The boys are ages which I like. The parents and I click. Child care is to be my one and only priority. We both decide to talk one more time. Maybe, maybe this is the one.

Cullen ended up accepting the job with the three boys.

AMONG THE CROOKS AND NANNIES

Okay, I'll admit it. I almost didn't include this category. Why? Because most of the publicity given to nannies lumps them in this category even though only a small number of nannies qualify. Movies such as *The Hand That Rocks the Cradle* and the *Baby-sitter* are not about the typical nanny. They dramatize the dangerous, the evil. True, the Crooks are Nannies from Hell. However, they seldom are truly evil. Some are just incompetent, others untrustworthy, still others are thieves. But most will not physically harm the children or their parents. And they are generally easy to spot. You'll know pretty soon that the nanny you have hired doesn't have a clue about appropriate, age-relevant behavior or discipline if she puts your infant in his crib and shuts the door just because he didn't co-operate. It won't take long for you to realize your child care provider is overly critical of the children, uses inappropriate language, or is abusive in any way. The response to these situations is clear and most parents do not have any trouble reacting appropriately, which is to get rid of the nanny.

The two signs that surfaced repeatedly in stories about Crooks were repeated lying and dishonesty about money. For example, one family told me about the six foot, three inch, incredibly beautiful woman they hired. They said, "She came with a thick folder of references, all saying she was terrific. She was only with us for three or four months, but almost immediately we noticed she lied. It seemed trivial in the beginning and we gave her the benefit of the doubt. She would do things like give the kids ice cream and then tell them not to tell us. She said she didn't smoke, but we found butts in the trash and in the nanny car. The grocery change was always short. I would miss my shampoo and notice a bottle exactly like it in her bathroom. There were a hundred little things. She left without notice and we later discovered she had hundreds of dollars worth of parking tickets, we had a huge overseas phone bill, and we were sued because she had been involved in a hit-and-run and never told us. We should have fired her immediately, but were afraid to hurt her feelings. We didn't have *real* proof she was lying or stealing. We've since decided that we will only hire and keep someone who is absolutely honest."

Another parent told me, "I automatically assumed that if I trusted someone with my kids, I could trust them with my money. And when I employed someone, I didn't want to offend the person by checking on them, such as asking for receipts or questioning where the household cash had gone. After the experience I had with one nanny, someone who worked for us off and on for two and a half years, I've changed my mind. She seemed to be a good nanny; my daughter loved her. She worked part-time for us while she was attending a culinary academy. She always arrived on time to our house and seemed to have a good head on her shoulders. She came from a large family and all of the children had gotten into trouble with the law. I thought she was different. Then she decided to move in with us; I later realized it was because she was in financial trouble. It was during a terrible time for me: my mom died, I had to commute out of state to help my dad, and I closed one of my businesses—a dress shop—and moved the inventory into my house because I couldn't cope with the stress. My second child was born premature and was on a heart monitor; I had to keep him near me at all times. So much was going on that I didn't realize I wasn't getting my credit card statements. Also, when I would meet my nanny's friends wearing clothes that looked familiar, it didn't dawn on me that they were from my inventory. Our nanny decided to move out and we lent her money for an apartment. Then she disappeared. I then got a notice that my credit card was being canceled for nonpayment. It took me several months to straighten out the financial mess and to reconstruct what had happened. It turned out our nanny had used my card number to buy a fortune's worth of stuff as well as to finance several out-of-town weekends with friends. We never prosecuted her, but I heard from other people other dishonest things she did. I still feel hurt when I think about it. I once considered her a friend."

But what if you don't actually observe deviancy? What if all you have to go on is a child's changed behavior? What do you do if you suspect your nanny is not telling the truth about something, but you don't know for sure? Or the children appear well cared for, but you are missing things from the house? How suspicious do you have to be before you take action? Not all Crooks are easily identifiable.

Crooks, whether they harm your possessions or your children and whether the harm is physical or emotional, are Nannies from Hell. You need to get them out of your house, away from your children as soon as possible. And if you only suspect, but don't know for sure, that you are dealing with a Crook, act anyway. This may be unfair advice for some nannies, but to use a worn-out but appropriate platitude: better safe than sorry. I never once interviewed a family who regretted terminating a suspected Crook too early. I talked to several who waited too long. Parents inevitably bend over backwards to give their child care givers a fair shake. You and your children deserve protection. If you have the slightest gut feeling things are amiss, take appropriate action and don't wait for "proof."

She Turned Our Family Upside Down

THE CHASES' STORY

Marcie Chase was pregnant with her second child. She hired a nanny who was older, thinking that all she really wanted was someone to hold the new baby, since their first child, Samantha, was due to start school. The person they hired came from out of state and was referred by an agency. She had raised a family and was represented as being very competent with children. Somehow her references checked out.

Marcie says she still does not know how this could be the case, because the nanny, Margaret, was simply awful. In the first place, she lied about her age. She had told the agency she was forty-eight, but when she arrived it was clear she was at least fifty-eight, wanting to be thirty-eight. The Chases were told Margaret was divorced, but when she arrived she told them she was still married, but that her husband was out of work and had financial troubles. She had agreed to do some housework during their phone interview. When she arrived she told Marcie she had rheumatism and couldn't do any. She also refused to cook, saying she was a terrible cook. Marcie decided that if the nanny loved her child everything else was immaterial.

From the first day Margaret came, the house seemed like it was in turmoil. Marcie couldn't pinpoint exactly what she did to cause this. It just happened. Margaret would do things like give Samantha a whole can of cola and then complain that she wouldn't eat lunch.

The grand finale came when Marcie was home on maternity leave. The baby was due in two weeks. She realized that Samantha was not on any schedule, despite her written in-

continued

structions that this be done. She found being home exhausting.

Marcie explained, "My picture of going into the hospital and having things be okay at home collapsed. Margaret had such a complicated personal life—her husband called all the time, she was worried about money, about the dogs she had left behind, about one of her sons who she couldn't find. She was an emotional basket case and I was rapidly becoming one too. I talked to her about her being distracted. I even suggested that she should consider going home to straighten out her personal life. She became immensely offended and insisted nothing was wrong.

"My due date came and I was exhausted. I had been working harder than ever caring for my daughter and the house since Margaret had arrived. The doctor gave me strict orders to slow down, but I just didn't seem able to because Samantha always ran to me when Margaret was around. David stepped in. He told Margaret, 'Your number-one priority is to let my wife rest.' He left for work and I went into my room to take a nap and heard Margaret and Samantha on the patio just outside my room. Margaret was on a mobile telephone talking to one of her children. Samantha was at my door, knocking and calling to me. I then heard Margaret come to the door and pull Samantha away, at which point Samantha cried loudly. I finally got up to see what was wrong. Margaret explained her crying by saying she was tired. We put her down for a nap, but when she woke up she continued to cry. After an hour of this, I realized something might be physically wrong. I called David and asked him to meet me at the doctor's because I couldn't carry Sam in.

"The doctor examined Samantha and said her arm was out of the socket and that probably somebody had pulled it too hard. He made an adjustment and after a momentary yell, Samantha was quiet. Needless to say we were furious, since the most probable cause of the injury was the pull Margaret had given her arm earlier that day. Not only was Samantha being

continued

hurt, but David's world was being turned upside down too since he didn't feel he could risk going to work.

"We decided to get rid of Margaret even though I really needed child care help. It turned out that getting rid of her wasn't that easy. I'll spare you the details, but suffice it to say that it took several days, we had to purchase an expensive airline ticket, and after she left, I realized she had cleaned out my wallet and taken all the money from our 'household emergency' money jar. I still get angry thinking about her."

Concluding her story, Marcie told me, "We have never had our life in such turmoil; we've never felt so much emotional exhaustion as we did with this nanny. And I *paid* her to do this to me."

David and Marcie switched their daughter to a family day care in their neighborhood. When their second child, a boy, was a couple of years old, they once again tried home child care. This time they hired a former high school friend who was looking for a way to supplement her income while she looked after her own child. They said the arrangement worked out great for everyone.

THE PARTY GIRL

She is pretty and she can be vivacious. She likes music, dancing, fast vehicles, and males of all ages. She's a Party Girl.

Not all pretty, vivacious, male-loving nannies are Party Girls. Party Girls are distinguished by one characteristic: The jobs they do are viewed as means to an end and the end is having a good time. Whether it is waitressing, retailing, or hotel clerking—all common work experiences for Party Girls—the job is viewed as a necessary evil in order to earn the money to enable her to have fun.

The males in your household will think the Party Girl is terrific, at least at first. She flatters, flirts, and takes good care of them. Your children may like her a great deal too. She is probably the type who will get down on the floor and play with them as long as they like. The Party Girl has components of a Nanny from Heaven, at least while she is able to focus on the job.

However, if the truth be told, the Party Girl usually turns out to be a Nanny from Hell. She seldom has the maturity to discipline appropriately (most are too strict, rather than too lenient), is too self-focused to be tuned in to the real needs of the children, and seldom stays long enough to form real attachments with your family. The mom in one household said, "I never could trust her completely with the kids. Her love life, her need for excitement, and her focus on men meant that the things I considered of most importance, namely my children, were forgotten in a flash if she got within ten feet of some guy she thought was cute. And her definition of cute was pretty liberal. Some of the men she went out with were pretty slimy looking. I worried that she was meeting them during her working hours. I really wouldn't be surprised if she selected activities for the children based on who she could meet there."

Party Girls share some characteristics with Perpetual Teenagers. They don't like any restrictions on their freedom. And they usually are not good at keeping commitments. One parent said, "I have employed the same summer nanny for three years and you would think by now I would know not to trust her assurance she will be on time and will not go away during the summer. I should know better. This year she once again promised faithfully that she would not take any trips, yet after she had worked for three weeks she informed me she would be away for a week. A new boyfriend invited her to go to Hawaii and she simply could not turn the invitation down." Another parent related, "I know I can't trust her to be alone with the children for any period of time. She just doesn't stay focused and often times she is late for work. The kids love her, however. She's fun. I'm not wild about some of the things she exposes them to—they hear the plots to all the latest adult movies and learn to sing the Top 40 hits and to dance the newest dances from her—but by and large she's harmless and they look forward to her coming."

Party girls are not their best in the morning. To be more precise, I'm referring to the morning hour when work starts. A Party Girl is in her best form at 2:00 or 3:00 A.M. when she returns home.

She also causes more than her share of banged-up autos. She often receives phone calls just after you've gone to sleep.

Employing a Party Girl is not all bad. After she's gone, you will appreciate a quieter, less bubbly type of child care person. Your children, however, might complain that their new nanny is not as much fun.

The Hanukkah Nanny

THE COHENS' STORY

Veronica and Irving Cohen hired a young woman named Linda. She was twenty-one and her main interest was where the next party was going to be held. The first weekend she was with the Cohens she stayed out all night on Saturday night and came back at 3:00 A.M. on Sunday, but stayed outside the house until 4:00 A.M. She needed to be up at 6:30 and so did the family. Needless to say, the Cohens were concerned.

The following morning, Veronica told her that what Linda did on her off-hours was her own business, but that she expected her to get enough sleep so that she could function effectively during the day. Linda was not delighted with Veronica's comments, but did say she would keep the instructions in mind.

The Cohens planned to visit Irving's family for Hanukkah at the end of December. They gave Linda the choice of coming with them or staying at home. She elected to stay home.

They needed to use two cars on the trip and Irving and the kids left several hours before Veronica. Veronica went to the store to get some last-minute things. While she was there she decided to buy a small Christmas tree to bring home to Linda. Their house was decorated with Hanukkah decorations and she thought that a tree would make Linda feel more at home while they were away.

Veronica came home to find that Linda thought she had already left on the trip. While she had been at the store, Linda

continued

had taken down all of the family's decorations and put up Christmas ones everywhere. It turned out she planned to have a party that night, a party she had never discussed with the Cohens.

Veronica finally decided that Linda had to go when she returned home from work early one day and found the kids were all outside while Linda was inside listening to music with earphones on. The kids were too young to be outdoors without supervision and Linda could never have heard them if they needed help.

The Cohens arranged for a cousin to live with them and handle child care. At the time they told this story, the cousin was about to leave and the Cohens had not yet found a replacement.

COUCH POTATOES AND ANTS-IN-THE-PANTS

The Couch Potato and the Ants-in-the-Pants are two opposite manifestations of the same phenomenon. Their predisposition to either inactivity or excessive activity is so great that it influences their abilities to relate to and care for children well.

The Couch Potato is usually hefty, but not always. She might also be a Queen Bee in addition to being a Couch Potato. What distinguishes her is her attitude or aptitude toward activity. She would prefer to read than to throw a baseball or play "chase." Watching TV or going to the movies is high on her list of enjoyable activities. She'll take the car rather than walk to the park even if it is close by. And she would rather stay at home than go to the park in the first place. If you insist she go out, she'll elect to sit on a bench and watch the children as they dart from the sandbox to the swings. Instead of climbing up a slide and demonstrating to a cautious youngster that it is not as scary as it seems, she'll offer verbal encouragement from the sidelines.

She can be industrious, dedicated, imaginative, caring—in other words, a good nanny, or even a Nanny from Heaven. She just doesn't move a lot. She is ideally suited to caring for infants, children who are "indoors" types, and children with special needs who require more than the usual amount of patience and emotional support or those who can't manage a lot of physical activity. On the other hand, the Couch Potato is not particularly well suited to active toddlers or older children who want someone to assist them with sports.

Couch Potatoes are fine for some families, less desirable for others. You need to be in touch with your own attitude about physical exertion and your beliefs about the strength of role modeling on children. If at least one of the adults in your household is physically active and encourages the children to be the same (if you think exercise is important in the first place) and you think this is sufficient role modeling, then by all means don't overlook a Couch Potato as a potential nanny. If you are a physically active person yourself who has little tolerance with others who are not, be prepared to modify your beliefs in this area or be continually frustrated by a Couch Potato.

An important consideration in deciding whether to hire or retain a Couch Potato is the needs of your children. Are they whirlwinds of activity who will get into trouble unless someone is physically running after them? Conversely will they endanger the health of a nanny who is unaccustomed to physical exertion and finds herself doing more of it than is comfortable? If so, better steer away from Couch Potatoes. Are your children at the stage where they spend most of their time with friends and don't need an adult to play with them? Do they enjoy projects that require fine motor skills, such as drawing or crafts, more than those involving large motor skills such as climbing, running, and jumping? Are their interests primarily intellectual rather than sports-oriented? A Couch Potato can make a fine caretaker for them.

The Ants-in-the-Pants is characterized by her propensity for movement and the activities she prefers. For the Ants-in-the-Pants, the more active a project, the better. She'll steer your youngster away from computers, books, video games (well, maybe not video games since many give the illusion of motion), TV watching, and art projects toward sports, nature hikes, bicycle trips, and the like.

She'll choose a day at the beach over an excursion to the library, a game of hopscotch over one of jacks. The Ants-in-the-Pants likes to be out of the house, doing something active. At the park she's the one at the top of the jungle gym right along with the children in her charge. She's the one who insists they learn to swim, often having been a swimming teacher herself. She also may have been a soccer coach, a track star, or an ace volleyball player before becoming a nanny.

The Ants-in-the-Pants can be a great companion to young boys and girls who like to play rough. She'll get down on the floor and get a kick out of tossing them around and letting them climb on her back. She'll do calisthenics in your living room and use the baby as a weight. She'll encourage your toddler to sit on her back as she does push-ups.

An Ants-in-the-Pants nanny can sometimes be distracted and may not be particularly well organized. In her hurry to get under way she might forget to take a snack along on excursions. But she will keep the kids so busy having fun that they won't miss the juice boxes she left on the counter at home; they'll happily drink water from the water fountain, something they would never consent to do with you.

The Ants-in-the-Pants and the Couch Potato are Nannies from Heaven for some families, Nannies from Hell for others. The main problem with both is their lack of versatility. Unlike Super Nanny who regularly reads and also wrestles or twirls around the room during pretend ballet, the Couch Potato and the Ants-in-the-Pants are limited by the strength of their respective needs to be sedentary or active. In an extreme case, the Ants-in-the-Pants will be unable to stay indoors at home even if the weather is rotten or the children are feeling ill or lethargic. Her need is so strong, she just can't table her plans to be outdoors. I've also known Couch Potatoes who simply couldn't rouse themselves to get a child interested in a physical activity even when the child would have greatly benefited from the experience.

Of course, few nannies are as extreme as the Couch Potatoes or Ants-in-the-Pants I've described. Most just have predilections one way or another. Just keep in mind these nanny types as you interview and select a nanny. Choose one that matches the needs of your children and your family's personality.

Ping-Pong Hires

THE DARLINGS' STORY

The Darlings have four children: three sons and one daughter. The children are all within six years of each other. Carla Darling explained that she originally looked for a nanny who was very energetic since the demands of looking after four young children are considerable. She found Millie, a twenty-two-year-old farm girl who loved sports. At first the family was delighted with Millie. She arrived in July and kept the children occupied playing with the hose outside, having picnics, and going to parks. By November, however, Millie's need to be on the go all the time didn't seem as terrific as it had in the beginning.

"Millie was so driven by her own needs she was unable to pay attention to mine or the children's," Carla explains. "It took me a while to figure this out because in the beginning the things she liked to do and the needs of the children tracked pretty closely. Then one day I heard crying in one of the children's bedrooms. I went in to find Millie putting my two-year-old, Carter, in a backpack in preparation for a hike and insisting to Jessica, my three-year-old, that she needed to leave her dolls behind. It was Jessica who was crying. She wanted to stay home to play dolls. It was windy and cold outside, hardly optimal weather for a hike under the best of circumstances. I pointed this out to Millie and said going out with the children was a particularly bad idea because Carter was sick. Millie insisted it would be good for the children since *she* was on a diet and needed the exercise."

Millie's need to be active and gone from the house finally conflicted so badly with Carla's desire to have the children close by and available led to a parting of the ways. Carla then sheepishly admitted she made the same mistake in hiring her

continued

next nanny, except that this nanny was driven by the desire to avoid exertion.

"The next person I hired was more of a homebody," Carla elaborated. "The only problem was she not only liked to stay at home, she liked to stay in one place. An ideal job for her would have been to stay all day in a rocking chair holding a baby. My children, on the other hand, are more the rocket-ship than the rocking-chair types. Although our nanny gave me assurances she was an active, play-on-the-floor type of person, she wasn't. I think she probably believed this and just wasn't insightful. This nanny, Dariene, was always on a diet. If I sent her grocery shopping she would forget to buy most of the food on the shopping list and mainly buy ingredients to bake chocolate chip cookies. She would then spend most of the afternoon baking cookies, basically ignoring the children who wanted someone to play with them. Guess who ate most of the cookies?"

At first Dariene didn't have an active social life and stayed home in the evenings. Then all of sudden there was a change and she was going out every night. The clue to her sudden popularity was discovered when Carla looked through a kitchen drawer for a recipe and found a clipping of a personal ad. It said something to the effect that a tall beautiful blond who liked walks on the beach was looking for companionship. It took Carla quite a while to realize that Dariene had written this ad. She was blond. If "tall" and "corpulent" (Dariene weighs at least 260 pounds) are synonymous, then Carla conceded Dariene was also "tall." But, "walks on the beach"? Forget it! Dariene never walked anywhere if she could drive instead.

Carla Darling is a freelance writer. She and her husband, Ben, a business executive, had seven nannies before they found a nanny who stayed with them for several years. They live in Minneapolis.

Evaluating Applicants: A Checklist

Here are some questions to ask yourself as you assess potential nannies so that you make a good match with your family. Remember that most nannies fall into more than one category.

These questions are merely suggestions. They aren't foolproof. More than anything, use your intuition in characterizing a potential nanny.

Is she a Princess?

1. *Does her past experience or training indicate an attraction to glamour?* Participation in beauty contests, cheerleading, modeling, fashion school, beautician school, etc., are clues.
2. *Do her long-term goals tend toward such jobs as flight attendant, model, movie star, or stage performer?* Women who aspire to these professions are not necessarily Princesses, but these goals are red flags. You need to explore the reason these jobs seem attractive. Are her aspirations realistic?
3. *Does she describe failures in previous jobs as always due to circumstances beyond her control? Does she blame former bosses as the reason jobs came to an end?* Princesses often lack the ability to be self-perceptive.
4. *Does the applicant have self-esteem problems that she attempts to solve by a focus on the external—namely, by an overemphasis on the way she looks and how important her job appears to others?*

Is she a Boss?

1. *Is the applicant a first child? Does she come from a substance-abusing or other type of dysfunctional home?* Bosses often grew up in households where they had to function prematurely as adults.
2. *In describing past experiences, does she use a lot of phrases like "I did it all myself," "I was in charge," "No one had to teach me, I picked it up on my own," "No one else was as good as me," "I told everyone how to do it correctly"?*

3. *In previous jobs was she in charge? Was she the manager of the dress shop, the head of the kitchen, the supervisor of the other salespeople? Do you get the impression that she will be happy only if she is head honcho?* Super Nannies also often like to be in charge. What distinguishes Bosses from them is that Bosses are not versatile. They cannot function in any other mode.

4. *Ask her about her favorite and least favorite jobs. Were the jobs she liked least those where someone told her what to do? Were the jobs she liked best ones where she could be independent (such as in sales) or in command? Is she very competitive? If so, will this stand in the way of her being a team player or is she willing to play whatever position is the best fit?*

5. *Is she empathetic?* Bosses often are not.

If you are not sure whether she is a Boss or just a very take-charge person (who could be Super Nanny), ask her former employers how she interacted with them. Did she ever defer to them? If so, was this done easily and graciously?

Is she a Queen Bee?

1. *When asked about what matters most in her life, do friends come near the top of the list?*

2. *What are her favorite activities or hobbies? Are most of them socially oriented?*

3. *Does she give out a lot of personal information about previous employers?*

4. *When asked if she would mind a job where she could not talk to her friends even by telephone while working, does her facial expression or verbal answer indicate this would be unacceptable?*

An affirmative answer to any of the questions above indicates you should be sure to question former employers when you do reference checks about whether this person has Queen Bee tendencies.

Is she a Perpetual Teenager?

1. *When asked about her parents, does she indicate continued conflict with one or the other? Does she admit to being estranged from relatives, siblings, etc., and refuse to discuss it?*
2. *When questioned about relationships with the significant people in her life does she give any indication that she is angry at many of the adults?*
3. *Does she describe former bosses as being totally at fault for the reason previous jobs ended?*
4. *If she has been in trouble, for example, was kicked out of school or got traffic tickets, does she blame it on unreasonable rules? Does any of her past experience indicate an unwillingness to abide by established rules?*

The Perpetual Teenager does not like to play by any rules except the ones she sets for herself. She also tends to be in conflict with many of the adults in her life.

Is she a Professional?

1. *Does she have a lot of long-term child care experience and describe each job in a clinical way, stating the statistics such as numbers of children or hours worked, without communicating any of the emotional aspects of the position?* Professionals often categorize previous jobs in terms of tangibles such as compensation or benefits, ignoring how enjoyable the children were or other intangibles.
2. *When questioned about former experiences, does she refuse to reveal what was wrong with any job, instead saying that all were okay?* Professionals rarely criticize former employers. They've learned that references are key to getting a next job and therefore always attempt to leave with relationships cordial.
3. *Does she have rigid demands about hours, duties, responsibilities, travel, holidays, etc., and also firm requirements about expectations (e.g., "I expect the parents to come home promptly and not be*

late")? Not all professionals are rigid about job conditions and pay, but most are.

4. *Even though she may be friendly when introduced to your children, do you sense genuine interest and warmth?* This is hard to determine. Go with your instincts.

Is she a Crook?

1. *Is there any indication the applicant has had trouble with the law? Does she seem overly and prematurely eager to work for you? Does she ask for the job and want to start immediately before asking any pertinent questions?* Crooks are often focused on getting away from their current situation and are anxious to be somewhere— anywhere—else immediately.

2. *Are there unexplained gaps in her job history? Does she attempt to hide some former employment? Is she vague about precise dates of employment?* A failure to give a complete job history, complete with past employer contact information, is a clue something might be wrong.

3. *Does she seem willing to leave a current employer with no notice? Does she say things like "They were mean to me, so they deserve what they get"?* Crooks often justify their antisocial behavior in terms of retaliation for real or perceived injustices.

4. *Are her references in writing? Does she give you excuses why you can't talk to any of these?* Crooks often get former employers to write them good references as part of a termination agreement.

5. *After you hire her, does she get phone calls asking for repayment of money? Are her phone calls suspicious at all, such as people repeatedly refusing to leave names or return telephone numbers? Are her possessions or lifestyle out of line with her stated salary history or current salary? Does she fail to account for money you give her, or repeatedly fail to give you the change?* These are red flags that you should be cautious.

Is she a Party Girl?

1. *Are her favorite pastimes dancing, going out, or entertaining friends?*
2. *Does she seem flirtatious with the males in your household?*

3. *Does she dress seductively?*
4. *When asked about what was good or bad about previous jobs, does she indicate the best jobs were ones that gave her the most opportunity to have fun outside of work (e.g., jobs that started late in the morning so she could sleep in, or ones that ended early so she would have a lot of time to get ready to go out dancing)?*

The Party Girl is more focused on outside enjoyment and her own needs than on her job. If you get a sense from what she says or how she acts in the interview that an applicant fits this category, be sure to probe employers about her attitude toward her job, and whether her job was adversely affected by after-work activities.

Is she a Couch Potato or an Ants-in-the-Pants?

1. *What are her favorite activities?*
2. *How would she structure a regular day with each of your children? How would she handle a day with inclement weather? When one of the children is tired or ill?*
3. *If she could spend the rest of her life doing one sport or hobby and make a living from it, what would it be?*
4. *How would her friends describe her: as an active go-getter or more as an easygoing, stay-at-home person?*

Couch Potatoes and Ants-in-the-Pants nannies are usually aware of their own proclivities and quite willing to tell you. Asking an applicant question 4 directly is a good way to get her to reveal her self-perception. I often ask applicants what they think other people, such as former bosses, their parents, or their friends, would say about them. A preference for being active and on the go or, conversely, for staying at home and being more sedate is not good or bad in itself. A problem arises only when the individual is ill-matched to the style of the family.

TABLE OF RED FLAGS

TYPE	CHARACTERISTICS	MOTIVATOR	%HEAVEN/%HELL
Princess	unrealistic expectations; self-involved	glamour	20/80
Boss	take-charge; competitive	control	50/50
Super Nanny	nurturing; versatile; supportive	desire to help	100/0
Queen Bee	gossip; center of attention	friends	50/50
Perpetual Teenager	angers easily; won't follow rules; passive aggressive	rebellion	20/80
Professional	reliable; skilled; lacks enthusiasm	money	80/20
Crook	dishonest; untrustworthy	none	0/100
Couch Potato/ Ants-in-the-Pants	activity level governs	differs	30/70

CHAPTER 6

Setting Up Your Home

MYTH
The only livable solution to employing a live-in nanny is to have nanny quarters that are separate from the main dwelling.

TRUTH
The key to a successful living arrangement is to know yourself and your needs for privacy, and to do your best to protect these needs.

The single greatest fear parents face after deciding to hire a live-in nanny is the prospect of sharing their "space." Whereas years ago the majority of families who employed live-in child care lived in homes or apartments that had "servants' quarters," today's employers usually have to make some adjustment in how their home is organized in order to accommodate another person. The good news is that you don't have to add a cottage or rent the apartment next door in order to attract a good nanny. Today's child care giver is flexible. There are some minimum requirements, however.

The number one rule in deciding how to organize your home to welcome a live-in nanny is to be clear on how much privacy you require in order to feel comfortable. The more privacy you would like to protect, the better equipped you should make the nanny's quarters.

At a minimum, nannies require a private, furnished room. Baby nurses who generally are only employed for the first few months of an infant's life, usually share the nursery. You will need to offer all other child care providers their own room.

The location of the private bedroom usually is dependent on what you have available. For those families with flexibility, placing the nanny the farthest distance from your bedroom generally gives you the most privacy. Rooms with a private entrance are also a big plus. As one dad confided, "It was a pleasure when we moved to a house that had an entrance off the nanny's room. She liked to stay out until after midnight whereas we go to bed early. Since we couldn't hear her go in or out, the hours she kept were not a problem to us."

Some parents place their nanny in a bedroom close to the children, especially if the children are young. That way she can be close to them even at night if they awaken. Most parents I talked to, however, felt that having a nanny sleep near the children was unfair to her and it impinged on their own ability to parent while they were home. One mom said, "Even though I feel terrible the next morning, I want to be the one to comfort my son if he has a bad dream. I want to be able to put him to bed, gaze at him as he sleeps, or just in general feel that he is close to me and me alone at nighttime. If a nanny were in the next room it just wouldn't feel the same."

In deciding which bedroom to call the "nanny room" don't forget that most nannies will want to have friends visit. Many families restrict friend visits to the nanny room. Do you want her friends in the main area of the house or as far away as possible? Arrange the nanny quarters accordingly.

Another consideration is the bathroom. Most nannies express a strong preference for having their own. One nanny told me she loved her job, but sharing a bathroom with the children was a real hardship. She explained that the children she cared for were young, and in order for her to feel comfortable she had to clean the bathroom every evening. "The oldest boy often misses the toilet, the middle girl loves to dig holes in the bath soap, and all three drip water everywhere. I'm tired when I finish working. I don't want to have to then start scrubbing toothpaste off a basin and wiping a toilet seat. Besides, I have to keep my shampoo, toothbrush, and other toiletries locked in a cabinet, otherwise the children play with them. It's a real pain."

The basics required in the nanny's quarters are a bed, linens, reading lamp, chair, desk, and accommodations for her clothing. If you can give her her own bathroom do so, even if it means giving up a guest bathroom or making other family members share. It will give your nanny more of her own "space," a consideration most nannies appreciate.

The owner of a nanny agency gave me a quick piece of advice to pass on to parents. She stressed the importance of having the nanny's room ready when she arrives. "You can't believe how important this can be to a young woman who has just arrived to live in a strange household and start a new job. If you have been storing extra clothes in her closet, have them cleaned out before she arrives. Have you told her the room has a desk, but you haven't bought it yet? Make sure it's there when she arrives. You can't believe how many families say the room is equipped with something and then take months and months to actually provide it. This may be a small thing in the eyes of the parent, but can be a big deal to the nanny. Avoid hard feelings and make her feel welcome by having her room ready."

Many families furnish more than the essentials both for the nanny's comfort and for their own privacy protection. In deciding what is reasonable to provide consider the following:

LUXURY OR ESSENTIAL?

Television Set

Should you provide your nanny with her own TV? That depends. Are you twenty-two, a couch potato who loves MTV, and generous enough to share your clicker with your nanny (and her friends)? If so, don't bother getting an extra set and ignore the remaining questions.

Do you view your home as your castle, your sanctuary from the thundering mobs you encounter every day, whose only purpose is to rob you of control? Skip the questions, get her her own TV, and spend the time you saved reading a good book.

What is your TV philosophy? Do you think of watching TV together in the evenings as family time? Do you allow your children to watch only selected programs? What message about TV do you want to communicate to your children? Your nanny is a role model for your children. Many nannies are in their teens and twenties. Do you want your children to emulate the TV viewing habits of someone from this age group?

Would you mind the TV set being on while you are home, but not watching? Would you mind your nanny's friends watching your TV with her in off-hours? If you and your nanny are both watching TV, who selects the programs? Is the TV set within hearing distance of your bedroom or your children's?

In our house we decided early on to provide our nanny with her own TV to watch in her off-hours. We issued strict guidelines for when she was allowed to watch the family TV during working hours: never.

VCR

Most families do not equip the nanny's bedroom with a VCR, but with the prices of VCRs coming down, it may become more common. Those families I interviewed who did, felt it was worth the one-time expense. As one parent put it, "It's hard to say no when your nanny says she's always wanted to watch the movie you've rented, could she join you and watch it too?"

If you live in a remote area and your nanny doesn't have much to do in the evenings, or if she is shy and hasn't made many friends, the use of a private VCR is a big plus for the nanny who enjoys movies. It can be a status symbol and a reason to invite "the girls over to watch a flick" for the nanny who is social. It is a real asset for those families who would prefer their nanny was safe at home in her off-hours rather than sampling the area's nightlife. And last but not least, it is more comfortable for the nanny who values her own privacy to watch a movie in her own quarters rather than in yours.

Kitchen Facilities

"You'll need to remodel this hallway and add a cook top and refrigerator," remarked an acquaintance as I was wrapping up a tour of the house I had just purchased. The hallway she was referring to led from the guest bedroom intended for use as nanny quarters to the kitchen. It was lined with cupboards and used to store linens. "But we're right next to the kitchen," I commented incredulously. "But obviously you lack cooking facilities for your nanny," was the emphatic reply.

What was obvious to this woman was not to me. And in fact, most families do not provide separate kitchen facilities. However, some people feel strongly that it's important the nanny have at least a small refrigerator and a hot plate[1] in her room. One dad explained, "When I get up at night to get a midnight snack, I don't want to have to get dressed before I go to the kitchen." A mom said, "I like to sit in my bathrobe and slowly read the paper during weekend mornings. I don't want another woman in her bathrobe sitting at the table eating her breakfast at the same time. It's my house; I don't want to share it with someone else on the weekends. Since our nanny has a hot plate, coffee maker, and refrigerator in her room, she eats her weekend meals there." Still another parent explained, "Dinnertime is family time for me and I don't want anyone other than family members there. Our nanny eats before we come home, and then if she wants snacks afterward, she has them in her room."

Sharing the kitchen with our nannies never felt intrusive to me. They always slept until noon during the weekends unless they had hot social plans, in which case they were up and gone before we got up. They also were either not nighttime snackers or courteous enough to pretend I wasn't, and never surprised me during an evening raid to the pantry. For me, providing a separate cooking facility is a luxury and not a necessity, but if you are a person who wants total distance from your nanny at mealtimes and during off-hours, you may consider offering it.

---

1. Hot plates have been known to start fires. If you decide to provide one, make sure it is in a safe place and that your nanny knows how to use it properly. She must be fastidious in turning it off.

Automobile

Urban dwellers and others whose nannies don't have to drive can ignore this section. All others, please listen.

Many years ago—in my B.C. (Before Children) era—I drove a small, inexpensive, but spiffy car. The second time I took it to a body shop in as many weeks to have the same smashed-in front bumper replaced, the car mechanic looked at me solemnly and said, "Lady, there is only one car you should be driving." "What is that?" I asked innocently, relieved not to be given the lecture I expected. "A tank," was the answer.

I offer the same advice to all families whose nannies drive cars. They should be provided tanks. Barring that, give the nanny the newest, safest car you own. Pay for her to have driving lessons (safety-minded parents insist on this even for those nannies who have been driving awhile), anticipate in advance that she will probably have at least one accident, and pray that it is minor and your children are not in the car.

This book was originally in danger of having a chapter titled "Bumper Cars." If you've employed a nanny, chances are you have a car story to tell. I've collected scores of them. One nanny totaled two family cars in one shot. She was a Nanny from Heaven in other respects; she just wasn't a good driver. (She was in one family car, following the other, and didn't stop in time at a red light. She hit the family's other car, which was stopped at the light.) Another nanny had an accident a week (none of them were her fault, according to her). I recorded a fair number of hit-and-run stories, where nannies left the scene of an accident and didn't tell either the police or their employers. One mother whose (former) nanny had done this was still so upset she found it hard to talk about the experience even though it had happened several years earlier. The accident had involved the nanny hitting a child, fortunately not seriously. The family didn't find out about the accident until their car was tracked down by the police. It took them months to straighten out the legalities.

There were nannies who toppled mailboxes, hit the same neighbor's car three times, and several who professed complete ignorance when confronted with huge gashes in the automobiles they drove. We had a favorite nanny who occasionally hit the garage door when she backed out of her parking space on the pavement in front of the garage. We look at these dents fondly; with the exception of her parking skills she was a Super Nanny.

The mix of an automobile and a nanny can not only engender great memories, they can also bring great adventure into your life and provide great entertainment to share at your next cocktail party.

One family hired a nanny who had recently been discharged from the military. The family did not check whether her discharge had been honorable (it was not; she had been released because of repeated drug usage). The only reference they got on the nanny was from her husband who was still in the military. He told them his wife was "great with kids." Harry, a single dad, decided to hire the nanny.

"About two weeks after we had hired this woman," Harry related, "I got a call from my daughter Mandy's preschool saying that no one had come to pick Mandy up. Our nanny was supposed to but didn't show. I left work, picked Mandy up, and then proceeded to call hospitals, police stations, and what have you to locate my nanny. I finally concluded that the nanny, my Volvo, and worse yet, Mandy's favorite stuffed animal, a little bunny named Snuggles, were missing.

"Snuggles had accompanied Mandy to school and had last been seen in the back seat of the Volvo. Mandy was inconsolable. The police said it was too soon to look for the nanny, but they would search for the car. Frankly I was just as concerned about the return of Snuggles. After a sleepless night with Mandy howling about Snuggles, I was willing to trade the car, the nanny, and some cash for the bunny.

"The next day, I got a call from the police that the Volvo had been spotted near the military base. I jumped in my car and met them there. There was some jurisdiction problem and I found a highway patrol officer, a sheriff, an assistant deputy, and military police at the scene. No sooner had I arrived than a bulletin came in that the car had been spotted elsewhere. I got in a police cruiser with two policemen and off we went. While we were driving, I spotted my stolen car going in the opposite direction. We did a U-turn, radioed for help, and set off on a high-speed chase."

Harry went on to describe the chase scene, complete with vehicles racing at daring speeds, flashing lights, sirens, and lots of suspense and action. The car was recovered and it was discovered that the nanny had "sold" it in order to get money for drugs. The nanny had grand theft charges filed against her. Harry had the time of his life. Snuggles was returned, unharmed, to his tearful owner.

A more typical scenario than theft for the nanny/car mix is the auto accident. The ones I heard primarily occurred when the nannies were off duty and luckily no children were in the cars. My friend and neighbor Randy told me this story about her nanny, a sweet and very nice girl named Donna.

"I got woken up by a phone call around 6:00 A.M. It was Donna, very apologetic about calling so early. She said she had had a little car trouble and could I come get her? She said that if I was too tired, she could walk home, but even though I was half asleep I had the presence of mind to say that either I or my husband Ed would come.

"Ed got up and went in search of her. He expected her to be by the side of the road with a flat tire or a stalled engine. Instead, as he went down the hill a half mile from our house he saw the hill ablaze with lights. There were police cars, fire engines, rescue trucks, you name it. We later learned that Donna, on her way to an early morning aerobics class, had gone around a curve at thirty-five or forty miles an hour when she should have been going no more than twenty-five mph. Her car missed the curve, flipped over, and fell fifteen feet to land upside down on a driveway. Our car was totaled, but she didn't have a scratch. She's a wonderful nanny in other respects so we didn't fire her, but now we don't let her drive the children anywhere, which is a major pain because I have to interrupt my business whenever the children need to be taken somewhere."

It is simply not practical for anyone other than the urban dweller to prohibit his or her nanny from chauffeuring the children. Indeed, in some families, this is the nanny's main task. So what do most families do? They try to limit their losses by furnishing their nanny with the smallest, least expensive, and most undependable car they own. Some nannies drive real clunkers. This doesn't make any sense to me.

The most valuable thing in your life is your children and you want them to be as safe as possible. If your nanny gets into an accident you want her and her passengers to have as much protection as possible, which translates into a large, late-model vehicle. Invest in the safest "nanny" car you can and require that your nanny, no matter how old or experienced she may be, take driving lessons.

Is an automobile a luxury or an essential? It depends on where you live and how much public transportation is available. If you live in an area where it's a necessity to have a car, do you need to furnish your nanny with her own car? About twenty-five percent of the suburban families I interviewed insist their nanny supply her own car.

Fifteen percent provide the nanny a car for use during working hours, but require her to share it with a parent during off-hours. This works well in some cases and leads to dissatisfaction in others. The key to success depends on both parties' maturity and willingness to be reasonable. The remaining sixty percent of families provide personal cars for their nannies and most do not follow my guidelines. The nanny tends to drive the oldest, least expensive, and possibly least safe automobile the family owns.

Telephone

Insist your nanny have her own. You pay for the installation (this extra line will come in handy when your children become teenagers) and furnish the actual phone. The phone service needs to be—and this is key—in her name.

Additional Persuasion for Those Reluctant to Follow the Telephone Advice

For all you doubters, below are responses to some common objections to insisting your nanny obtain a private line.

- *"But my nanny is new to the area; she won't have anyone to call. It's unfair to require her to pay for something she doesn't need."*

Offer to pay the base monthly cost of her phone for the first few months she is in the area. Her long-distance charges are hers to pay.

- *"But she makes so little; it doesn't seem fair to expect her to pay for her own phone."* Raise her salary sufficient to cover the monthly cost for basic phone coverage. In most areas this is less than $10 a month.
- *"But she is here illegally. Doesn't this prevent her from getting a phone in her name? Also, I don't want to jeopardize her employment."* All she needs to give the telephone company in order to get a phone is a passport number. Even visitors to this country can get phone service. You don't need to be a citizen. And as far as I can tell, although getting through to a customer service representative can sometimes feel as cumbersome as reaching a government official, there are no tie-ins. The telephone company does not inform Immigration or any other government department on the visa status of their customers.
- *"But she has promised to pay for all her calls."* Would you be interested in investing in a bridge in Brooklyn?

Here is a little quiz. Choose any one of the following that applies to you:

1. Do you have a hidden desire to function as a receptionist during your off-hours?
2. Do you like to be awakened in the wee hours of the morning by your nanny's current boyfriend, her ex-boyfriend, or her ex-ex-boyfriend from abroad who doesn't understand time zones?
3. Do you enjoy being surprised by the police showing up on your doorstep because your mother has called them? She's sure something is wrong because your phone has been busy all day; no one could talk *that* long.
4. Do you want to be shocked at how high a phone bill can be?

Pick any one of the above four and you win the grand prize of a shared phone.

If you have the other phone, believe me, when your Nanny from Hell leaves in the middle of the night without notice, you may be left with brokenhearted kids, mounds of laundry, and the prospect of spending your vacation time at home recruiting child care, but you will be spared the added aggravation of handing over your vacation savings to the phone company. It was a rare family that I interviewed who allowed their nannies to use their phone for personal calls who didn't get stiffed at least once. Some of the amounts ran into the hundreds of dollars. One mom anguished, "She was only here two months. How could she have run up a $782 phone bill?" If the phone had been in the nanny's name, it would have been the phone company's problem and not the family's.

Insist every nanny you employ, no matter how responsible, mature, or wonderful she appears during the interview, have a phone in her own name. No need to send me heartfelt letters of thanks when this advice pays off for you. Buy extra copies of this book to give to your friends who employ nannies. That will be thanks enough.

Telephone Answering Machine

I am a marshmallow when it comes to this item. Many families don't provide it. I, however, feel that even though it isn't an essential, it's nice to give your nanny one.

Remember how it felt to be single? In the days before answering machines were commonplace (not that I'm old enough to remember this, but I have heard stories . . .), wasn't it torture to wonder if Mr. Fantastic had called when you weren't home? How many evenings did you stay home waiting near the phone? Most nannies spend their days in the company of children and would like to spend their off-hours with adults. They want to be in contact with their friends.

While your nanny is working taking care of your children, you don't want her to run to her room every time her phone rings, and yet it isn't fair to insist she ignore the ring. The solution is the answering machine. She gets to find out at the end of the day who called her and you get a nanny who is not distracted by personal calls during working hours. An answering machine is not very expensive yet it can be an important social lifeline for a person who works in the home.

SUMMARY

1. Organize your home to ensure that you protect the amount of privacy you need to be comfortable.
2. Although you do not need a separate cottage in order to attract a Nanny from Heaven, at a minimum you must provide a private furnished bedroom. Her own bathroom, TV, VCR, telephone answering machine, private entrance, and kitchen facilities will contribute to your privacy as well as to your nanny's comfort.
3. Your nanny needs to have her own telephone in her own name.
4. If driving is a requirement of your job, make sure your nanny drives the safest car you can afford.

CHAPTER 7

Managing a Home Employee

MYTH

Managing a home employee is the same as managing any other employee.

TRUTH

The management basics are the same, but, boy oh boy, is the situation different! For insight, ask yourself how well do you "manage" your parents, spouse, or children?

Maintaining a healthy, mutually satisfying parent/employee relationship is similar to riding a two-person bicycle. The parent is in front and determines the direction the team takes. The speed the bicycle travels is dependent on both participants pedaling together. The success of the outing, and the fun of doing it together, comes from both being motivated. They each end up less tired because they have pedaled as a team rather than as competitors.

Unfortunately, some parent/nanny relationships end up with one or both parties emotionally and/or physically exhausted either because they lose sight of their common goal (the children's well-being), they haven't agreed up front what speed feels right for both, or in some cases, they don't agree on who should be steering. When any of these things occur, a crash is inevitable.

Sometimes the crash is the parent's fault. Consciously or subconsciously, some parents don't want their nannies to succeed because of feelings of guilt, jealousy, or fear of being supplanted. Just as often, nannies are at fault, also sometimes for reasons they themselves don't understand. Some of them feel competitive with the parents, or have confused their employers with their own parents or own children. We'll talk about these situations and what you can do about them later in this chapter.

However, more often than not, the team is a good one. Both people want the partnership to succeed, both are good people, both want to pedal together. What they lack is structure. They need rules and a communication system so they can make adjustments along the way.

HOUSE RULES

The phrase "House Rules" reminds me of a long-ago conversation with some college friends who represented a mixture of cultures and ethnicities. We stayed up late one evening telling each other stories from our childhoods.

The discussion led to reminiscences about food. One of the girls told the group that she had been brought up kosher, sort of. Sort of? she was asked. "Our house was kosher," she said as though that made things perfectly clear. Pressed to clarify, she explained that all food prepared in her home was kosher and while eating at home everyone observed kosher rules; however, when they dined out they ate pork, shellfish, and other nonkosher foods. Her family wasn't kosher; their house was.

We introduced House Rules after we hired our first nanny and quickly found out that what our nanny and we considered normal car maintenance differed. ("Oh, the red light means the car needs oil? I didn't know.") We lost a car engine, but gained an institution, House Rules. Strictly speaking, we should have called them Car Rules, but our car usually behaves itself better than our house does.

Smart families will be proactive and anticipate potential conflicts before they hire. We weren't so smart and our guidelines were developed *after* each nanny problem occurred. We would discuss the problem with her, come to an agreement on how the situation should be handled in the future, and write the new rule on a yellow legal pad, which we kept in a manila folder labeled "House Rules" in a drawer in the kitchen. After a while our list became quite extensive.

We came to use our house rules as a test for a prospective nanny. Watching an applicant's reaction to reading House Rules can be quite revealing. Those young women whose primary motive for becoming a live-in nanny is to get away from the restrictions their parents give them at home can't flee from your home fast enough after reading your house rules.

House Rules are intended to cover the issues that can arise out of the "roommate" portion of your relationship with your nanny. The beauty of House Rules is that they are impersonal. Labeling the rules "House" suggests the rules aren't yours, they belong to the house. And how can a person be mad at a house? Furthermore, the rules are impersonal because they are not directed at any one person. They are rules for anyone who works and lives with you. They communicate and protect those lifestyle essentials that make your home a comfortable place for you.

Below is a sample list of House Rules, a compilation of some of the house rules I heard about during my interviews. It is offered to start you thinking about what works for you. After some of the rules, I've included additional information in brackets to give you insight into the situation that provoked the development of the rule.

Each family is different and therefore will have a very different list. One couple I interviewed had a problem with their au pair showering after 10:00 P.M. Her bathroom was over their bedroom and hearing the running water woke them up. The solution to the problem—a house rule that baths or showers in the upstairs bathroom had to take place before a specific time—was simple. Unfortunately, it took several days of the parents being grumpy, the nanny sensing something was wrong (but not knowing exactly what), and everyone thinking everyone else was inconsiderate, before one of the parents remembered about House Rules and used this mechanism to communicate about the problem.

House rules, even though they are not meant to be personal, can be negotiated with each new nanny. A good time to discuss this is during your second interview. You can also leave it until after the nanny starts work. Make sure you retain rules that are important to you even if your nanny thinks they are silly. The importance of lifestyle issues in a happy parent/nanny relationship is not to be underestimated, either for the parents or the nannies. Good nannies have lost their jobs and sorrowful children have lost nannies they liked, because the "roommate" portion of having a live-in didn't work even though the "care giver" aspect worked fine. As one nanny employment agency owner told me, "Most nannies get fired not because of their child care competence, but because of personality or lifestyle issues."

House Rules

Visitors

Nannies are allowed to have up to three guests visit during her off-hours in the evening. We would like to be introduced to all persons who are invited. Men are not allowed, unless it is a boyfriend of long standing and we have given our express approval. Please make sure that your guests leave by midnight during the week.

Guests should stay primarily in the nanny's quarters, but may use the family room as long as noise is kept to a minimum. You may offer them refreshments, but please be reasonable.

No overnight guests are allowed normally. If you wish to have an overnight guest during the weekend, please obtain our prior consent.

During working hours, no visitors are allowed with the exception of other nannies who care for children that are close in age to ours. You may invite them to lunch when a parent is not home. Please tell us in the morning if you plan to have friends over that day.

Our children are prone to ear infections. We try to minimize their exposure to colds and other illnesses. Let your friends who are bringing children to our house know that we would appreciate their not bringing any child with a runny nose (regardless of the reason) or any other sign of illness.

continued

During the days when a parent is at home, we would prefer you not invite other nannies over. If a parent decides to stay home unexpectedly and you have prior plans to have other nannies come over, we can discuss it.

During weekends when we are not at home and you are, you may have company, but *no* parties. The same rule applies if you house-sit. [Most families will attempt to define "party." Even the best of definitions will not stand in the way of the nanny intent on having the bash of season.]

If a family member of yours wants to visit and stay with us, we will discuss this on a case-by-case basis. In no event is the person to live with us for more than two weeks. [Considering the fact that our own relatives are only allowed to stay three days, this is quite generous.]

Visiting Others

We do not allow our children to go in the homes of people we do not know. They are also not allowed to go to any home with a swimming pool even if we do know the parents. If you need to stop by another house to pick up a nanny and/or children, please make the visit extremely short and keep our child by your side at all times. Better yet, have the nanny meet you outside or meet at the park or other destination.

Food

Food is to be eaten in the kitchen and eating area only while the children are awake since this is a rule that they must follow. After hours you may eat food in your room.

Please do not drink soft drinks, chew gum, or eat junk food in the presence of the children.

We will provide you with special foods and snacks to a reasonable degree if they are healthy and not overly expensive. We do not cover the costs of frozen diet foods, exotic or

continued

gourmet foods, or sugared cereals. However, if there is a food you particularly enjoy and it is not something we normally eat, we will be glad to provide it for you. [One mom said she felt fine buying bottled water for her nanny, even though the rest of the family drank from the tap, but she really resented paying for sodas, which she felt were a waste of money. Another family told me they allowed their nanny to purchase whatever she wanted for herself when she shopped for the family, but were amazed at the bill when she started to live on frozen diet foods.]

The children are not allowed to have candy and other sweet snacks more than once a day. They are not allowed to eat hot dogs or other processed meats except occasionally. Please act as a role model while in their presence.

We do not like dishes in the sink. Please put all dirty dishes immediately into the dishwasher.

On weekends, if you will not be eating with us, please tell us in advance.

Liquor is not considered part of "board." Please do not use any of the family's beer or liquor. ["What about in cooking?" asked one nanny applicant. She wasn't hired for missing the point.]

Your Room

You are responsible for maintaining your own room. Please do not accumulate dirty dishes or leave open food containers or anything else around that would attract insects. ["We normally don't go into the nanny room and don't care how it is kept, but the exterminator told us we better start caring," one dad told me.]

We would appreciate it if you would maintain your room in such a way as to be a good example to the children.

Please don't put nails or thumbtacks in the walls or paint anything. You may use sticky tape to hang mementos or use the bulletin board provided. If you don't like the paintings

continued

that are already up, you may remove them and give them to us for storage. You may also move the furniture around to suit your tastes. [One nanny put posters up with thumbtacks on every wall and the ceiling. She was hurt the family was less than enthusiastic about her decorating.]

Automobile

If you feel ill or are on any medication that shouldn't be combined with driving, please don't drive the car. We will make other arrangements to transport the children to their activities.

Please clean the car at least once a month.

Check the oil at least once a month. ["And refill if needed," one parent forgot to add. Their car was traded to the towing company in exchange for towing fees.]

Fill up the gas tank when it reaches a quarter tank.

Let us know immediately if you hear any unusual sounds or if the vehicle is acting strangely in any way.

We pay for all gas except if you go on a long trip (more than fifty miles) or use the car *extensively* during your off-hours, in which case we would appreciate your filling up the tank.

If you have an accident, it is not sufficient to exchange phone numbers and insurance information with the other party. You must call the police immediately. Then call us. *Never* leave the scene of an accident.

The same procedure applies if you hit an unoccupied vehicle.

If the accident was your fault, we will expect you to pay for the insurance deductible to a maximum of $500.

If you are involved in a hit and run, in other words, you do not acknowledge you were in an accident, it is cause for immediate dismissal.

continued

You and all passengers are required to wear seat belts. Young children are to be in child safety seats at all times. If you are tempted to get out of your seat belt to retrieve a toy, turn around and look at a child or some other reason, don't. Stop the car and then take care of what you need to; don't do it while you are driving.

You are allowed to stay out overnight, but our car isn't. If your situation is such that you can't return the car in the evening, please discuss this with us in advance.

Water

When going swimming, we require one adult per child who is a nonswimmer. If the children are a mixture of swimmers and nonswimmers, the rule is one adult can watch one swimmer and one nonswimmer, but no more. If all the children know how to swim, one adult can watch a maximum of three children.

Toilet lids are to be kept shut in every bathroom. Toddlers have been known to drown in toilets.

No buckets of water are to be left around for the same reason.

The plastic inflatable pool must be emptied after every use.

Children under the age of three are not to be left in the bath unattended *ever*.

We try to conserve water so please do not let faucets run unnecessarily.

Telephone

You may receive only emergency calls on our phone.

Please take messages completely and place them on the pad next to the phone. If you do not have time to take a complete message, let the phone answering machine take the message. Please do not write on the walls. [One nanny, intent on taking messages every time the phone rang regardless of

continued

which room she was in or what she was doing, wrote messages on the wall since she often didn't have paper handy.]

Money

The money in the emergency fund is for household emergencies only. Please do not borrow this money for personal use. If you are short of cash and need an advance, ask us.

If you need money for an outing or some other work-related reason, let us know in advance. If the need is unexpected, please pay for it out of your own funds, give us the receipt, and we will reimburse you immediately. [Some families have household funds for this reason and the nanny withdraws cash and puts receipts in. Others give their nannies a monthly allowance for such purposes. Still others allow nannies discretionary funds for purchases such as children's clothes and toys up to a certain limit. *In no event should you give your nanny a credit card in your name, or give her access to your ATM.* I have the sad testimony of several families who did so to their profound regret. Even supposed Nannies from Heaven were found to abuse this privilege to the tune of thousands of dollars. The families had little recourse because they couldn't prove it was theft.]

Privacy

Please do not discuss our personal affairs with anyone else. We will not gossip about you [except to pour our hearts out to a certain author of nanny books].

Our bedroom is off-limits unless you are invited in. We consider your bedroom the same.

Please do not read any of our personal letters even if they are in the trash. [I know of one nanny who gave editing suggestions to her author employer even though the author had never shown her the manuscript. The nanny was reading discarded copy from the wastepaper basket.]

continued

Habits

No smoking is allowed in our home, car, or grounds. We do not want the children to ever see you smoking.

No drinking alcohol during working hours. No driving and drinking ever.

No use of illegal drugs is condoned anywhere.

Although you have no curfew, we would appreciate your getting enough sleep so that you are refreshed in the morning and have patience during the day.

If you are ill, please let us know immediately. [One nanny, just returning from a ski vacation, bravely emptied the dishwasher and made the children's breakfast before telling the family she had the flu. Needless to say, everyone else got it too.]

Please say "please" and "thank you." We want our children to be polite and they will emulate your habits. [A magician performing at a child's birthday party asked his young audience to say the magic word. Expecting a response of "Abracadabra," he heard a chorus of "please" instead.]

Please keep your window closed during wintertime except for brief periods to air out your room. If the temperature in your room is too hot or cold, we will correct it by setting the thermostat. [One family's enormous jump in heating costs was explained when they discovered their nanny was attempting to heat up Manhattan by keeping her window open all winter.]

Please wear clothes when you are out of your room. [Yes, one family did find it necessary to have this house rule, prompted by a nanny the children loved who had some unorthodox ideas about what was appropriate attire.]

Emergency

Although your social life is your own business, if you plan to be away overnight, please leave a telephone number and address where we can reach you in case of an emergency. You

continued

may enclose this information in a sealed envelope and we will not open the envelope unless we need to reach you. [If we open the envelope and find it empty, we will tell your parents—who inevitably call to tell you some important news when you are away and we don't know where—that you've gone off with an ex-con biker with spiked hair and tattoos.]

Also, for your safety we would like to know if you are going to be away overnight. [This rule gives some families important practice parenting a teenager: their nanny. Good luck!]

Additional house rules can pertain to conduct, usage, charging privileges, etc., in respect to family memberships at country clubs, health clubs, video stores, and other perks sometimes provided for nannies. They should be tailored to your individual situation.

I'll admit that the above example of House Rules is somewhat long and compulsive, but I've come full circle in this respect. I used to think that rules were unnecessary if all parties were mature and respected each other. I now know that even mature, respectful individuals can vary greatly in what they consider "normal" behavior. You can save a lot of aggravation if you communicate up front what you consider normal in your household.

About the list being a sign of compulsivity . . . It's true confessions time. I used to complain about my husband being too compulsive. I brought this up for the first time during our honeymoon (I'm a genius at timing). He obliged by deciding to no longer triple-check and confirm our flight arrangements.

We missed our flight out of Madrid because we thought the plane left an hour later.

It took years for him to stop reminding me of this, but eventually he did. Not one to learn a lesson easily, I found another opportunity to accuse him of being much too compulsive. This time we were in the process of building a house and he was typing a list of the builder's responsibilities. "You don't need to list everything," I complained. I can hear the moans from all you home builders who know better.

Develop an extensive list of house rules. Don't worry about being accused of being compulsive by your spouse, your nanny or any other misguided soul. After all, they are not *your* rules, they belong to the house.

WEEKLY MEETINGS

Most business management books discuss the importance of regularly scheduled meetings to discuss the progress of key projects and to identify and solve problems. Regularly scheduled meetings are not important with a home child care worker—they are essential.

The purpose of the weekly meeting is twofold: to discuss issues pertaining to the children and to resolve any issues between the parents and the nanny. Conversation about the children is self-explanatory so we will focus here on what should transpire in the more emotion-laden and difficult portion of the meeting, that which covers the nanny-parent relationship.

Most families agree on the importance of open communication with nannies. "I've told her to be free to come and talk to me about anything, anytime," more than one parent told me. Why is it, then, that when a nanny quits, the most frequent response from the parent (according to one nanny agency owner) is, "I didn't know she was unhappy." Most of the nannies I spoke with admitted that they had left jobs for reasons that, in retrospect, would not have been that important had they been dealt with in a timely matter. By the time the issue was raised, the nanny was so frustrated or enraged, there was no going back.

The onus for scheduling and leading the meeting is the parent's. Most nannies are not as well educated, sophisticated, or experienced in life as their employers and don't know how to raise issues of potential conflict. Many have never attended a formal business meeting. Most are intimidated. They find it simply too hard to speak up about something that frustrates them. It is the parents' responsibility to solicit information from their nannies about what may be sore spots. Parents should also use the weekly meeting to acknowledge what has gone well. It's a good time to formally acknowledge the nanny's contribution to your family and say "Thank you."

Leanne

The Smiths' Nanny

Leanne was with a family for five years over a six-year time period. She left after the first year to work someplace else, and she stayed with the new family six months. She then went to a third family and stayed three months. She then returned to her first family, the Smiths, and stayed four more years until they moved out of the area. She explains the job changes this way:

"I guess after I left the Smiths and worked other places, I realized they were not such a bad family and they realized I was a good nanny. The first year we were together was a learning experience for both of us. I was their first nanny and they were my first job experience. Neither of us realized until we had tried other situations that we were a good fit.

"The issues that seemed so great at the time I left didn't seem so important later on when I had been in jobs where I was *really* unhappy. At the Smiths' I was respected, my contribution was appreciated, and I was a member of a team bringing up Karen and Vanessa, their two children. I didn't realize this at the time because I focused on what went wrong, instead of what was right. They asked me later why I didn't tell them what was wrong, but I just couldn't. I felt strange criticizing them. It was just easier to leave.

"When I think about the issues that upset me the first year, they were things such as lack of privacy, long hours, and extra work that was not in my contract. Like, for example, I was asked to do food shopping, which wasn't part of my job description. I found this really hard because I wouldn't know what to do if something on the list wasn't available. Should I substitute something else or forget about it? When we talked

continued

about my coming back to work I finally mentioned this and Jane, my boss, told me she thought I liked food shopping which is why she asked me to do it. She thought it would give me a chance to get what I wanted for myself. But she had never told me this before.

"I realize now that the things that drove me crazy and that kept me up at night thinking about them were issues that could be discussed and negotiated. I was too immature to talk about them.

"When I talked to them about coming back, we covered all my concerns and they changed the parts of the job that were hard for me such as sharing a room with one of the children. They even paid my share of an apartment so I could be a live-out nanny. The first year, I was too inexperienced to work things out any other way than leaving. Now I know better."

Leanne worked as a nanny for a total of seven years. She currently works as an administrative assistant for a well-known management consultant. She says that working as a nanny was excellent background for her present job. She regards her employer as a grown kid. She is careful about his ego, compliments him a lot, and occasionally puts a Tootsie Roll lollipop on top of his pile of mail to sweeten up the task of responding to it. He says she is terrific.

In the Meeting

In our house we hold our meetings weekly, on Monday evenings after dinner. We compensate our nanny for taking the extra forty-five minutes the meeting typically runs, by allowing her to leave early on Tuesdays. Some families I interviewed paid for the extra time, others didn't, some conducted it during normal working hours.

Evenings work best in our household. Other parents say that everyone is too tired at night to have a meaningful discussion. Schedule the meeting whenever you like, but schedule it in advance and make sure it happens every week, whether or not you feel you have something to say.

Our meeting usually starts off with a conversation about the children: progress they've made, problems, special needs, and so on. We attempt to limit this discussion to ten or fifteen minutes because otherwise we run the risk of talking just about the children.

After we are "warmed up" talking, my husband or I will ask our nanny if anything happened during the week that she would like to discuss in terms of her own employment. She knows by now that if she complains or is angry we will not react by jumping down her throat or becoming defensive. We listen quietly, rephrase what she said in order to be sure we understood correctly, and then we discuss it, attempting to understand her point of view and expressing ours. If our actions during the week were wrong, we apologize. Often the problem results from a miscommunication. This is a good time to explain what was going on in your head when you used an inappropriate tone of voice or failed to acknowledge a job well done or wounded her feelings by reversing a decision she had made. Use this chance to nip small problems before they blossom into humdingers.

Were Weekly Nanny Meetings Conducted More Than a Century Ago?

Early on in my research I discovered a reference to a child care provider problem in a journal written in the 1800s. The notation said that a wet nurse complained she could not feed the baby properly because her own ale allotment was inadequate.

She must have become a very wet wet nurse, since it was noted her ale allotment was increased threefold.

The weekly meeting is a good time for you to learn how your nanny likes to be managed. Different management styles work better than others with different personalities. For example, some nannies like precise instructions; others thrive better with a looser hand. Listen to your nanny. If she feels the reins are too tight, decide to loosen them, or explain why they need to be tight for the time being and develop a time frame for giving her more responsibility and freedom. Is she uneasy because she's not sure what to do or how to do things your way? This is a good indication you need to be more involved, more directive.

Many nannies suffer from loneliness, some from homesickness; being a nanny can be a hard, isolated job. There aren't coworkers with whom to socialize or trade gripes. The weekly meeting is a good chance to ask her about her feelings. And she will probably need to be asked.

In a typical job setting, asking employees how their social lives are going or whether they are happy is inappropriate and, in some instances, might be construed as sexual harassment. However, when that employee also lives with you, the situation changes. You need to know whether or not she is content with her life outside work as well as at work; it affects her job. A nanny who loves her job, your children, and everything about the situation *except* that she is lonely or misses home will probably not be with you long. You need to find out what is going on and, if necessary, help her correct the situation.

In addition to finding out your nanny's feelings, you need to express your own. The weekly meeting is a good place to formally tell her you appreciate her efforts. Be specific. "You're doing a great job" is not as meaningful as "Wednesday when I came home and saw all the children working together on the art project, I was so grateful you were our nanny." If anything happened during the week that you want corrected or eliminated, also be specific: "Our three-year-old is singing about passion and love again. I want to remind you that when she is in the car, I would prefer that you put her tapes on instead of your own music."

PROCEDURE MANUALS: YES OR NO?

Some families are so organized they have computerized menus and daily schedules. Others, like mine, operate more informally (my motto is: If the children are still alive by bedtime, the day has been a success). However, I do have to say I was intrigued when one of the families I interviewed proudly showed me their procedure manual. Having been a businessperson for many years, I have read more than my share of procedure manuals and have even—I blush to admit this—developed one or two masterpieces myself. A procedure manual is a book or a collection of pages that tell a new person how to do things the company way. The advantage of a family procedure manual is that you can hand one over to a new nanny and not have to train her, or so the theory goes.

The manual I looked at was full of information on how to handle the family's household: their recycling process, how to do laundry, how to do dishes, how to do compost, where to put things (a paper pile, a book pile, a toy box). . . . It was all down there on paper. Amazing.

I told the mom how impressed I was. "Thanks," she responded. "But it doesn't work. No nanny or housekeeper we have ever hired was able to get the hang of how we do things by reading the manual. I've had to tell them verbally, watch them, and give feedback."

Whew! Was I happy to hear that! I declined to question any of the other families who told me they had developed procedure manuals whether they were worth the effort, so I can honestly say that one hundred percent of the families I *did* query reported they were a waste of time.

PRAISE PUBLICLY (AND OFTEN)

Several years ago a book called *The One-Minute Manager* was published and became an instant success. The advice this book offers is still relevant and is especially useful with a home employee. One of the things the authors of this book advise managers to do is to catch their employees doing something good and then praise them about it. The praise should be specific ("I like the way you helped the children resolve their argument. You really understand five-year-olds."). It should also be immediate. Frequent praise, said out loud in public, improves self-esteem and job performance and enhances the employee/employer relationship.

Many nannies lack self-esteem. Our culture does not, for the most part, value the job of child rearing. The nanny profession is not looked upon as prestigious. The people who go into it do so primarily because they love children. They know they will not get rich or gain peer prestige. They can, however, gain the satisfaction that their job is important through observing the impact they have on the children in their care. But children rarely acknowledge this. It is up to you, the parent, to do so on their behalf.

The more you can observe your nanny performing well *and tell her you've noticed,* the more encouraged she will be to continue to perform well. Praise is motivating.

When you need to correct your nanny, do so in private. If at all possible, do so just before she is about to perform the task again. If you correct before an act, it gives the individual a chance to do it well the next time. Criticism, done properly, serves to teach and correct. Once the person has done what you wish, then you can praise, to motivate them to keep trying.

MAKING IT LAST: THE ROLE OF ROLES

Annual nanny turnover has been estimated at forty-two percent, which is about the same as turnover for other child care workers. Conventional wisdom says turnover is high because the job is low-paying; therefore, many in it consider it transitional employment rather than a profession. Yet, some nannies stay with the same families for years, raising children from infancy to at least high school. I secretly envied these families. How nice it would be to have the "child care" problem taken care of permanently! Your children would have continuity with someone, you would have someone you trusted . . . I need not go on with the picture. It's an almost universal dream of those of us who need child care.

After umpteen years as a personnel executive I knew the key to low turnover in a business setting. If you hire well (i.e., someone with the skills and personality that fit the job to be performed) and you then manage well (i.e., pay properly, give regular feedback and appreciation) employees respond by staying on the job. Yet the same strategy did not seem to be as effective with a home employee.

I asked myself why it is that some of the most screwed-up families seem to keep nannies forever and other families—trying their best to follow good hiring and management practices—go through nannies as if they were getting frequent-flyer miles for each hire.

I asked every nanny, parent, and expert I interviewed what was the key to that ultimate match: the family made in Heaven teamed up with the nanny made in Heaven. They gave me answers—all different.

The nannies said that good management practices were the most important ingredient to longevity. They told me the key was mutual respect, appreciation, and fair pay. "I'm paid well, treated as though my work is important, and often given unexpected but appreciated tokens of their gratitude, like tickets to a concert or a gift certificate at a music store," one nanny told me proudly. She had been with the same family for six years and had every intention of staying for as long as she was needed. Her thoughts were echoed by most of the others with whom I talked. They said they remained with the same family because they loved children, believed they were making an important contribution, *and* their feelings of self-worth were bolstered by their employers.

"If you don't manage well, then you don't stand a chance of keeping a good nanny, but even if you do, it's not enough. The most important ingredient to employing a Nanny from Heaven is to choose wisely up front. Spend the time you need to find the right person, even if it takes you longer and you have to spend more money than you expected. It will pay off with a long-term, high-quality care giver." The person who told me this is the owner of several nanny agencies and a parent herself. Being a former personnel executive who made her way up the ranks through being a hiring specialist, I couldn't agree more with her. If you make the right selection in the first place, managing that person is easy. Hire the wrong person and all the management skill in the world will not make this relationship work well.

"Training is key," a researcher, college professor, and pioneer in the emerging modern nanny profession confided. "Trained nannies view themselves as professionals and have the skills to do the job well. Because they know about child development, they can offer children what they need regardless of the child's age. Therefore, they have the skills to stay with the same family as the children mature. Some nannies without training function well with only selected ages. For example, a nanny who is wonderful with babies might be a disaster with a teenager. Therefore, the same nanny might not be competent enough to function well for the family over time."

"Nope," said a well-known psychologist to whom I posed these answers as the key to nanny longevity. "Training, careful screening, good management practices all are necessary, but they aren't enough."

"Then what is?" I asked.

"The nanny's 'fit' into the family's dynamics is the single most important reason some nanny/family matches are good and others aren't. The 'role' an employee plays while at work needs to mesh with the 'role' the employer plays. When the two roles are complementary, all parties are happy. When the roles clash, it's just a matter of time before the relationship falls apart."

"Whoa," I replied. "This book is supposed to be a light-hearted look at how to get the best home child care. How am I ever going to explain this stuff about roles?"

"You'd better," was the reply. "It's vital to understanding long-term employment in any job and yet almost no one talks about it. Do you want to take the short and easy route or do you want to give your readers the real scoop?"

So, here it is, folks: the real banana, the whole enchilada, the big shebang. The envelope please . . .

The answer to keeping a nanny for ever and ever, or at least until next year when you won't be so desperate, is that all four components mentioned by the experts need to be there: the selection must be good in the first place, the person needs to be skilled and willing or flexible enough to adjust as the family changes, the compensation (both monetary and psychic) must be fair, and the "fit" of the nanny into family dynamics must complement and not clash. These same four factors apply to any job in any occupation—with one difference. The difference is in the weight each of these factors has.

In a normal workplace, compensation is often the most important of the factors. The other factors may be off: The person may hate his or her boss, may not excel skillwise, and probably shouldn't have been hired in the first place, but will continue with the job because the pay, monetary or psychic, fits his or her needs.

Because a live-in child care job is so personal, so intimate, the major factor spelling the difference between long- and short-term employment is the relationship of the nanny with her employers, the parents. The other factors—selection, compensation, and skill match—play a role, but do not have anywhere near the significance of the relationship factor. The nanny not only works, but often lives at her job site, therefore it is key that she fit in comfortably with the family dynamics. This "fit" is probably the most important reason some nannies and families seem to match hand in glove, key in lock, baby in diaper. While others—families who are good, fair employers who try to hire and manage well—have a more difficult time finding someone for the long term.

The odd thing about all of this is that sometimes the families who are dysfunctional—that is, in which one or both of the parents has unresolved issues from childhood that prevent the parent from functioning as an emotionally mature adult—have the easiest time finding nannies who fit well with them. Why? I think it is because a number of nannies themselves are dysfunctional and fit right in. Lest this line of reasoning provoke you to take a crayon and scribble all over the page in a rage, let me defend myself by saying I am sharing with you the *impression* I gathered during my conversations with nannies and the families who employed them. The dysfunctional nanny/dysfunctional family theory of long-term employment is by no means a scientifically researched, documented conclusion.

If you think about it carefully, my theory should give us all some hope. After all, how many of us are *not* dysfunctional? Who among us has reached emotional maturity? If my premise is correct, all of us emotional babies have a chance at finding a nanny who will care for our children and us in perpetuity. We just have to find a nanny whose neuroses complement our own.

As a consolation prize to those few parents and nannies who are emotionally healthy: When you find each other, the result is pure bliss. Children who are raised in the resultant environment of appropriate care and good modeling are indeed fortunate.

In the spirit of fun inquiry, the following section looks at the roles people commonly adopt in a work environment. These roles are different from the types covered in the chapter "A Gallery of Nannies," which categorized various personalities. The roles discussed below are temporary roles people sometimes assume when they are dealing with issues of power and control, something that occurs regularly in the workplace.

If you want your next nanny hire to be your last, or if you have problems with your present nanny and don't quite understand why, or if you are a nanny who is continuously unhappy regardless of the family you work for, read on. You may find an insight or two here that could help you steer onto the right path.

On the other hand, if you think someone who views psychological analysis as fun deserves to end up under analysis, or if you've just had a sleepless night with a sick child, or if you are just plain uninterested in exploring the psychological underpinnings to parent/nanny relationships and conflict, skip the psychology and jump to where we discuss sex.

POWER, CONTROL, AND RELATIONSHIP ROLES: SOME BEHIND-THE-SCENES PSYCHOLOGY

Three axioms in business management psychology have particular application to a home employee:

1. Conflict, regardless of the stated reason, almost always has to do with issues of power and control.
2. The way in which we relate to issues of power and control is usually the same way we learned to deal with them in child-

hood. One way people gain a sense of control is to fall into the role that felt most comfortable growing up.
3. Employees (probably subconsciously) often view their bosses as parents.

Control, even if it is an illusion, helps us feel safe. This is especially true in times of stress. When we feel good about ourselves, we may try out new behavior and take risks. However, when we are stressed we tend to fall back on tried and true behaviors, which almost always are ones from our childhood.

Therefore, it should not surprise you to learn that people who work together often deal with issues of power and control by falling into the context of family roles, such as: parent, child, sibling, friends, and so on. For the purposes of this discussion, I use a simplified model (recognizable to anyone who is familiar with transactional analysis) with three participants: parent, child, and adult. In this model:

1. The parent holds the power, makes decisions, and is the nurturer.
2. The child is powerless, follows direction, and is dependent.
3. The adult shares power and decision making but does not become emotionally involved to any great degree.

Role selection has nothing to do with age. A person selects the role he feels gives him the most control over his life, the one that feels safest. There aren't good or bad roles per se, although the role of "adult" is the most psychologically healthy. In real life, most individuals switch between several roles many times every day as different situations arise and they encounter other individuals also playing roles. In my simplified version, we will assume that employers and employees stay mainly in one role.

The fun begins when "roles" interact and have to work together. Certain combinations blend well. Combinations that are complementary tend to satisfy the parties involved and are stable. Therefore, when the parent/nanny role combination is a good one, the chances that the nanny will stay with the family for a protracted period of time is enhanced. The most common pairings that work well are parent/child (with nannies this is usually mother/daughter), child/parent (daughter/mother) or adult/adult (partners). These pairings are remarkably stable and can spell long-term satisfaction for all involved.

Some parent/nanny combinations lead to inevitable discord. In a parent/parent combination both the mother and the nanny want to be the boss, both want to lead and make decisions. In a child/child relationship, both want to be taken care of. The prognoses for these relationships are not good.

STABILITY OF ROLE COMBINATIONS	
COMBINATION (EMPLOYER/EMPLOYEE)	STABLE
Parent/Child	yes
Child/Parent	yes
Adult/Adult	yes
Parent/Parent	no
Child/Child	no
Adult/Parent	no
Parent/Adult	no
Adult/Child	no
Child/Adult	no

Parent/Child Combination

If you are a person who likes to be the decision maker, you function best in the "parent" role. You will pair best with a nanny who likes to follow orders, get specific direction, and receive advice (sometimes in personal as well as work matters), that is, a nanny who likes to play the "child."

Parents who find themselves at home a lot either because they are stay-at-home parents or work out of their homes or work part-time, often team best with nannies who are used to having an employer close by and who welcome this proximity. Some nannies do not want to be fully in charge; they want the parent's direction on a frequent basis. They look to the parent as a role model, an authority figure, a leader. They are helpers, assistants, apprentices. Teamed with a mother who has a strong personality and a desire to be present and actively involved in the raising of her children, the combination is a good one.

In a parent/child relationship, the parent often finds herself caring for the nanny. She nurtures the nanny by giving encouragement, advice, and direction. This sometimes extends to the nanny's personal life, with employers introducing their nannies to friends or dates. Some employers research and arrange continuing education for their nannies. Sometimes they spend long hours counseling about boyfriends, appearance, health, and so on. This is not bad as long as both the parent and the nanny like the arrangement. It can become burdensome, as in the situation where a nanny crosses the line and instead of viewing her employer *like* a mother begins to believe subconsciously that she really *is* her mother (remember the Perpetual Teenager) and acts out an unresolved childhood drama in an effort to get resolution. But for the most part, if the employer likes to nurture and the nanny needs nurturing, the relationship can be satisfying for a long time.

Nannies in households where they play the "child" role often also carry this role in their relationships to the children. They function as playmates, friends, allies, confidants. This can be highly beneficial as long as the nanny is also competent in maintaining safety and security and is mature enough to discipline appropriately.

Child/Parent Combination

If you don't like to supervise, don't have confidence in your own parenting abilities, or don't have the time to do either well, you might enjoy relating to a highly competent, self-starting, and "in-charge" employee. An inexperienced, passive, or dependent nanny is not right for you. You need a nanny who can plan the children's activities, make independent decisions, and who thrives in a loosely managed job. In a working relationship such as this, the nanny assumes the "parent" role and the parent the "child" role. This is not to say the nanny is your children's mother. It's just that in a work setting she functions by exerting control; she likes being boss and decision maker. She likes things to be done her way or no way.

At times, the parent is the one who needs nurturing. Sometimes the mother feels isolated. She may be living in a neighborhood where people do not speak the same language as she, either figuratively or literally. She might be a person who is not very social and who prefers relating to people singly and in the safety of her own home. She may be an inexperienced parent who welcomes the direction a more experienced person can give her or she may be overwhelmed by the dual demands of working and parenting and decide to delegate parenting to someone else. In all of these situations, a nanny who likes to be in control will be a good match for this parent who wants nurturing.

The roles "parent" nannies assume in relationship to the children in their charge tend to be as surrogate mothers or second mothers. They don't replace the real mother even in cases where the real mother is incapacitated due to illness or absent for some other reason. They function as an additional mom.

Parent/Parent Combination

The parent/parent combination occurs when the parent and the nanny both like to be the head honcho. Remember the eruption of Mt. Vesuvius in Italy? Of course you don't; it occurred in 94 A.D. Although some historians might dispute my account, I believe the Roman gods set off the volcano to illustrate to the mothers in the area what would happen if they hired other "mothers" as their child care providers. Since everyone in the vicinity was covered in lava, the lesson was unfortunately lost on them. Don't let it be lost on you.

Employers who function as "parents" ultimately collide with employees who function as "parents." If your nanny seems highly competent, the children love her, the household is running smoothly, and yet even being in her presence drives you crazy, ask yourself if maybe this isn't a case of two "mothers" in the same house. I've never been in a house large enough for a mother/mother pair.

To illustrate how our role adoption has its genesis in our own childhood and how this is then manifested later on, I offer my own case. My mother (not my *real* mother, of course, because she would not speak to me again if she thought this was *really* about her) likes to have things her own way. She likes to be in control. Her ideas are the right ones; what is good for her is good for me.

I like to control things, too (perhaps it's clear who I learned this from)—simple things, like what I name my children (no, Mom, I still haven't forgiven you for interfering in this area), where I live, my profession. . . . I'm willing to share these decisions with my husband because we have worked out mechanisms to do so smoothly. But beware the nanny who comes into my house and unilaterally tries to change things. She instantaneously takes on my mother's face, I feel like I am being forced into a "child" role and I don't like it (yes, I, too, have unresolved conflict from my past). She and I will immediately lock horns as we battle to see who will play "mother." Nannies who are control junkies need not apply at our residence.

Adult/Parent
Adult/Child

What happens when an "adult" employer teams with a "parent" employee or a "child" employee? As in a parent/parent pair, the result is discord.

Initially the pairing of an "adult" with a "parent" can function smoothly because the "adult" often just overlooks the transgressions of the "parent." However, the "adult" employer is bound to get annoyed eventually. "Parent" employees annoy because they usually do not respect appropriate boundaries, consistently step on the "adult's" toes, and often are opinionated and controlling, insisting everything be done their way. The "parent" employee may take over jobs that aren't hers, conceal information, or sometimes even lie in an effort to maintain control. She may also invade the family's privacy or pry in an attempt to know everything. The only stable pairing for a "parent" employee is with a "child" employer or with an employer who is absent.

The pairing of an "adult" employer with a "child" employee doesn't work well either. If you find that your nanny's personal problems are draining you and you are constantly feeling sorry for her or trying to help her (wasn't it *her* job to help *you?*), then she may be the extra child you didn't want because your mothering plate is full. You do not expect to have to nurture another adult in your household; you want to work alongside someone who is emotionally mature and competent. "Adult" employers tire of the emotional demands of their "child" employees, while the "child" employee often feels abandoned, unloved, or unappreciated by her "adult" employers.

No Relationship

Occasionally nannies and their employers have no apparent relationship at all. Even though the parent/nanny relationship is a work relationship, it should have *some* emotional component. When there is none, it can mean that either or both of the parties have trouble with emotional closeness. Parents who view nannies as no more than servants, or who have abdicated the role of parenting so completely they are not interested at all in the care their children receive, fall into the category of "no relationship."

In order for a "no relationship" situation to be stable, both the parent and the nanny must feel comfortable working with no input from the other. This is more the exception than the rule. Nannies who reported working for families who didn't want to relate to them at all usually didn't stay long. I would like to believe that nannies who flourish in a "no relationship" environment can relate to the children in their care by adopting the role of "real" mother, where they raise the children almost exclusively.

Unfortunately for the children, the literature seems to indicate that it is more customary for caretakers in a "no relationship" arrangement to act as mere custodians, not emotionally investing any more in the child than they do in the relationship with the parents. We've all heard stories of the "poor little rich child" raised by servants who had no real interest in the child.

Enmeshed Relationships

At the other end of the spectrum are those parent/nanny relationships that are so enmeshed that almost no components of an employer/employee relationship remain. This happens when a parent becomes best friends with the nanny or the nanny becomes a confidant. Lonely moms sometimes turn to their nannies for companionship and understanding. Mothers and nannies need to be emotionally involved to some extent; after all, they work and sometimes live together. However, if the relationship between the two crosses over the boundary of being a work/personal relationship and becomes almost exclusively personal, it becomes a problem. When the mom finds that her *only* or *best* friend is the nanny, she should review her life to see if this is appropriate or healthy. Dads and nannies can also develop emotional and sometimes sexual bonds that change the relationship from employer/employee to one that is overwhelmingly personal.

The enmeshed relationship may be remarkably enduring if all parties are happy in their roles. Indeed, some parents (dads) I interviewed cemented their relationships with their nannies by marrying them (and divorcing their spouses). More often than not, however, one of the parties is unhappy that the relationship is too enmeshed and tries to change the role played, and the relationship becomes unstable and falls apart.

POWER MODEL IN EMPLOYER/EMPLOYEE RELATIONSHIPS	
Parent/Child	Power is uneven
No relationship	Parent holds power
Adult/Adult	Power is shared
Enmeshed Relationship	No one holds power

Partners

The healthiest relationship pairing for all involved has two or more adults caring for the children in partnership. In this pairing, all the parties are emotionally mature and view each other as child rearing partners possessing complementary talents to offer the children. The parent(s) and nanny have different skills to impart. One may be more patient or more creative or more fun. Another may be a better disciplinarian, teacher, or sports enthusiast. In my interviews I talked to several families who function as partners or teammates with their nannies. A spirit of mutual cooperation and the common goal of rearing decent, competent children unite these teams. I solicited quotes from them to share with you in the epilogue.

Finding a nanny who is capable and able to be a partner is not simple. Emotionally mature young women are not beating the bushes to be nannies. However, judging from my interviews, age does not seem to be as much a predictor of maturity as does the nanny's own upbringing. Even some very young women are able to function well as partners. They usually have been raised in nurturing, warm families.

The other element vital to a successful partnership is parent(s) who are willing to share power and control over issues related to the children. Some parents feel guilty about their absence during the work day and compensate by being dictatorial about what transpires while they are gone. Just as many, for the same reasons of guilt, abdicate all responsibility to the nanny, thinking "I am a bad parent for not being around, therefore I don't deserve to have a part in making decisions with her." Still others feel hopeless: "I can't control what goes on, so why try?" Still others take the "she is so competent and wonderful, there is nothing I can add to the equation" approach. All of these attitudes need to be analyzed and changed before a true partner relationship can succeed.

Developing a partnership takes time. In this relationship power and control tend to be fluid and to shift from one person to the other depending on the situation. In order for this to happen, mutual trust needs to develop. And developing trust takes time.

In a partnership the parents are in charge, but their desire to do whatever is best for the children overrides feelings of proprietorship. As one parent explained to me, "When I see how my children thrive with Annette's love and attention, the momentary jealousy that leaps into my awareness is quickly smothered by gratitude she is in our lives. I am an older mom, and although I only work part-time and am at home quite a bit with the kids, I'm just not as good as she is at engaging them in activities. She is so playful. And so very patient. I find I'm not very good at handling children when they are tired or whiny. She hardly ever loses her temper. On the other hand, my children almost always come to me when they need reassurance about themselves or help solving a problem. They seem to instinctively know who is best at what and seek out that person."

A nanny named Wendy who now works in an office, but who for several years partnered with a couple in raising their three children, told me, "We always worked as a team. We talked a lot about what to do, disciplining, habit changes, et cetera. When the parents were in the room, they would generally discipline the kids and when I was alone, I would. However, we reinforced each other. If the children misbehaved again after their parents left I would say something to the effect of 'Did you hear what your parents said?' and the parents would do the same, saying things like, 'Are you listening to Wendy?' We agreed a lot about parenting philosophy. We trusted each other and communicated well." (Incidentally, later in the interview when I asked Wendy about compensation she admitted she was earning less take-home pay as a receptionist and office assistant than she had as a nanny, but explained, "I think that's proper. Phones aren't as important as children.")

Partnerships, once established, can be stable. In the effort to find the right person to participate in such an arrangement, however, the family may turn over several nannies. It is extremely difficult to tell during an interview whether or not the interviewee has the capacity to be a good partner. Unfortunately, it may take a few hires before you find a real partner. That is why sometimes the best parents, the ones who are the most emotionally healthy, have the hardest time settling down with a care giver.

So, the next time your snotty neighbor who has had the same nanny for umpteen years comments on the fact that your house has a revolving door in regard to nannies, smile inwardly to yourself. It's just possible that you are one of the myriad healthy families who just hasn't had the good fortune to find an equally emotionally sound child care giver. Your neighbor's family, on the other hand, might be dysfunctional. We all know that it is easy to find a dysfunctional nanny.

PROTECTING YOUR NANNY FROM HEAVEN

We know the importance of keeping our children safe. If you are the employer of a Nanny from Heaven be advised that your nanny is much more in danger of being snatched away than your children. Every day, all across America, nannies are stolen. They're being approached by other parents at the park, accosted in supermarkets, and intercepted as they push strollers in malls.

If you employ a Nanny from Heaven, protect her as fiercely as the Louvre protects the Mona Lisa. The market for good nannies is an active one. And like fine art, the price paid for an experienced nanny can spiral out of control. You may not be able to afford to keep what you have unless you are careful.

How can you protect your nanny from being taken by a family who thinks they need her more than you do? You cannot forbid your nanny to go to places where nanny-needing moms are lurking, since these are usually the places you hired her to visit in the first place: the children's school, playgrounds, sports events, and private lessons. You also can't stop her from socializing with other nannies. They inevitably exchange information on salary, working conditions, and available job openings. So what can you do?

Presumably you are already taking care of the three "pay" basics:

1. You pay the market salary rate, even if your nanny doesn't request it.
2. You pay attention to personality types and workplace "roles" when you make hiring decisions.
3. You pay attention to your nanny's emotional well-being with good communication, such as weekly meetings and frequent feedback.

Now you must consider the finer points of nanny protection.

1. IDENTIFY WHAT IS UNIQUE ABOUT YOUR JOB.

One of the best ways to protect against someone offering your nanny a better job is to structure your job in such a way so that it is not easily reproducible. Remember, not all compensation is monetary. There will always be someone desperate enough to pay more than you for the services of the nanny you treasure. Being able to give her some of the benefits she enjoys with your family might not be as easily accomplished. Some suggestions are:

A. *Unique scheduling*

Some families are able to structure the timing of their child care needs to blend well with the time needs of the nanny. For example, a nanny who wants to go to school during the morning or some other specific time knows that this advantage is not easily duplicated. Perhaps you can offer a four-day week or time off in the summer for the nanny to travel or some other scheduling advantage that is unique to your situation and the nanny's needs.

If you can manage it, give your nanny time off during the day. This adds remarkably to the quality of her working day. Some employers who take for granted that they get a lunch hour forget that most nannies, like most stay-at-home moms, don't even get to go to the bathroom alone, let alone a chance to eat a normal meal.

B. *Unique incentives*

Actions speak louder than promises. When you give your nanny something important to her, you communicate that she is valuable. Figure out what is meaningful to your nanny and provide it if you can. If she loves exercise, offer to pay half of a gym membership. Or, if you can, buy the membership and arrange for her to use it as long as she is employed by you. If your nanny loves movies get a monthly movie pass for her, or make sure she has her own VCR and video rental membership. If candy is her weakness, arrange to stock her favorite kind. Label a shelf with your nanny's name on it and keep the candy there. Silly? Maybe. Effective? You bet. Worth it? Ask anyone who has lost a nanny they liked: absolutely.

C. Business perks that can be passed on

Does your or your spouse's business give you some advantage that you can pass along to your nanny? This could be in the form of medical, dental, legal, or business assistance. Identify ways to let your nanny know you are thinking about her.

2. BONUSES, BONUSES, BONUSES.

Nannies usually become more valuable the longer they are with you. The children grow to depend on them, and they become acclimated to the family routine. If you can't pay above market wages, but still want your compensation package to stand out, figure out how much it would cost to replace your nanny. Be honest in your evaluation. Figure out the cost of advertising or an agency. How much will temporary baby-sitting cost you? How much work will you have to lose while you search? Add these numbers together. Figure out the psychic cost of saying good-bye to someone you and the children trust, and then tack on ten or twenty percent or more to the result. Offer this amount to your nanny if she stays for a specific amount of time. A typical amount of time is one year, but you can tailor it to your needs. We suggest that the timing not be more than a year. And the amount? In our household, it is at least equal to one month's salary.

3. ADULT PLAY.

Include your nanny in your vacations even if it costs more to do so. And let her know way in advance the traveling plans for the next year. When you are on vacation, stay home some evenings and baby-sit and let your nanny go out and explore the local nightlife.

Take her out to dinner, with or without the children. You can use your weekly meeting as an excuse. Or just say you felt you all needed adult time away from the kids to relax. A nanny's job should not be all child play and no adult play.

4. NURTURE YOUR NANNY'S PROFESSIONAL AND PERSONAL GROWTH.

We have sent our nanny to child development classes and invited her to join us when we attended lectures on child rearing issues such as limit setting. And we paid her overtime while she attended these. This communicated that we viewed her job as being important and that we were willing to invest in the improvement of her skills.

We also regularly tell her when we know of activities she might enjoy attending and we give her time off to participate in those that excite her.

Assist your nanny with career planning. Most nannies only stay in the occupation for a few years. Help her plan the next step in her career and assist her in gaining the necessary education. One lucky family had a nanny who initially had the long-range goal of wanting to open a restaurant, but then decided she wanted a career in catering. They financed her cooking classes and ate all the homework. When they no longer needed her nanny skills, she continued to cook dinner for the family in addition to her job as a full-time caterer.

5. TREAT THE OTHER PEOPLE IN HER LIFE WELL.

If possible, get to know her close friends and relatives and be nice to them. Invite them to your home. Let them know you are good people who want the best for everyone in your household, including your nanny.

If your nanny is offered another job and she can't decide what to do about it, she probably will ask people she knows about their opinions. More than once the advice given by a parent or mature friend has stopped a nanny from leaving a job that she basically likes to go to an unknown one that offers more money or seems more glamorous. This won't happen for you unless you have your nanny's family and friends on your side.

6. CHILD REARING PARTNERSHIP.

I discussed this in the previous section about roles, but am repeating it because it is so important. Develop a real relationship with your nanny. Get to know her as well as you can. Treat her as a partner. She probably is spending at least as much time as you do with your children and will have an impact on how they develop as human beings. Involve her in decisions concerning them, especially ones that affect both her and them.

Stick to your end of the work agreement in the "little" things. Be considerate. For example, if you have stipulated that it is not her responsibility to do dinner dishes, don't leave them in the sink overnight and repackage them as leftovers from breakfast. It may seem small to you, but partners make mutual agreements and changing one unilaterally opens up the possibility the other partner will feel resentful.

7. EGO MASSAGE.

Being a nanny can be a lonely job. It's hard work. And seldom do nannies get the reward of finishing a project or closing a sale or seeing their work come to completion. Children usually don't show appreciation for the things we do for them. For nannies, it is up to the children's parents to pass along the thanks. One nanny, a Professional who had worked for several families, said her present employers were the best she had ever had. When asked to be specific she explained, "They are never late, they keep me informed of changes way in advance, my paycheck is ready on time, they are very organized, they show their appreciation in tangible ways: they bring me flowers, brought me earrings when they returned from a trip, gave me an Easter card and an Easter lily, a Christmas bonus and once, when they heard me say I liked a certain rock star, brought me tickets to his concert. They say in a lot of ways that they like me."

I already advised you to give your nanny plenty of positive feedback. I recommended that you thank her often and point out frequently the positive impact she is having on the kids and your family. I would like to add that you should occasionally do this in writing. It will help her to have something tangible to look at on those days when everything seems to go wrong and she is most vulnerable to someone offering a change of scene.

One day I came in and all the children were happily involved in different activities. One was feeding the rabbits. The other was working at the computer. A third was being tickled by our nanny and was laughing. "This is such a happy place. It's so nice to walk into a house where everyone seems content," I said more to myself than to anyone else, but fortunately out loud. Our nanny overheard the comments and said, "Thank you. It's nice to hear you feel this way." I made a mental note to express my thanks more often for what she was doing for my family and that evening wrote her a thank-you note that the children decorated and then taped to her door.

As I reflect on my life as a former personnel executive, I realize that the secrets to protecting your nanny from nannynappers are no different than those used by smart business managers who want to stem employee turnover. Often, though, we seem to forget that caring for our children is a profession worthy of respect and admiration. We need to assist our nannies in feeling good about themselves and the job they do. If we are successful, they will not only continue to do a good job, but will also be less vulnerable to promises of a job in greener pastures.

TERMINATING THE NON–NANNY FROM HEAVEN

Termination. It's a harsh word, bringing up images of bodies disintegrating in midair. Yet, it is a fact of employment. Sooner or later every employer faces the end of a relationship with an employee, either through retirement, mutual consent, firing, or quitting (which is tantamount to the employee firing the employer). Like death, taxes, and the fact that your child will get the chicken pox the day you are supposed to go on vacation, you can't avoid ending the nanny relationship. You can only hope to make it as smooth as possible for you, your children, and the nanny.

Time for Nanny to Go

Sometimes the writing you see on the wall is not washable. It is written in indelible ink and clearly states that the time has come—your nanny is no longer suitable for your family. She has broken a vital rule and been caught in a major infraction (stealing, a hit-and-run car accident, drug use, physical or emotional child abuse) or continues to commit minor violations (being consistently late in spite of multiple warnings, disregarding house rules). All the signs point to one exit and that exit leads out. If this is the case, you are lucky. You may feel sick to your stomach, anguished at the thought of all the disruption this decision will mean to your life, but at least you know you have to do it. A change must take place.

Equally lucky (I use this term loosely) are those families who lose their nannies. Sometimes the nanny gives plenty of notice, more often than not she doesn't, and sometimes you are even the last to know she is gone (the kids knew last night, the neighbors knew last week, and the post office has had her change of address card since last month when you decided to give her another chance after she swore she'd never come home drunk again). You, believe it or not, are also fortunate because you can go into gear, into high action, into full search mode for a replacement without any ambivalence.

Most families are not so lucky. These are the families who suspect they should be looking for a new nanny, who have a feeling things aren't supposed to function as they are, *but* . . .

There are a million "buts." For want of space and time we will list just a few:

1. I know she is shortchanging the grocery money, but the children love her.
2. I know she isn't telling the truth, but she's acting more like a teenager than a sociopath and she hasn't told lies about anything important.
3. I know she's totaled the car, but it scared her and she will drive more safely in the future.
4. I know she isn't working out, but I have this really important project at work that has to get done.

5. I know she really should go, but it's so hard to find someone.
6. I know the end is near, but if I let her go, I might get someone worse.
7. I know I need someone else, but she knows our schedule and I don't have time to train someone else.
8. I know she isn't the right person, but our vacation is coming soon.
9. I know she shouldn't stay forever, but maybe she can just stay until summer ends and school starts.
10. I know she isn't good with the kids, but she is so good keeping the house clean.
11. I know sometimes she is terrible, but sometimes she is great.
12. I know she is unreliable, but when she comes she is wonderful.
13. I know she is wrong for us, but we've had so many changes in our life I don't want to make the children go through another one.
14. I know she is wrong for us, but the agency guarantee just ran out.
15. I know my intuition tells me to act, but I need actual proof.
16. I know the children aren't fond of her, but I enjoy having her around; she's so much brighter than others we've had.
17. I know she is crazy, but she knows our routine. If I fired her she might come back and seek revenge.
18. I know she is wrong for us, but she needs this job so badly.
19. I know she is terrible, but letting her go could destroy her.
20. But, this is a terrible time to have no child care!

Real, live parents just like you have told me every one of the excuses listed above. These parents are caring, educated, dedicated parents who want the best for their children. However, faced with the dilemma of no child care for even a brief time versus inadequate but certain child care, we sometimes hide our faces ostrich-like in the sand. Unless the situation is clearly black and white, such as when your nanny leaves or you have to fire her because you catch her red-handed in a major infraction, it can be hard to make the decision to change. Parents often delay terminating a nanny for two common reasons:

1. They feel as though they are being held hostage.
2. They don't trust their own instincts.

Being Held Hostage

You hire a new receptionist at work and find she's all thumbs. After two weeks on the job she is still losing calls, misspelling names, and seems continually befuddled. What do you do?

Easy decision, right? You terminate her. It's best for the company and ultimately best for her to find a job more suitable to her talents. The situation I outline before you, however, was not as easy for the manager of a Madison Avenue advertising agency. One of his best clients, Mr. Berkowitz, had been disconnected for the third time. Mr. Berkowitz was calling from a phone booth several blocks away and finally decided the only way to reach his ad agency was to walk there. He was not happy about this.

The manager was not happy either. He knew the receptionist wasn't working out, but she was the daughter of his closest friend. She was a high school student, filling in while his normal receptionist was on vacation. The personal connection with this receptionist, a girl he had known since birth, put him in an emotional bind. He was being held hostage.

That receptionist was me. My father's friend ultimately took me out to lunch at a fancy restaurant, told me I shouldn't waste the remaining two weeks I had promised to work for him indoors in a boring office, paid me for the time, and sent me to the beach. I never did find out if he kept Mr. Berkowitz as a client. (It has been over twenty years and I can still hear the pleading voice, "Darling, this is Mr. Berkowitz again, *please* don't disconnect me.")

Once you hire a nanny and bring her into your home, you become vulnerable to being an emotional hostage yourself. More often than not, it takes time for you to decide that the nanny is unsuitable. Usually by then you've invested time and energy training her, she knows the household routine, and, most important, she is part of your children's lives. They have attached to her, which makes you reluctant to take her away.

Sometimes, we know almost immediately that we've made a

mistake. You've extended an offer, the nanny accepts it, and suddenly she reveals a side of herself that gives you reason to be concerned. Or she starts work and within the first few days it dawns on you that she might not be the right person. Yet, even those wise families who stipulate a trial period sometimes don't terminate a nanny who appears as if she is going to cause them heartache, and instead tell themselves it's too late. Why? Because they are emotional hostages to the fear that it is just too difficult to find a Nanny from Heaven. They settle for what they already have. Elaine Swartz did just that. She got insight into the fact that she had probably made a hiring mistake the first day her nanny arrived for work, but told herself it was too late to act because the nanny had already unpacked. In hindsight, Elaine wished she had acted sooner.

Never Hire Someone Right before Christmas

ELAINE SWARTZ'S STORY

"When my son was about six and my daughter was five months old, our nanny, Jenny, decided to get married. We had lots of nannies before her and each time I had found them through newspapers ads. I always had a very good response to my ads and it had always been easy, but this time it was just before Christmas and very few people answered.

"I now know that nobody in his or her right mind is looking for a new job just before Christmas and no one who is stable is looking for a new home at that time either. When I got the poor ad response, I should have waited until the new year and advertised again. Instead, I lowered my requirements and interviewed people without direct child care experience or references.

"The only reasonable response was from a thirty-two-year-old woman named Robin. She walked into the house and at first seemed interestingly artistic, perhaps a little flamboyant. She was quite pretty. She was tall, wore a long black skirt, and had chestnut hair. She had some interesting ideas about projects

continued

---

that she could do with the children and she seemed innovative and warm.

"The interview was much shorter than usual. We both had commitments and for some reason that I don't exactly remember, I didn't take my normal amount of time getting to know her.

"The first day Robin moved in, our former nanny, Jenny, was visiting to pick up some of the things she had left behind. She and I were talking upstairs while Robin was downstairs unpacking. Robin suddenly came rushing up the stairs saying 'I know you're talking about me!' I didn't know what to say because, of course, we weren't. So I reassured her we weren't. She countered, 'I can always feel the vibrations when someone is talking about me. My skin feels tingly.' She then returned downstairs.

"Jenny left and I went downstairs to talk to Robin. I said, 'I don't know what the problem is, but I've been friends with our former nanny for years now and I hope that someday you and I will become friends too. We didn't even bring your name up in our conversation.'

"Robin answered that she was sometimes too sensitive and when I asked her why, this terrible history of how she had been abused as a child came out. Well, I knew right away that was a bad sign. But there I was; she had already unpacked her bags. What could I do? I was hard up. I didn't have any alternatives. Even though in my heart I knew I was worried, I hoped I was wrong and she would turn out to be okay."

She didn't. Robin turned out to be horrible. She was so sensitive that anytime Elaine gave her any direction she would burst into tears. Elaine increasingly felt as though she had to walk on eggshells every time she was around Robin. The emotional tension was terrible. But, she reasoned, by now she had invested the time to train Robin. Besides, how could she advertise for a replacement while Robin still worked for her? It was an extremely busy time at work and Elaine rationalized that when things slowed down . . . One night Elaine returned

continued

home to find that Robin had moved most of the family's living room furniture out in order to move in her own furniture, which had been in storage. She had at one time vaguely mentioned the desire to move in her piano, but that was all. Now a huge baby grand piano, a strange sofa, and several chairs had been placed in the living room while Elaine's furniture was scattered among other rooms and the garage. Elaine still didn't fire Robin, figuring that she was strange, perhaps even crazy, but nice to the children and therefore should be tolerated.

Elaine's work schedule changed and she was forced to request that Robin adjust. When she refused, Elaine terminated her. Robin came back a week later. Elaine was feeding the baby and upon hearing Robin's voice the baby vomited.

Elaine said she wasn't sure if the vomiting was coincidental, an indication of the baby's feelings, or of Elaine's own discomfort being transmitted to the infant, but the act was a clear reflection of how everyone in the family felt.

Elaine said that a bad experience with a nanny is like labor pains, you eventually forget the intensity, you forget many of the details, but you never completely forget the experience. Elaine's next nanny was a Nanny from Heaven.

Most often, when faced with a nanny who isn't totally, obviously, significantly terrible, we come up with "buts" to rationalize why we can't make a change now. The real reason we don't make the change is that we don't want to face the emotions involved in terminating one relationship, deciding upon another, and then reinvesting ourselves. We fear that it will harm our children to ask them to say good-bye. It is very uncomfortable for us to say so ourselves.

I speak from personal experience, my own and that of dozens of families. The feeling of being held hostage, of somehow not being able to act even though you know you should, is very common. To date, I have found only one antidote, one key that unlocks the fetters. That is the belief, the firm belief, that you can do better.

Visualize the nanny who is perfect for you. Visualize her in detail. She is out there. Everything you need to do and know in order to find her has been covered in this book. If you have a nanny who is not a good match for your family, let her go in the knowledge that she needs to go on with her life to find her perfect job. You need to be free to find a Nanny from Heaven.

Faced with the bonus of two free weeks after I left the ad agency, I reactivated my Red Cross Water Safety Instructor license and landed a job as a lifeguard. I made a little less money, but met several good-looking guys (what a trade-off!). I don't know who the ad agency hired to replace me, but I guarantee she was better than I had been.

Rationalizing Away Your Instincts

Sometimes—most times—your nanny is not all bad. In fact, she probably is good or even great in certain respects. When does the bad outweigh the good? Is one very important thing going wrong reason enough to fire an otherwise well-performing employee? Does it take ten minor infractions for you to decide to cut the cord? How does one decide to trade in a semidefective model for a new and unknown one? Do you act on intuition even if you don't know for sure? These are not easy questions.

The best advice I can offer is don't explain away your intuition. Trust your "gut feeling." The problem is most of us don't. The pit of our stomach says "She's not right; she's not right." Our head counters with, *"But . . ."*

You are going to have to get some agreement between body parts here. Tell your head to remember what I suggested in chapter 2, that you can reasonably and realistically only expect three things from a nanny: that your children be kept safe, that your children are happy and thriving, and that the nanny diminishes the stress and tension in your household rather than adds to it. If any of these have been violated, you need to say "good-bye" to your "buts" and take action.

When is it a good time to get your "but" in gear and make a change?

Rule #1: There is no good time to have a baby, go on vacation, or replace your nanny.

Rule #2: There is no need to ponder when is it a good time to change child care; it usually isn't under your control.

Rule #3: There is a cost to taking action; there is also a cost for not taking action and sometimes this is the greater cost.

Rule #4: Even under the worst of circumstances (and this author has heard some stories about pretty bad timing), everyone survives.

It is *never* a good time to have a disruption in child care. So do it sooner rather than later. Do it even if it is inconvenient, expensive, or emotionally wrenching. Your children deserve the best care you can provide for them, no ifs, ands, or "buts" about it.

Notice

If your nanny is the one who has decided to leave, you don't have much control over how much time you have to get a replacement. Nannies from Heaven tend to leave because they intend to get married, go away to school, or retire. In these situations you are usually given several months' notice and the opportunity to arrange an overlap, which is wonderful for everyone involved. Nannies from Heaven sometimes also leave because of sudden events like family illness or their own illness. In this case, you won't have plenty of notice, but at least you can look forward to the children and you being able to continue contact with her sometime in the future. Dwelling on any of this is pointless, because it is not controllable.

Nannies from Hell love the intrigue of plotting a secret getaway. They have been known to give notice the day before you leave on vacation or to decide they are much too talented to be nannies and give you two days to find a replacement (during which time the children have the flu and you have a critical project to finish). Once again, you don't have much say, so there is no use discussing it here.

If you are the one who has made the decision, it is a different ball game. The rules of this game are simple. Be decisive. Be as nice as you can monetarily. Be swift if she is a Nanny from Hell. Take your time with others.

If the nanny has been with you for less than one month and you have stipulated up front that the first month is a trial period, you may let her go with no obligation to pay severance pay. Some families pay some anyway to maintain a good relationship with a person who now knows their children and where they live.

If the nanny has worked for you past the trial date, you will need to honor the notice period you listed on your work agreement. Most nanny work agreements specify two weeks' notice from either party. Two weeks is not a lot of time to find quality child care, nor is it often sufficient time for a nanny to find another job and place to live. However, the facts of life are that in ordinary workplaces, hourly employees are usually asked to give two weeks' notice and in the home, if you get notice at all, it probably will only be two weeks or so.

Some parents negotiate one month's notice up front. This works well if your nanny is a good one and respects agreements. It backfires with a Nanny from Hell. She is not likely to honor a one-month notice period, yet if you fire her, you are obligated to give her one month's salary in lieu of notice. Even so, I suggest you consider asking for as much notice as you can and paying the penalty of having to pay a person off if she turns out to be wrong.

If she is indeed a Nanny from Hell, you will want her out of your home as soon as possible. Savvy employers pay their employees the salary due them plus the salary for any notice period and ask Nannies from Hell to leave immediately, even if they have no back-up plans. If she really is a Nanny from Hell how do you think she will act now that she knows in a few weeks she will be gone? Families who wanted to be "nice" to caregivers who they knew to be bad news were often sorry.

Be nice financially to anybody you terminate. Pay for goodwill. Pay more than your work agreement stipulates, just to get her smiling. However, if you are terminating a Nanny from Hell, make sure you are edging her toward the door as you hand over the cash. If at all possible (and sometimes it's not), make the parting pleasant even for caregivers you hate, but make sure they leave swiftly. If she has nowhere to go, pay for temporary housing or a hotel room. Collect all her keys before she leaves.

If you are dealing with someone who is less than a Nanny from Hell, you will want your children to have as smooth a transition as possible. Walking a nanny to the door and asking her to leave immediately is disruptive not only to the nanny, but also to your children, so you do not want to do this unless it is *absolutely* necessary. Children need time to say good-bye and to process the loss of a caregiver. Most of the time a nanny quits because she didn't get along with a parent (usually the mom), not because she didn't get along with the children. Likewise, when a nanny is fired, it is frequently because she has violated the trust of the parents, not because the children didn't like her. Children often love nannies their parents hate.

Relationships often sour at the end and you may find yourself angry at a nanny who has performed an adequate job until now. Or she may have not done a good job and you find yourself tempted to get even for her transgressions. You would do better to swallow a little pride and take out insurance for the future. You will want this person out of your life permanently and the best way to ensure this is to guard against her leaving feeling she got a raw deal. Nannies have been known to seek revenge for real or imagined hurts.

Provided she is not a Nanny from Hell, let her work out the two weeks or other agreed-upon notice period. Let her even think it was her idea to leave in the first place. Let her "take advantage of you" by offering to give her extra money for a smooth transition. The theme is that a nanny who leaves happy is less likely to cause trouble for you in the future. This is not always possible to arrange, but if you can manage it, do so.

What to Do

When you have made the decision that your nanny must go, sit down and talk to her in a private setting. If the decision can wait until your regularly scheduled weekly meeting, then let it. If not, make sure you have a quiet place to talk that is not in earshot of the children.

Without placing blame, cover the reason you have come to the decision you have reached. Leave room open for discussion, but be decisive and do not imply that whether or not she stays is open for negotiation. Be nice, but firm. Be honest, but don't belabor her weaknesses. Some parents try to salvage the nanny's feelings by saying things like, "We've decided we don't need so much child care" or "I'm going to stay home with the children" or "Our wonderful nanny who was with us before has decided to come back." You can give excuses like this if they are true. Don't if they are not. It is much better to find a nonemotional but true statement like, "Our styles of disciplines don't mesh well together," or "You would be terrific with younger children who like to play a lot because you are so good at finding fun things to do, but right now we need someone who is a more careful driver since the children mainly need chauffeuring." Respect the nanny's feelings by leveling with her, in a kind and gentle way.

Discuss severance pay, the final work date, and how to handle references. Cover what you want said to the children. Agree on what explanation will be offered to her friends and family. Get her focused on the next step in her life. Expect her to feel hurt, sad, angry, or relieved. Expect to feel so yourself.

One nanny told me about a parting of the ways she had had with a family. She had worked for this family for several months, most of the time at loggerheads. She explained she tried to hang on because she felt she had made a year's commitment, but she was miserable most of the time. "The mom told me how to do everything, like how to properly boil an egg. I've been cooking for ten years and I know there are lots of different techniques for cooking eggs, all of which get you the same result. But this mother didn't just care about the result, the process had to be the same as hers. So, you can imagine how much direction I got in child care! I'm a career nanny. It was hard for me to be treated like a perpetual trainee. We eventually agreed to part. The mom kept reminding me that she wanted no emotion about the decision, especially on the last day. I thought to myself, "This is an emotional occasion; when I give the child I have cared for a last hug, I will feel sad. But I resolved to not show my feelings in compliance with the mom's wishes. The last day came and I said good-bye to my former charge. She and I hugged and were fine. The *mom* burst into tears."

Transitions can go smoothly, as the next two stories illustrate.

Time to Go

THE BENTLEYS' STORY

The Bentleys have five children, all boys. When their youngest reached kindergarten, they decided that their long-term nanny no longer suited the family's needs. She was very warm, loving, and nurturing. She didn't drive, however, and she didn't discipline well. Tanya Bentley explained, "We loved Connie. We all did. The boys loved her, my husband and I loved her, even the cats considered her bed the preferred place to sleep. For almost a year, I made other arrangements to get the boys to their activities after school. For awhile I was able to get a college student to chauffeur them around, but as soon as finals came up, the arrangement fell apart. I constantly was on the phone asking other parents to give my kids rides.

"We couldn't afford to hire an additional person to handle our child care needs while Connie was at home doing household duties, which were of secondary importance to us. Plus we had another problem. She was way too easy on the children. If one of the boys didn't want to do his homework, Connie didn't insist. If another wanted to watch TV despite our insistence that there be none during the day, she'd look the other way. She'd give her life for these boys, but she didn't have what it takes to handle the discipline part.

"It all came to a head when one of our sons broke his arm for the second time. He had been jumping from the top bunk of his bunk bed. Connie had told him not to and he disobeyed. She couldn't get him to a doctor because she doesn't drive. My husband was out of town and I was at an off-site

continued

meeting, an hour and a half away. Getting my son to the doctor was such a production, I realized we couldn't put off making a change.

"We talked to Connie and explained the situation. We asked her to think about what she wanted to do next and promised to support her in her choice. She decided that she wanted to work for a family that had younger children. We agreed on a termination date.

"I don't know who was more upset, me or the kids. But everyone agreed with the decision. We made plans for Connie to baby-sit one evening a week and to work one weekend day for a few months. We scheduled it before she left so that everyone could feel there would be some continuation. The last weeks were hard, even though we found someone who was perfect for our current needs. This new person, a guy actually, wasn't Connie. Once the boys got used to him, however, they really enjoyed the special advantages he offered. He was a good sports coach, a musician, and a computer whiz, all interests of my boys. Whereas they viewed Connie as a second mom, they came to see our male nanny as an older brother or second dad.

"We're lucky, I guess, because Connie stayed in the area. She has become an 'aunt' to our family. We don't see her that much anymore, but she is still part of our family."

The Bentleys, a Chicago family, said that their first grandchild was named Constance in honor of this favorite nanny.

It Was a Great Year

FRANCINE DAILEY'S STORY

"I had an au pair from France who was great. She was still a child herself and loved to sit on the floor and play Barbies with Gaby, my daughter who was four at the time. When

continued

Evette, the au pair, had to return to France, I was worried how Gaby would take the news. I am a single mom and Gaby had had too many losses in her life thus far. I didn't want her to lose Evette, but there wasn't anything I could do about it. To make matters worse, my new child care person wasn't going to start immediately so I couldn't arrange an overlap between her and Evette.

"I told Gaby two weeks beforehand that Evette had to return to her own mommy in France. Both Evette and I reassured Gaby that she was loved, that she was a joy to care for, and that the leaving had to do with Evette's need to go home. Evette put up a big world map and drew a line between her city and our own. She then pasted pictures of her home around the border so Gaby could see where she was going.

"Evette and Gaby talked a lot about the separation. They practiced on a toy phone talking to each other. Evette made a tape of herself reassuring Gaby that she cared for her and would miss her. She finished the tape by reading a book that the two had often shared.

"I won't say that Gaby didn't miss Evette. I know that she did a lot. I let her listen to Evette's tape as often as she wished. In the beginning it was several times a day. After a week, it settled down to once every three or four days. I also invested in long distance phone calls, not every time Gaby wanted to talk, but at least one a week for about three weeks. When I had to tell her we weren't going to call, I encouraged her to draw a picture we could send to Evette.

"Gaby is now twelve and doesn't remember Evette. But at one time in her life, this young woman was very important to her and I'm glad that I was able to make the transition as easy as possible."

Shortly after their interview Francine and Gaby visited Evette and her family in France. It was wonderful trip for everyone. Gaby recently won a statewide French language competition.

SUMMARY

1. One key to maintaining a healthy working relationship is structure: develop house rules, praise frequently, conduct regularly scheduled weekly meetings.
2. Family dynamics play a pivotal role in the nanny/family match. Dysfunctional nannies do best in dysfunctional homes. Functional nannies stay with functional families.
3. Employees often adopt work roles based on familial patterns. The pairing with complementary employer roles is crucial for long-term satisfaction. Some role pairings, like parent/child and adult/adult, are stable. Others, like mother/mother or child/child, are unstable and will result in either the nanny, the parent(s), or everyone becoming unhappy.
4. Termination is a fact of life. Terminate the employee you suspect is a bad fit sooner rather than later. There never is a good time to lose child care, so don't wait.
5. Protect and nurture your relationship with a Nanny from Heaven. Nannynappers are lurking everywhere.

CHAPTER 8

The Triple-A Approach to Life with Nanny

MYTH
Our child care worries would be over if we could just find a nanny who is wonderful with our children.

TRUTH
An old proverb says, "Be careful what you wish for, you just might get it."

Most families I interviewed were happy with their decision to employ a nanny. No other child care option offers so many pluses, except perhaps care by an extended family member. Then again, considering the prevalence of mother-in-law jokes in our society, my vote remains firmly cast for nanny care. The reality of kindly Aunt Julia or sweet Grandma Rosalie peacefully cooperating with us to raise our children is more fairy tale than truth. (And if you've read any Brothers Grimm fairy tales in their original form, you'll know that the authors' last name was appropriate.) Parents and grandparents who themselves were raised by relatives living together told me entertaining but harrowing stories of colossal family fights over such important child rearing issues as whether the children should be allowed to bathe with the garlic strands they wore around their necks in summertime to protect against disease.

Do you think the plastic dishes in your cupboard were originally designed for children? Heavens no! How many times have you actually seen a child drop a dish? Plastic ware was invented to prevent the loss of dinnerware hurled to the ground to emphasize an opinion during a family discussion about child rearing.

Compare this with the calm discussion during the weekly meeting I advised you to have in chapter 7: a lot of praise, a little correction, everyone drinks tea, the children are peacefully asleep or watching a video, sometimes there is a tear or two, but usually issues get resolved and everybody reaches closure at the end. If not, you can always fire the nanny or she can quit. Try to sever the ties this easily with a blood relative. I rest my case. Give me an *N*, give me an *A*, give me an *N* and an *N* and a *Y*. Yea . . . Nanny!

This book's primary goals are to give you all the tools you need in order to find a Nanny from Heaven for your family and to address the main questions that surface for first-time nanny employers and for those families who have made bad hiring decisions in the past: What do I really need? How can I find the right nanny? How will I decide? Hopefully, *The Good Nanny Book* has answered these questions for you and given you the courage and the expertise to proceed. You *can* find a Nanny from Heaven. If you don't immediately, keep trying. You will be successful.

A secondary goal has been to equip you to manage and live happily with the nanny in your life. We've talked about the mechanics—a weekly meeting, a work agreement, compensation that enables you to keep the Nanny from Heaven in your life or get rid of a Nanny from Hell. However, one subject remains to be discussed. What do you do with a nanny who is good with your children, but who is problematic for you? She isn't Super Nanny—wonderful for the whole family—but she's not a Crook either.

Why devote a chapter to discussing problems, when I am so firmly committed to nannies as a fantastic method for sharing child rearing? Because every solution brings forth its own set of problems. And even though I would rather deal with the problems generated by nanny care than any other form of child care, saying a nanny employer will automatically live happily with his or her nanny is tantamount to advising a pregnant woman that if she tells her fetus often enough to sleep through the night after birth, it will (I tried this, and he didn't).

PROBLEMS—REAL AND IMAGINED

It is very common for a parent to worry about bringing a nanny—whether for the first time or the tenth— into his or her family. If you find yourself with fears, don't push them away or, worse yet, worry about your worries. Allow them to surface; recognize them as being valid. Instead of saying to yourself, "I have nothing to worry about," tell yourself instead, "No matter what comes up, I can handle it." In this chapter, I will teach you how to solve any problem that may arise from life with nanny.

If you do not have any fears regarding a potential nanny or problems with a current one, skip this chapter. I once bought a book for one of my children in an effort to combat a nightly worry about scary shadows on his wall. It had a good title, something about there not being any monsters or ghosts, but if I had read more than the first few pages in the store, I wouldn't have bought it. Page after page, it covered all the scary creatures a child did not have to fear. Many of them even I had not previously known about (ghoulies?). I have to say, shadows were never again my child's scariest nighttime concerns. I unwittingly introduced him to several other much scarier options.

As you think about a specific problem you may be having with a current care giver, or confront any apprehensions that hamper your hiring a new nanny, consider the following points:

1. No form of child care is painless, including (*especially* might be a better word) the decision to stay home and provide all the care yourself. Day-care centers, family day homes, and other arrangements all have their own set of fears attached to them.
2. An emotion, regardless of the circumstance, is real. The first step is to face the feeling and admit it is there. Parents who did this were the most successful in resolving their situations.
3. Put yourself in the other person's shoes. Think about the nanny's apprehensions. She often has at stake a job, a place to live, a reputation. She doesn't have your resources should things not work out.

One mom confided that, faced with taking care of her firstborn alone after the departure of a baby nurse, she was reduced to tears. The nurse's parting words were, "Remember you're bigger than he is." I offer you similar advice. You're "bigger" than your nanny.

Enlisting the aid of a nanny to care for your children can be an immensely rewarding experience. The psychic payoff for doing what is best for your children by itself can be tremendous. Even parents with horror stories often also had inspiring experiences of wonderful women who continued as honorary family members long after they ceased being employees, because they had meant so much to the family. It is worth the effort to find an excellent nanny and to live happily sharing child care responsibilities.

THE TRIPLE-A APPROACH: WHAT TO DO WHEN LIFE WITH A GOOD NANNY PRESENTS A PROBLEM FOR THE PARENTS

No one should continue to employ a nanny who is not good at child care. If you have read this far, I hope you know how strongly I feel about this. Don't compromise, make excuses, or delay in terminating a nanny who delivers anything less than very good care for your children. You should be satisfied with her warmth, her manner of discipline, the way she speaks to your children, her attention to safety, her ability and willingness to nurture each one of them in the individual manner the child requires.

However, there are nannies who do a good job with children, but are unsatisfactory in others ways. Their lifestyles, their habits, their attitude toward adults—in myriad ways a "good" nanny for the kids may not be good for us parents. If you should find yourself in this situation, what should you do?

Some parents adopt the attitude, "She's good at child care; that's all that's important." Or they say to themselves, "My children will be happy if she is happy, so I don't want to say or do anything to risk her becoming unhappy; I'll overlook the behavior that annoys me." Many parents—too many, in my opinion—accommodate to situations that make them feel uncomfortable, telling themselves that is the price to pay for harmony with their care givers.

At one time I was guilty of acting this way. I no longer do. Just because our children are our first priority does not mean that nothing else counts. A nanny is employed to make the *entire* family function better. If your children are happy with her but you are not, you must make some changes.

Faced with a nanny whose behavior bugs us we have three options:

1. Alter the behavior.
2. Accept the behavior.
3. Avoid the behavior.

I call this method of dealing with problems the AAA (or "Triple-A") approach. It was developed by Dr. Virginia Price. AAA is an acronym of the three positions you can take: to *a*lter, *a*ccept, or *a*void the problem. Any of the three responses is acceptable as long as it achieves peace of mind, which is your goal. Remember, a nanny is supposed to decrease the tension in your household rather than add to it. If you don't want to change the nanny, it may be in your court to decrease the tension by learning how to do so unilaterally.

The AAA Approach: Alter the Behavior

If you are like me, you automatically choose the first option and, when faced with someone who doesn't do things the way you prefer, you try to change the person.

I simply can not understand why my children can't turn off lights when they leave a room, why the toilet seat is left up, and why no one in my home except me thinks it is important to keep belongings in their proper place. I tell everyone this often enough; it's beyond me why very little changes. However, I haven't stopped trying. So it shouldn't surprise you when I admit that when the nanny in my life does something that bothers me, or doesn't do something I think she should, I automatically choose the first option. I ask her to change.

Most nanny employers do the same. Even those who have a hard time knowing when something *really* bothers them, or difficulty in articulating their discomfort once they figure it out (put me in both categories), eventually tell their nanny they disagree with something she is or is not doing. Hopefully, most of us do this during the weekly meeting and in an unemotional manner that completely and fairly communicates the problem and doesn't damage our nanny's self-esteem. However, even under the best of circumstances and with the best management practices, sometimes some of us fail. There is no change.

Yet, some parents *are* effective. They ask for a change of behavior and get it. They articulate their needs and, presto, the needs are met. What is their secret? Is it in the way they communicate? Their tone of voice? Their ability to choose the right time? The words they selected? (In searching for the answer I had great hopes of using it to finally get everyone in my family to flush the toilet.) So what is the difference between failure and success? Why are some parents able to solve problems more effectively than others?

The reason some people are more successful than others at altering their nanny's behavior has to do with the nanny in their lives and the nature of the problem. That's the secret. Some nannies are better at change than others. Some problems are more amenable to being solved than others.

It's a little like parenting. If you have more than one child, you know that some children are easier than others. Some kids make us feel like great parents and others don't. Or to be even more precise, the same children, at different stages, allow us to feel more or less competent, depending on the stage.

Sometimes the nanny is amenable to your suggestions. For example, our current Super Nanny, when asked to change the way she does something, smiles sweetly and says "Sure." She makes me feel like Super Boss. Yet, a previous nanny we had, when asked to do something very similar, would nod in agreement during the weekly meeting when the issue was raised, promise to implement the change, and then either continue or escalate the offending behavior. My management techniques were the same with both nannies. The results differed.

If the reality of life with your nanny means that although she is wonderful with your children, some of her behavior is troublesome to you, and your efforts to change the behavior have failed, you are left with the choice of continuing to feel aggravated or to try one of the other options in the Triple-A approach: acceptance or avoidance. Why? Because if she won't change, the only way to deal with the negative feelings the behavior generates is to either change the way you view the behavior or avoid the behavior entirely. If you change the picture in your mind, you can change the feelings associated with the picture.

The AAA Approach: Accept the Behavior

When you switch your viewpoint and accept behavior so that the behavior no longer bothers you, you are displaying acceptance. This is not resignation, where you swallow your feelings and harbor bitterness. It is not approval, where you condone the behavior. Instead, you reformat the picture of the behavior in your head so you feel okay about it.

For example, a woman at a playground initially was angered by two children who were playing roughly and bumped into her child. She complained to their nanny and was told that the children were out of sorts because their mother had died the previous day. Upon hearing this, the woman immediately pictured the children's behavior through a different lens. She instantaneously stopped feeling irritated and felt sympathy and understanding instead.

Likewise, a father was initially bothered by his nanny's recent and unexplained inability to carry through on household assignments, when he arrived home unexpectedly and found his children and the nanny deeply involved in practicing a play intended to be a birthday surprise for him. He changed his point of view. He realized the nanny was spending her time well and changed from feeling annoyed to feeling grateful. He *accepted* her behavior.

One way to move to a position of accepting another's behavior is to explain the behavior in a way that takes away its emotional sting for you. You don't have to agree with the behavior; you simply reinterpret it in a nonthreatening way. You can trivialize the situation ("It's really not a big deal"), detach from it ("It's not directed at me"), or depersonalize it ("It's an affliction"). For example, one family had an au pair who was out of sorts in the mornings. She would walk through her duties as if half asleep, would yell at the children if they gave less than one hundred percent cooperation, and generally was not the best person to relate to before 10:00 A.M. The parents counseled her to get to sleep earlier, tried to persuade her to try vitamin supplements and light therapy to change her internal clock . . . nothing worked. At all other times except early morning hours when she was Attila the Hun, she was fantastic. Everyone loved her.

Realizing their au pair couldn't change, the family tried to alter her schedule and duties so she could sleep in. It was a major disruption, and they found themselves unable to get to work in time, so they returned to the old schedule.

Finally, the family concluded that the only way to deal with the situation was to adjust their thinking. They explained to the children that the au pair was not a "morning person" and didn't feel well until she had adequate time to wake up. They reminded their children how it felt to be sick. The whole family practiced compassion and understanding rather than condemnation. The children came up with ways they could be more self-sufficient in getting ready for school. Everyone tried to be extra considerate first thing in the morning. In retrospect, the parents were glad they had been faced with the problem. They felt their children gained a lot in moral fiber in learning how to cope with it.

The AAA Approach: Avoid the Behavior

Another family had a nanny who was fantastic at every aspect of her job except food selection. This presented a huge problem for the mom whose career was as a nutritionist. Before the nanny (whose name was Erisa Zarwuela—the children called her by her initials) was hired, the family ate whole grains, lots of organic vegetables, and very few sweets. After Erisa became the nanny, the children's eating patterns changed. Erisa was a terrible cook, but a great baker. She baked a lot and encouraged the children to eat what she had baked, sometimes to the exclusion of less sweet and more nutritious choices. One day the mom came into the kitchen and noticed the children were breakfasting on pancakes covered with chocolate syrup. She questioned them about this and they replied, "Mom, we don't call her E.Z. for nothing."

The parent in this case decided to avoid confronting E.Z., to not discuss it further with the children, and to not face it herself. She simply stayed away during the meals provided by E.Z., bought vitamins for the children, and made sure the meals she herself cooked were nutritious.

She explained to me, "Erisa was wonderful, truly wonderful. She was also very sensitive. I chose to avoid a discussion with her about food because I knew that neither of us would be able to change our point of view. Erisa simply did not like to cook—I think she was afraid she would burn the food—while I felt she should attempt to cook healthy food no matter what. On this one issue, I decided to back away because she was head and heels better than anyone else I ever had who worked for me."

Another family chose a different form of avoidance. They told me about one nanny who was good at child care. The problem was that she continued to smash their cars up. The dad explained, "She took an old classic Porsche we had because her own car was at the body shop being fixed. She drove the Porsche out of the driveway right into a Mercedes parked on the street. She asked the body shop to please fix the car before we came home, but of course that was impossible. We forgave her that time, but two months later, she backed out of the driveway into a brand new Corvette. She not only had a problem with cars, she was also always breaking things in the house—dishes, knickknacks, the VCR, the children's toys. Even though she was great with the kids, we fired her. We simply couldn't live with the knowledge she was such a bad driver."

THE THORNIEST PROBLEMS

The four problems we will address in the remainder of this chapter are not necessarily the most common problems parents face when employing a nanny (Nanny trying to steal Dad is extremely rare). But they are the situations parents *worry* about the most, especially with a live-in nanny. In my interviews, when I explored the nitty-gritty of what really scares some of us—both actual and potential nanny employers—about home child care, the child care itself was not a primary apprehension. Nor was concern about cost. Or worries about loss of privacy.

We parents are afraid a nanny, especially a great nanny—the only kind any of us should employ—will replace us and make our own role redundant. We reason over and over again with our children that there is no big, bad wolf who will come and eat them while they sleep, but we lie awake nights agonizing about whether a nanny will steal our children or our spouse's affections.

Beautiful women confessed self-consciously to me that they didn't want to hire a nanny who was very attractive. Competent professionals shared fears about being outclassed by nannies who were "too" skilled. Almost universally, the dads said they would not feel comfortable with a male nanny.

The fear that a nanny will cause the loss of affection of our spouses (usually husbands, but not always) or our children is important to discuss. I counteract my own fears in any situation by visualizing it as though it were really going to happen and deciding how I would handle it. I am able to relax about a situation if I know that if the very unlikely worst case were to become true, I still will be all right. Therefore, I discuss here some real-life situations where the nanny does indeed have the potential for replacing the parent, not because I believe it will happen to you, but in order to let you know that you could handle it if it did.

Does competition for affection present a real problem for most families? Rarely. What *can* be a major hassle are limit setting and boundary issues. Parents don't usually worry about this, yet it is the single most difficult problem many parents face. No discussion about life with nanny would be complete without a look at boundary violations.

Finally, the problem of a nanny getting a case of raging hormones and letting this interfere with her job performance because she is so distracted (or pregnant) also occurs often enough to bear discussion (besides, I promised you a discussion about sex). I heard almost as many stories with this theme as I did about car episodes and large phone bills.

Raging Hormones

Many nannies are young (my definition of "young" is anyone younger than me, so in this case it is someone in their twenties and thirties) and most are single. The combination of young and single equals raging hormones. Not for all nannies, but for a significant portion of them. What does this mean for you the employer? Entertainment and cause for amusement, or extra trips to the drugstore for antacids. It's your choice.

You definitely cannot alter the behavior. You can require your nanny to be home at night by a certain hour during working days. You can have fifteen house rules all saying in different ways that men are not allowed to sleep over. But can you really alter in any significant way behavior driven by raging hormones? This is a rhetorical question.

What you can control is your reaction to the fact that your nanny spends her off-hours on the hunt. You don't need to tolerate her breaking any of your house rules, if she does that. Insist that she respect those. But do so from a position of amusement as opposed to one of anger or aggravation, which parents whose views are strictly moralist and nonapproving often feel.

One couple I interviewed smiled when they told me about an au pair who had worked for them many years ago. They spoke fondly of this young woman who went out every evening in search of romance and enlisted everyone's aid in deciding which outfit she should wear during her nightly excursions. "She would bring our daughter into her room and ask her opinion about what she should wear. When they had both selected the perfect clothes, she would waltz through the house to show it off," the mother told me with a twinkle in her eye.

"All the neighbors' heads would turn as she walked our daughter to school," the dad told me. "She always wore very tight-fitting, sexy clothes. And she would sometimes show up for work exactly on time, but having come from spending the night elsewhere. She was really entertaining. We loved her exuberance and got a kick out of how focused she was on finding a man."

Raging hormones can be nothing but trouble unless you adopt

the attitude of the family above or choose to avoid the situation entirely. Many of the families I interviewed explained that their nanny's interest in members of the opposite sex caused stress in the family through the nanny either becoming pregnant; engaging in behavior during work hours that had the potential for her to get pregnant ("I don't care that she and her boyfriend were intimate," one exasperated parent told me, "what I was angry about was that he was visiting her in the afternoons when she should have been watching my children"); or not being able to perform her job because she was spending so much time trying to meet Prince Charming.

Some of the families I talked with were still upset about their nannies' behavior. Others kept clear in their minds that the nanny was not their daughter, they were not responsible for her behavior during nonwork hours, they were not to blame if she got into trouble, and they were not angry. I remember one parent in particular who told me about his nanny who had been a diligent churchgoer, had come from a very strict home in a rural environment, and yet who had gotten pregnant after moving to a big city to work for his family. She arranged an adoption for her baby and continued as a well-loved nanny for four more years until she married and moved away. What I remember more than the story is the parent's tone of voice and attitude. There was amusement as he remembered his very pregnant nanny assisting at dinner parties and the guests pretending not to notice the pregnancy. There was compassion as he spoke about how the nanny had not been able to confide in her own family about the situation, how the members of her church deserted her, and how the father of the child moved away rather than acknowledge his responsibility. And finally, there was gratitude as he told me what a wonderful nanny she had been during the five years she worked for him.

The bottom line is that you will have as much success altering a case of raging hormones as you will getting your children to eat anything green. Write down the details of your experiences with your nanny with raging hormones and turn it into a screenplay for a soap opera or a romance novel. Make money, not waves.

Competition: Will She Steal My Spouse?

Raging hormones by themselves can complicate the parent/nanny working arrangement. When they take the form of a nanny becoming flirtatious with a parent (usually the dad), the result can make sitting through a presentation of the *Nutcracker* with two-year-old twin boys who have ear infections seem enjoyable by comparison.

To all the parents who know that employing a nanny is the very best care they can offer their children, yet who secretly worry, "What if the nanny I hire is prettier than me?" listen closely. *Nannies stealing husbands almost never happens.* However, I would be remiss if I didn't admit that nanny replacing mom does *occasionally* happen and not just to celebrities like Robin Williams, who married his nanny. (You're not getting any sleep anyway—why not leave you with the tiniest bit of concern to agonize over?) One woman I approached for an interview assured me that she could give me both perspectives, that of an employer and that of a nanny. She explained that she had been her husband's nanny before he divorced his wife and married her and had a baby. They now employ a nanny to care for their baby and her two stepchildren. Two other families made up of nannies who married their male employers declined interviews.

Have you ever asked a nanny what is her favorite movie? A surprising number name *Sound of Music*. "It has such a happy ending," one nanny told me with a sigh. It wasn't until later, when I thought about the ending, that I realized what she meant. Maria, the pious, beautiful, and talented nanny ends up with a career in the entertainment field, a ready-made family (seven children and no stretch marks!), and handsome, noble, and rich dad.

Jane Shacker employed a nanny who had *Sound of Music* aspirations. The nanny was a Party Girl with an enormous case of raging hormones directed at any male in sight, including Jane's husband. Jane's story was not unique, but in other stories I listened to about nannies who made advances to their employers, the inappropriate behavior did not affect the families as much as it did the Shackers (story follows). It usually was accompanied by other inappropriate behavior that was much more unacceptable. One dad told me that his family's nanny, who had been drinking, had come into his at-home office, thrown her arms around him, and said, "I like you; I *really* like you." She kissed him, left, and went into the bathroom and threw up. The family fired her because of her drinking and because they suspected she was stealing money. The dad explained his immediate thoughts after the nanny had kissed him. "My first thought was that she was probably trying to lift my wallet." He and his wife later laughed that this had been his primary concern.

Acceptance of a behavior does not mean you can't take any action. Just because the nanny making a pass at the dad didn't cause the family any emotional turmoil, it did not mean they weren't going to react. The family terminated the nanny because they didn't trust her; the fact that she had made a pass at the dad was a minor consideration. They simply didn't take the pass seriously.

The story below is one in which the nanny's flirting did cause considerable discomfort for the family. The situation was tricky because the nanny took excellent care of the children, and because the parents disagreed on how seriously they should take the nanny's interest in Martin, the husband.

Nanny Is After Dad and Dad Doesn't Have a Clue

(P.S. NANNY LOOKS GREAT IN A STRING BIKINI)

Jane Shacker hired a young woman, Honey, to care for her twins. When Jane interviewed her, she wore her blond hair in a ponytail and had glasses on. When she showed up for work, Jane's husband Martin answered the door. As soon as Honey saw him, she removed her glasses and let down her hair. She never used her glasses when he was around.

The family was having dinner when Honey arrived and Honey was asked to join them. It was clear from the start that the only person she wanted to talk to was Martin. She asked him questions about his job, his interests, his background and oohed and aahed at his answers. He thought she was great and was optimistic she would be a wonderful nanny.

Every morning Honey would watch from the window as Martin drove off, and she would sigh. And she mentioned to

continued

Jane's best friend that Jane thought Honey was trying to steal her husband, even though Jane had never said or done anything to give Honey this idea. When the friend mentioned it to Jane, Jane did indeed start to think this. As Jane explains, "The comment was self-fulfilling. After I heard it I did start thinking Honey's actions weren't innocent."

The Shackers went on vacation on their boat and took Honey with them. The arrangement was that she would work her normal hours. In her off-hours she sunbathed. During this vacation it was extremely obvious to Jane that Honey was taking a huge interest in Martin. She stayed in a string bikini the whole time. She followed him everywhere. She would reach out and touch his arm. She expressed tremendous interest in everything to do with the boat, which was his baby. And in the evenings she did a lot of drinking and giggling, especially in response to anything he said that was even remotely funny.

Jane told me, "My husband simply did not get it. After watching Honey's actions on the boat, I confronted him and gave him examples where I thought Honey was coming on to him. He said it was just her nature to be friendly. She was an army brat. He said that children who grow up in the military learn to be friendly and make friends easily. It didn't convince me, but I did have to admit the kids liked her a lot more than our previous nanny and I dreaded having to look for child care again.

"Honey was very active in putting together a social life for herself. She asked everyone we knew to fix her up. And when she didn't have a date she would go out, probably to bars. The liquor in our house disappeared at an alarming rate. I found cigarette butts in the trash even though she claimed she didn't smoke. Then I started finding marijuana roaches. I never knew where she was or with whom. She sometimes would come in the door at 7:00 in the morning.

"I tried to tell myself that she was good with the kids and I should be content with that. I told myself that her being flirta-

continued

tious with Martin was how she related to all men and did not mean she was specifically out to get him. But no matter how I tried to rationalize, to accommodate, or to accept the situation, I was troubled. Finally, my boss at work said, 'Jane, you're a wreck. Get this handled.' I need to tell you, I am not a jealous person. We have had several beautiful girls work for us and I have never had a problem with them. There was something different about this one.

"So, I ended up firing her. I really racked my brain first, wondering if I had done everything I could do to make the situation better. I started questioning all the decisions I made in life. Should I quit my job? Should I give up my career? Child care was such a huge hassle.

"By the way, Honey asked Martin to drive her to her new job. She was visibly disappointed when I went along in the car."

The Shackers both agree that removing Honey from their home was the best solution. They found a terrific nanny to replace Honey, even though it was an expensive process because they both had to alternately take unpaid leave from work during the time they searched. When I explained the Triple-A approach they said that avoidance was ultimately the only option for them. Whether or not Honey was really out to take Martin's affections away from his wife was not the issue. Her behavior caused the family stress and they were unable to either accept or alter it.

Competition: Will the Children Think She Is Mom?

When you introduce another person into a family, some kind of competition does frequently become an issue. Even if the competition does not actually occur, there often are competitive feelings. We fear that there may not be enough love or time or other life-sustaining ingredients for everyone. These fears often surface when a new baby enters the family. No matter how welcome the addition, siblings and spouses tend to worry about this new family member. The worry often takes the form of the question, "Will there be enough left for me?" This sets up an environment where competitive feelings may surface.

It should not surprise us then that the introduction of an additional adult—in this case a nanny—also creates an environment ripe for competitive feelings. Even the most secure parents sometimes worry that by bringing a nanny into the fold of their family they might lose something in the process, maybe even their children's affections. Competitive feelings can take different forms. Parents sometimes are jealous that their nannies get to stay home and play with their children. They may envy the nanny's relative youth and freedom or, if she is older, the fact that her own family responsibilities are over. The nanny's ability to take weekends off from the children may also be a source of irritation for overworked and harried parents.

Nannies sometimes envy their employers. Nannies may be jealous that the parents get to be "adult": to wear nice clothes, talk to other adults, be away from home. It's human nature to want what you don't have.

Is it any wonder that competitive feelings sometimes arise between adults who share the child care job? We expect our nanny to care for our children day in and day out, in sickness and in health, and to *not* daydream about them being her own children. We want our nannies to be totally involved with our children, but to relinquish them to us the moment we walk in the door. We want them to love our children, but not *too* much. We want our kids to love their nannies, but not *too* much. Although we strive to work with our nannies as partners, we sometimes end up as competitors because the situation is so personal and so important.

The truth is that there is enough love, work, and reward in child rearing, whether it be one child or five, to keep several adults occupied on a full-time basis. Cultures that share child rearing among several adults as a matter of course know this. We as a culture have forgotten it. However, just because it is a fact that children who love their nannies don't stop loving mom and dad it doesn't mean we stop worrying about the possibility.

We have already discussed an unlikely yet troublesome apprehension, that of losing your husband to your nanny, so we turn now to another dynamite-filled situation to see if it raises your blood pressure: relinquishing an infant to the care of a nanny. Will an in-

fant cared for primarily by a nanny view the nanny as more important than Mom or Dad?

The answer to this question is quite straightforward in regard
to children nurtured by nannies. I was told over and over again
during my interviews with experienced parents and child development researchers that *even the very best child care providers do not replace parents in children's eyes.* Even very young children who do not
see their parents as much as they see child care providers know who
"Mama" and "Dada" are and love them in addition to whatever feelings they have for their care givers.

Infants present a different picture when considering whether or
not affection for a parent will be supplanted by a care giver. An infant starts to recognize someone as a primary caretaker at around
four months old (as with all child development milestones this is
merely a guideline; children develop at different rates). By six
months old, the infant clearly shows a preference for the person who
has been interacting with him or her most intensely up until then. If
a care giver spends more time than a parent nurturing the infant, especially between three and six months old, there is a real possibility
the infant will regard the child care giver as being primary.

The good news is that few infants this young can say "Mama" so
you don't have to deal with the pain of this endearment being uttered to someone else. The really, really good news is that the infant
uses his primary attachment to form others, and by approximately
nine months will be branching out making many attachments. If
you enable your infant to make a primary attachment, whether or
not it is initially to you, you have done the best you can for him or
her. He or she will also attach to you. Unlike your nanny, you have a
lifetime to cement the relationship you have with your child.

However, how do you handle your feelings? You love that little
alarm clock who goes off every few hours all night long, and feel
that you deserve the most smiles. Your heart sinks when you see her
face light up when she sees your nanny. You want to feel happy she
likes her nanny. Your baby's reaction to her nanny is proof you've
got a good nanny. However, instead of the happy feeling you *should*
be experiencing, all you hear is a loud voice inside your head
shouting, "The baby is mine. Get your hands off her."

If only we always felt the way we should. Reality is that we often don't. We feel what we feel. If we can't alter the situation that faces us, we still have control over how we handle the emotions it provokes. Here are some examples of how different parents, utilizing the Triple-A approach, handled the fear that their infant would love the nanny more than them.

My Child Loves My Nanny More Than Me

(INFANT YOUNGER THAN SIX MONTHS OLD)

Acceptance

Marlene Fitzgerald is the single mother of twin boys who are now six years old. When they were four weeks old, she returned to work as an attorney. She loved her job, but her love for her children caused her to seriously consider giving it up so she could stay home to raise them. She explains, "I reviewed my finances and realized that the only way I could swing staying at home was to get a loan from my parents. I didn't want to do that. Besides, as much as I didn't want to leave my babies, I also didn't know if I could cope with staying at home all day without the stimulation of my career. I made the decision to return to work and to find the best nanny I could. The woman I found was wonderful and my boys smiled every time she came to work. To tell you the truth, I sometimes worried that they might love her more than me.

"Every time I felt what my mom used to call "the green-eyed monster" rising in me, I reminded myself that a parent's job is to do the very best for her children. Had the children's father been around, I would have gladly let him take care of the kids, not been jealous, and felt there was room enough in their hearts to love both of us. I'm a little embarrassed to admit it, but once I thought of my nanny as the kids' father, everything fell into place for me. I felt peaceful with my decision to continue my career."

continued

Debby Marshall is a hospital administrator. She returned to work six weeks after her daughter Chloe was born. Debby had mixed feelings about returning to work. She loved her job and was anxious to get back to it; at the same time she was unprepared for the magnitude of her feelings for Chloe. It was torture to hand her over to the nanny she shared with another single mom who had a toddler. "I had tears in my eyes all the way to work," she explained, "but I knew that was normal. The part that troubled me was that I hated the nanny. I hated her because she got to spend all day with my baby. I hated her because I knew that even if I could afford it, which I can't, I wouldn't feel satisfied being at home all day. I was terrified that Chloe would love her more than me. And then on top of this, I hated myself for being jealous of this kind, wonderful woman who was taking excellent care of my baby."

Debby shared her feelings with the support group of single moms to which she belonged. The others in the group had similar fears. One woman did not have competent child care and expressed envy that Debby did. She told Debby she should feel grateful she had good care and should count her blessings. Although Debby knew it was true, it didn't help her feelings of jealousy.

It was the feedback of a second woman that helped Debby. She suggested that Debby do some reading about child rearing in other cultures and other times. Very seldom did women do it alone. It was far more common for extended families—related or not—to care for children. "You are giving your baby a gift," this woman reassured Debby. "You are giving her the gift of your love plus someone else's. This someone else isn't going to be there forever, but you will. You will be the constant in your daughter's life. How nice it is that you are teaching your baby at this early age that there is more than one loving person in her life."

Debby began to view her nanny as a partner who was temporarily helping out. She made a mantra out of the words *temporary gift* and repeated them to herself whenever feelings of

continued

jealousy would arise. She didn't try to drive the jealousy away, she just let it coexist with feelings of gratitude.

Debby did another thing that other parents do to counter bouts of the "Will I Be Replaced?" Blues. She retained certain aspects of child care that she didn't share. She always put her daughter to bed. Even if she had night meetings she would come home to do this. She also always shared breakfast time with Chloe.

Several parents told me they reserve nighttimes as exclusive times. Even when they have nanny help available overnight, they opt to be the sole one to soothe nightmares away or to care for a child who is ill. Others made different choices as to what aspect of child rearing would be theirs and no one else's.

Avoidance

Dan Moreno was a single father. His wife died while giving birth to his son. Dan needed to return to his work as an architect in order to support his normal lifestyle. He explained, "I needed to go back to work so I got a wonderful older woman to watch Manuel. Every day when I left him he seemed happy to see her, but I wasn't so happy. By the time I arrived at my office, I felt so depressed I just couldn't face going in, but I forced myself. After four months I finally decided that Manuel was the most important thing in my life and I didn't want to miss a single moment of his growing up. I quit my job, terminated the nanny, sold my house and bought a smaller one. I took care of Manuel by myself until he was eighteen months old and paid my bills with the savings from the house sale. Then I launched an at-home architectural career earning a fraction of what I had been used to, but adapting by spending less money. I hired a part-time person to help out while I am working, but I plan to be a full-time dad with only minimal outside help.

Parents of older children who have been raised by care givers since they were young know that even the most wonderful care givers—the only kind you want caring for your children—did not become "Mom" or "Dad" in their children's eyes. If you are a first-time parent or the parent of very young children, this statement may not be enough reassurance but use it as a starting point. Examine the specific positives of the child care arrangement you have selected and remind yourself of it. If your fears about being replaced by a nanny are overwhelming, perhaps you should reexamine your decision to employ a care giver. Some parents, such as Dan Marino in the story above, adjust their lifestyles and delay a return to work. Some two-parent families decide that one parent will stay home while the other continues working (in our preschool, two dads became house parents while their wives continued working). Several parents I interviewed decided to work part-time instead of full-time while their children were young. Others elected to put professional goals on hold and stay home full-time.

One course of action that is *not* good for your children is to change care givers so that your children don't become too attached to any particular person. If you have the impulse to fire a good nanny just because you fear your child is getting too attached, fight the impulse. Use the Triple-A approach to handle your feelings.

Children need continuity. They need to attach to adults. For this reason, regularly firing nannies, or switching an infant to a day care center or to a family day care home just because you think the child will be less likely to love someone more than you is a bad decision. To rob an infant of the one-on-one love he or she is getting from a nanny because you are feeling jealous is to let your fears get in the way of your child's well-being. Work on the fears rather than on the arrangement. There is no limit to the amount of love in the universe. Your child's ability to love his or her nanny increases his or her ability to love you; it doesn't diminish it.

The competition for a child's affections is not a new phenomenon. It's easy to imagine the following tongue-in-cheek exchange between a nanny and a mom who have come to King Solomon to resolve their dispute.

Who Is the Child's Real Mom?

NANNY *(young woman dressed in sweat pants, Mickey Mouse watch, and T-shirt that reads: KIDS ARE NATURE'S WAY OF SAYING YOUR HOUSE IS TOO CLEAN):*
Mr. Solomon, Sir, this child belongs to me. I've changed his diapers, played with him, and watched countless hours of "Sesame Street" and "Barney" with him. He is mine.

MOTHER *(older woman, drawn expression on her face, dressed in wrinkled business suit):*
Your honor, this child is mine. I bore him. I get up with him at night. I work all day to support him. This other woman is a care giver to whom I pay a king's ransom—if you pardon the expression—and she won't even do laundry without objection.

NANNY *(her long eyelashes flickering over youthful, expressive eyes):*
Don't listen to her, King. I'm the one who spends all day with this child. He thinks I am his mother because she doesn't spend enough time with him. *(That ought to get her goat. Serves her right! I shouldn't be asked to do laundry; I'm a child care professional.)*

MOTHER *(slightly unkempt hair framing pale, taut face):*
Your honor. Her compensation includes three weeks' vacation and a membership in a video dating service. Now she wants to add the guilt package too. It's too much. Please don't take away my child as punishment for my trying to earn a living.

KING SOLOMON *(looking rather bored—he's listened to a lot of these stories recently):*
There is only one solution. We will split the child in two.

NANNY *(When I came to work here she did say she expected me to be mature and work out problems by compromising):*
Sure. She can have the half that poops.

Boundary Issues

Nations go to war over boundary issues and so do parents and nannies.

When we include any person in our intimate lives, whether it be a spouse, children, a close friend, a roommate, boundary issues will inevitably surface. Whether the precise situation involves space, privacy, or what have you, the emotions evoked typically are quite strong. It's fortunate nuclear bombs are not allowed in the hands of nuclear families.

Some nannies make great partners, sharing the children and your home with great respect for your rights as principal owner. Others are not as considerate, either because they don't know better or because they can't control their impulses. Faced with this kind of nanny, sooner or later, no matter how generous or patient a person you may be, you will feel as though your territory is being threatened. Never underestimate the magnitude of a parent's emotions when invaded territorially. If you delay in facing up to the problem and brush aside the feelings, eventually a war will erupt and it will be a war with no prisoners.

Several types of boundary issues can arise with a nanny, particularly a live-in nanny.

- *Privacy:* She comes into my room, she reads my stuff, she uses my things . . . [This sounds like sibling rivalry but it can occur between unrelated adults.]
- *Sensitivity:* She calls the children away while I am spending time with them, she changes my rules, she's unsupportive of moms working outside the home and lets the children know it . . .
- *Role confusion:* She gives me orders, she sides with the children when I punish them, she sits at my seat at the table, she grabs the paper before I have a chance to look at it . . .
- *Lack of consideration:* Her friends are always here, she turns on loud music while I am trying to work, the TV set is on full blast while the children are trying to sleep, she uses our car as a taxi for her friends, she invited her family to stay three weeks and we're supposed to foot the bills . . .
- *Possession confusion:* She lends out items that don't belong to her, she invites her friends over for meals without asking, she painted her room without permission . . .

- *Social obligation:* She thinks I am responsible for her happiness [Or, "I think I am responsible for her happiness."]. I have to introduce her to friends, take her everywhere with me, make sure she has enjoyable things to do in her off-hours, lend her clothes and jewelry . . .

The single most surprising thing about the boundary issues that parents I interviewed told me was the length of time it took many families to deal with the situations they faced. On paper, the stories seem unbelievable. How could the families have allowed the situation to continue? Many of the parents in these families seem to be thoughtful, smart adults. Quite a few are in management positions. No business would tolerate some of the boundary crossings that the parents chose to accommodate. Why? My theory is that most families find that getting through each day is hard enough without confronting their child care giver about a boundary violation and risking losing their child care. Of course, eventually the accumulation of trespasses becomes overwhelming and the parents end up exploding. But in the meantime—if my theory is correct— it seems easier to turn a blind eye than to acknowledge the offending behavior.

Parents told me about nannies arriving for their first day of work with a surprise friend (or two, or gerbils or a parrot or a dog and seven puppies) just for a "few" days. Others had boyfriends, cousins, parents, siblings, best friends who "showed up" and were allowed to stay, sometimes indefinitely. One nanny, after reassuring her employer that she did have a car to use to transport the children, failed to report that she didn't have seats in the car. Well, after all, she hadn't been asked that. The family gave her a month to get seats in her car and meanwhile rented a car for her. Other parents functioned as their nanny's therapist, social worker, matchmaker, best friend, and banker, even though they felt uncomfortable in the role.

Many, many families continued to accommodate nannies who violated reasonable boundaries long past the point they should have. Don't do this.

If you are faced with a boundary issue with your nanny, own up to the fact that *your comfort sharing space with her is as important as her performance caring for your children.* Nannies from Heaven are great at both. The nanny who is good with kids but not with adults will eventually look like a Nanny from Hell to you.

When a boundary issue arises, try first to change your nanny's behavior. Tell her what bothers you and explain why the behavior is a problem for you. Ask for a resolution. Jointly come up with one if she doesn't have the wherewithall to come up with one herself. Sometimes this works. Boundaries you think are self-explanatory may not be. Some nannies need limits spelled out for them.

If the behavior continues unchanged or if it metamorphoses into the same behavior taking a different form (the nanny who is asked not to open your mail starts to read discarded letters in your trash can instead) use the Triple-A approach. Persistent boundary violations usually result in the third technique, avoidance, being the course of action selected. Nannies who continue to violate boundaries usually get fired or quit in frustration if their employers persist in firmly defending limits.

The Mystery of the Proliferating Coffee Cups

THE ESMALIS' STORY

Shari and Tyler Esmali told me about a nanny who had no sense of boundaries in respect to their things.

"It probably would have taken us several more months to realize she was exchanging our belongings with her friends if it hadn't been for the coffee mugs," Shari related.

"Missing coffee mugs we might not have noticed. Coffee mugs that had proliferated to the point where there wasn't enough room on the cupboard shelves, even we couldn't miss."

"Why are you buying so many coffee mugs?" Tyler asked Shari one morning while they emptied the dishwasher.

"I'm not buying mugs," was Shari's surprised answer. "I thought you were bringing home mugs you've had at the of-

continued

fice for a long time. And by the way, look at our spoons. We seem to have lots of different patterns."

Shari continued with her story: "The realization that something strange was happening in our kitchen came on the heels of several weeks of questioning where the children's toys, tapes, stuffed animals, clothes, and even one time a crib blanket were hiding. Sometimes we couldn't find them for days at a time. Other times they were lost for good. Most of the items were fairly inexpensive, but many were irreplaceable in the eyes of the children.

"In an attempt to solve the mystery of the coffee mugs, we decided to enlist everyone's aid. The children, our nanny, and even the dogs were brought into the kitchen and asked to help solve the Case of the Extra Mugs. Much to the children's disappointment, our nanny immediately knew the answer."

"I drink tea when I go visit my friends," she explained, "and sometimes I'm not finished when it's time to leave, so I take the mug with me."

"Do you take spoons, too?" Tyler asked.

"I guess I sometimes do," she answered.

Tyler continued, "We insisted she take all the mugs and spoons back to their original homes. If she happened to find any belongings that looked like they might belong to us, we suggested she bring them back. Later that day, a big stack of our tapes and other belongings were put on the family room couch. Apparently, as our nanny made the rounds returning mugs, she also recovered some of the things she had 'lent' to others. When we questioned her actions, she seemed genuinely surprised that we should be at all bothered by the exchanges she had been making."

"When one of my friend's children are sick," she explained, "I take them videos and books and maybe a stuffed animal to make them feel better. Or if one of my friends likes something they see here, I let them use it for awhile. What is wrong with that?"

continued

Explanations about the Esmalis' point of view weren't understood. To this day, they don't think she was dishonest. She just was a generous, somewhat confused person who thought their things were hers to give away.

Shortly after this episode, the nanny and the Esmalis parted ways. She left in the middle of the night, taking from her room a lamp and an alarm clock that belonged to them, but leaving her fish tank with three fish in it (but no food or other supplies). They still have at least a half dozen coffee mugs that never found their way back to their rightful owners.

The Esmalis sometime later hired another nanny who had boundary issues, not only about possessions but about her role. She bossed everyone around and insisted things be done her way, and only her way. They say now that no matter how much the children love the nanny, if they find they have made this hiring mistake again, they will act quickly to terminate her if she does not have a good sense of limits.

Conclusion

The truth of the matter is that very few nannies are out to steal our children, our spouses, or our space. They come into our lives because they have chosen to earn their living caring for children, and living with us is a component of the occupation. Their motivations are often the same as those of nurses, teachers, doctors, social workers, and therapists. They want to help, to care for, to assist. Most want to do the very best job they can.

Nannies worry just as much, or possibly more than parents do about boundaries being crossed on the job. One of the most common fears is that a parent will take advantage of them in one of many ways, perhaps even sexually. One girl from the Midwest who had this apprehension decided to combat it with a foolproof plan. She informed the agency that was placing her that she would only work in a single-female-parent home. She was placed with a family comprising a divorced mom and her daughter in a large city.

When the nanny arrived at the family's home, she was surprised to discover that the mom, listed by the agency as an illustrator, exclusively drew pictures of nude women. When she asked the nanny to pose for her, the nanny politely declined, mumbling something about it not being in her job description. Her employer stroked her arm and told her she understood.

The next evening when the mother appeared in the nanny's room to inquire whether she would like a back rub, the nanny gave notice.

SUMMARY

1. Every form of child care—including the decision to take care of your children exclusively yourself—can evoke feelings of apprehension and fear.
2. Some of the most common apprehensions experienced by parents who choose nanny care are fears of competition and of being replaced by the nanny in the eyes of their children or their spouse.
3. The most common problems nanny employers usually face are the nanny's raging hormones and boundary violations.
4. The Triple-A approach to problem solving is very effective in dealing with real or imagined competitiveness, raging hormones, boundary violations, or any other problem that may arise. Choose to either alter, accept, or avoid the situation confronting you.
5. Choose the most competent, most wonderful nanny you can and don't be afraid you will be loved any less for it. The amount of love in the universe is limitless.

Epilogue

Some of the testimonials I heard during my search for the secret to employing a good nanny are very inspiring. The process of gathering the following quotes gave me the psychic fuel to continue on my own, sometimes frustrating search. I would listen to the children's voices on my tape recorder telling me how important their nannies were to them and get renewed energy in my endeavor to bring the same gift to my own children.

We did find our good nanny, a Nanny from Heaven. When she left in order to pursue further education, I found another to replace her. Once you know what you are looking for and how to look, it's not too difficult. I am glad to say that some of the following quotes come from my own children. Like all the other contributors to this book, my children's specific identities have been hidden, but despite the disguise, their voices ring out loud and clear in tribute to the nurturing they have received from nannies.

CHILDREN TALK ABOUT THE GOOD NANNIES IN THEIR LIVES

NICK (age 2 1/2): I love Avery. She is the best in the whole wide world. She is so nice. I'm going to marry Avery when I grow up.

NATHANIEL (age 3): Maria takes care of me. She plays trucks. I like trucks. She plays trucks a lot. We play trucks all day.

NICOLE (age 3 1/4): Chemain is my best friend. She helps Mommy take care of me. It's really fun when Chemain is here. Chemain brushes my hair and I brush Taffy's [her doll's] hair.

TARA (age 4): We have lots of people who love me at my house. Mama and Daddy, Obie [the nanny] and Kim [a snake].

MARK (age 4 1/2): I'm lucky. When Mommy is at work, Veronica and I make dinner and I get to choose. We go to the park and I hurt my knee and Veronica gave me thousands of kisses.

SIGFRIED (age 5): We have had lots of nannies, but I like Bonnie [present nanny] a lot! She tells me I have to clean up my room, but if I'm really slow she comes and helps me. She never yells. And if I eat all my lunch, I get dessert.

JORDAN (age 5 1/2): Chin is my aunt. She's not really my aunt, but she has taken care of me since I was a little, little baby. She gives me hugs and lets me touch everything in her room except I'm not supposed to turn on her TV.

JILLIAN (age 5 1/2): Flo Flo picks me up at school. She came to my play and helped me with my costume. I made the best costume. Flo Flo got the eye patch and sewed the costume, but it was my idea. Everybody at school thought I looked cool. Flo Flo and I have good ideas.

SUSAN (age 6): My nanny's name is Susan too, so we call her Sue. She taught me to ride a bike. I didn't want to do it, but she made me try. I cried but she said she cried too when she was little and she kept trying and trying and then she learned. I can ride a two-wheeler now. It's so fun.

GENE (age 7): My mommy used to take care of me but then she had to go to work. I was sad, but now I like being with my nanny. She and I do artwork together. We make pictures for my mom. I'm going to be an artist when I grow up.

STAR (age 8): Lisa lives with us. She is there when me and my brothers come home from school. She takes care of my little sister while we are in school. She makes the best chocolate cookies! I run into the house to get some right away. If I do my homework without being asked, she lets me read comic books. She made a rad house for my Barbie. It's a ski chalet.

ALEXANDER (age 9): The best nanny we had was Lynn, but I like Brooks too. He teaches me neat things like how to make a basket with only one hand. My friends like to come to my house to play because I have a man nanny who plays sports with us. My dad teaches me piano on the weekends.

JASON (age 10): Our nanny lives in the room next to me. She is really nice. She takes me to judo and helps me practice. I once kicked her and she didn't tell anyone, not even my mom and dad. It really hurt but she said it was an accident. No one knows about it.

JAGGER (age 11): Ashley picks me up at school and takes me on trips. We never have to go straight home unless I have a lot of homework. She invites my friends over. I missed her when she was gone last Christmas. She is getting married. I hope she stays our nanny forever.

RUDOLF (age 12): Simba teaches me all about her country. I am learning her language. We did a project about the ecology and the rain forest in her country and it won first prize.

CODY 9 (age 13): I like my nanny a lot. She helps me. She told me what to say to Shannon [a girl friend] and now Shannon likes me.

CRISTINA (age 14): Mika lived with us since I was five. She now comes and visits and I take care of her baby, Philip. She was my best friend. She told me we will always be friends. She said that once you make one friend you can make others. I have three friends now. I used to be shy.

KELSEY (age 15): Ruth taught me how to sew. She also taught me how to swim. My mom swims, but not very well. When I baby-sit I try to do the things that Ruth did. I never felt lonely or missed my parents with Ruth. She was strict, but really fun too. And she listened really well.

PEYTON (age 16): Adrianna was my nanny. She moved away but I talk to her at Christmas and she always calls me on my birthday. I went to visit her last year. We had a great time. She reminded me about the time she tickled me so much I wet my pants and then blamed it on the dog. I used to be embarrassed about that but now I am grown up.

CARSON (age 17): I am captain of the soccer team. Elizabeth taught me to play soccer. No one else in our family knew how to do it. Elizabeth made me practice and practice. She even gave me a trophy for most effort in the whole world. I thought it was made of real gold. I was kind of young.

ALIYA (age 18): My parents are divorced. I lived with my dad and my sister lived with my mom. Emilis took care of me while my dad was at work. She helped me with all my problems. She was like an older sister. Everyone should have an older sister who is nice and understands how you feel.

CHARLES (age 19): Irene Rose lived with us and helped my parents. When I think about her I remember singing. She was almost always happy. She was also strict. I could never get away with some of the things during the week that my parents let me get away with during the weekends, but I didn't think too much about it at the time. Irene was very fat. She used to joke about it. I'm sorry now that I used to joke about it too. She died last year and I'm still sad.

MICHAEL (age 20): Growing up we always had nannies. I don't remember anything particularly bad about any of them; most of my memories are about cool things we did. I think one of them must have been bad because I remember my mom and dad and the nanny screaming and then she left all of a sudden. For awhile I was really into models. I built this very special fort—I must have been eight or nine—and the dog ate part of it. I was extremely upset. Our nanny Kathy rebuilt the whole thing by the next morning. She must have stayed up all night. I've had excellent experiences with nannies. I'm lucky. Each one brought something unique into my life.

RHIA (age 21): As kids, we used to look forward to the nights our parents would go out. We had such fun with Maxine, who was our nanny. Sometimes we turned the house into a spa. The girls would do their hair, paint our nails, and things like that, and my brother would pretend he was at a gym and do exercises. Maxine always had great ideas. We would camp in a tent in the living room, we once put on a circus using all our stuffed animals, we put on plays, did dancing. She was terrific.

GOOD NANNIES TALK ABOUT THEIR JOBS

JAMIE: I can't think of another job where work is play. I feel blessed to have raised almost a dozen children without having a single labor pain. I've received more than a million kisses and probably kissed just as many bruises.

HUNTER: I was a nanny when I was in graduate school getting my Master's in Education. I hadn't realized how expensive it would be to live out of state and so when I saw an ad for a live-in male nanny on a bulletin board at the university I applied and was hired. Can you imagine me sitting at a little girl's birthday party with a birthday hat on? [Hunter is 6'4" and has a football player physique.] I loved the job and still keep in contact with the children, a boy and a girl. It's a long story, but their mom was a housekeeper who abandoned them at her employer's home. The employer adopted them and wanted a male figure in their lives. I became Uncle Hunter. I don't think I've had another job that was so rewarding, where I could see the difference I made right there in front of me—and I've had a lot of rewarding jobs. I'm a dad now and I know the difference between having your own children and raising someone else's but I still wholeheartedly love those kids I cared for.

REBECCA: I'm a career nanny. I've done this for twelve years and expect I'll do it for the rest of my life. Look at these babies [Rebecca specializes in twins]. Aren't they adorable? I feel like I'm the luckiest person in the world. Sure it's hard work. I like feeling I'm making a difference. I have a talent and I'm using it. I like the parents I work for a great deal. I won't accept a job unless I like the parents. They are the ones I am working for; I'm helping them. When I get tired, it helps to think about how you are helping nice people.

PAIGE: I am working as a nanny while I go to school. I want to be a teacher for children with special needs. The boy I take care of now is in a wheelchair. He has trouble doing most things you and I take for granted. He is one of the most wonderful people in the world. I really admire him. I learn as much from him as he learns from me.

MALLORY: I used to work for a family that was going through a divorce. The children lived with their mom for one week, then with their dad for the next. I stayed with them. It was hard on all of us. Sometimes I used to cry at night it was so hard. But we all made it. I stayed with the family because the kids needed me. They needed stability in their lives and I was it. I don't regret it at all even though it was the hardest thing I've ever had to do.

ELSA: I'm eighteen and I've just finished my first year as a nanny. I want to go college someday, but not just yet. I have a lot of responsibility at my job and I like it. It's a big responsibility taking care of children. I like the woman I work for; she has taught me a lot. When I have children of my own I will know what to do. The best part of my job is when the children tell you they love you. I also like watching them learning new things. They are so happy when they have learned to do something new. This is a great profession. I'm glad when the person I work for comes home because I'm real tired. The kids are happy to see their mom so it's not too hard for me to leave to go to the gym to work out. How do parents raise kids alone? There is so much to do.

NANA: My kids call me Nana even though that isn't my real name. I'm sixty-seven years old and I've had a lot of kids, more than I can tell you about. I worked for the Smithboks for twelve years and then for friends of theirs, the Grosses, and then for another family. You should come here at Christmastime. My house is covered with cards from my kids. I never did get married, but I've had all the blessings and none of the hassle, if you know what I mean. God put children on this world to love. My kids had their parents and me to love them. You can never have too many people loving you.

PARENTS TALK ABOUT THE GOOD NANNIES IN THEIR LIVES

DENNY AND COOPER: We have been really, really lucky. We both have busy careers that mean a lot to us. It has given us great peace of mind to know that the children are not only well taken care of while we are at work, but are getting benefits we can't give them. We are older parents and, frankly, don't have the patience our nanny has.

ROSS AND EMILY: I don't know what we would do without our nanny. She is fantastic. The children love her and so do we. She is the key to making our family unit work. We moved here from the Midwest and she came with us. We might not have moved if she hadn't agreed to come with us.

MARGARIT: I have a couple from China who live with us. They have been with me for six years. Frankly, I can't imagine life without them. I don't have any family close by that I trust to help me with child care. My children are now bilingual in Cantonese and English.

LENNY: My daughter has been cared for by au pairs for the last ten years. She has had insight into several different cultures and learned so much that she wouldn't have otherwise. I've enjoyed bringing these young women into my life too. There have been some problems—in life what is problem-free? But by and large it has been a very good experience.

ADAN AND SOCORRO: You have to find someone with heart, someone very kind. Children are the most important thing in life. We have a very kind woman caring for our children. The woman before her was also kind. I have nice children. I think this is partially due to the nannies who have been with us.

A FINAL WORD

The people in our lives are all that matters. Other things are important, perhaps even vital, but nothing comes even close to our relationships.

I have been blessed with children. I have been further blessed with assistance in raising them. My husband and I offer everything we are capable of offering to our children. Our nanny does too. Some of her offerings are redundant with ours, a few are in conflict, most are additional. She doesn't quite bleed along with our children in the same way that we do when they experience heartache, but we can't offer the sustained companionship that she cheerfully provides. She and we have different wisdom. We all do our best.

It's hard to be a nanny. It's hard to be a parent. It's also hard to be a child. If we all help each other in the spirit of love, maybe together we can make it less hard.

In-Home Child Care Definitions[1]

Au Pair (Foreign)

Foreign national in the United States for up to a year to experience American life. Lives as part of the host family and receives a small allowance/salary and helps with child care and housework. May or may not have previous child care experience.

Baby-sitter

Provides supervisory, custodial care of children on an irregular full-time or part-time basis. No special training or background expected.

Governess

Traditionally an educationally qualified person employed by families for the full-time or part-time at-home education of school-age children. Functions as a teacher and is not usually concerned with domestic work or the physical care of younger children. Hours of work by arrangement.

Nanny

Employed by the family on either a live-in or a live-out basis to undertake all tasks related to the care of children. Duties are generally restricted to child care and the domestic tasks related to child care. May or may not have had any formal training, though often has a

---

1. The International Nanny Association developed these definitions.

good deal of actual experience. Nanny's work week ranges from forty to sixty hours per week. Usually works unsupervised.

Nursery Nurse

Title used in Great Britain for a person who has received special training and preparation in caring for young children, in or out of the home. When employed by the family, may live in or out. Works independently and is responsible for everything related to the care of the children in her charge. Duties are generally restricted to child care. Work is usually fifty to sixty hours per week. In addition to specialized training, the nursery nurse will also have passed the British Certification examination of the National Nursery Examination Board.

Parent/Mother's Helper

Lives in or out and works for a family to provide full-time child care and domestic help for families in which one parent is home most of the time. May be left in charge of the children for brief periods of time. May or may not have previous child care experience.

APPENDIX B

The Work Agreement: Worksheet and Sample

The easiest way to develop a work agreement is to start with a worksheet. Use only those sections that apply to your situation. Add additional categories pertinent to your needs. Fill it in with a pencil. Discuss it with a new hire and negotiate those specifics on which you are flexible. When you are in agreement, you can develop a final document that both of you can sign. Following this worksheet is a work agreement you can use as a sample.

Period of the agreement: From _____ To _____

Workdays (circle): Mon. Tues. Wed. Thur. Fri. Sat. Sun.

Work hours: _____

Rest periods: _____

Trial period: _____

Compensation: _____

Pay period (weekly or monthly): _____

Handling of taxes: _____

Overtime pay: _____

Travel or 24-hour pay: _____

House-sitting pay: _____

Vacation (how much and when to be taken): _____

Performance reviews (when given): _____

Sick days: _____

Holidays: _____

Benefits: _____

Automobile policy: _____

continued

257

Duties in Addition to Regular Child Care (Check Applicable):

SPECIAL DUTIES

____ Involve children in activities such as (specify)
____ Transport to school and activities
____ Tutor or assist with homework
____ Arrange play dates for children
____ Take children to appointments such as doctor and dentist
____ Maintain daily log including activities, skills learned, food eaten
____ Other

HOUSEHOLD MAINTENANCE

____ Make beds (children's only) (family's)
____ Straighten up after (children only) (family)
____ Cook (children's meals only) (family's meals)
____ Wash dishes and clean up kitchen (breakfast) (lunch) (dinner)
____ Clean children's rooms at least __ times a week
____ Clean other rooms in house (specify) at least ___ times a week
____ Laundry (children's) (family's)
____ Ironing (children's) (family's)
____ Maintain children's clothes, toys, furniture, and equipment
____ Periodic heavy cleaning (polishing silver, cleaning closets, cleaning refrigerators and stoves, etc.)
____ Pet care
____ Errands (children's only) (family's)
____ Family entertaining tasks (preparing, serving, etc.)
____ Management of other staff
____ Home management (arranging for repairs, bookkeeping, etc.)
____ Plant maintenance
____ Gardening assistance
____ Other

continued

Family policy on food (elaborate):

Family philosophy on discipline (elaborate):

Family expectations for children's daily activities:

Who is expected to hire back-up baby-sitters if nanny is ill or can't work extra hours? _____

When is weekly meeting scheduled? _____ Is overtime paid for this? _____

Will nanny eat with family? _____

Termination policy (notice period, pay in lieu, how nanny's outstanding debts to be handled):

Sample Work Agreement

This agreement is between Sally Mayer and the Rodriguez family. It covers the period July 10, 1996 to July 10, 1997.

Sally Mayer agrees:
1. To provide full-time child care from 8:00 A.M. to 6:00 P.M. from Monday through Friday. On Wednesdays she will baby-sit until 10:00 in the evening as part of regular hours. Full-time child care consists of (but is not limited to) waking and dressing the children; feeding them nutritious meals and snacks during the day; bathing them; planning and involving them in activities that promote their emotional, social, and intellectual development; supporting the children's special interests; nurturing and promoting feelings of warmth and security; scheduling daily times to read to them; caring for them when they are ill, being empathetic and actively helping them achieve solutions to problems.
2. To comply with parents' child rearing and discipline philosophy and to daily communicate with the parents on issues related to this.
3. To read any child-relevant material supplied.
4. To maintain a cheerful and helpful attitude and to be a good role model.
5. To be reasonably flexible in times of emergency or unusual circumstances.
6. To communicate with the parents as soon as possible about any problems, issues, concerns, etc., related to the children or to her own employment.
7. To maintain her own room and the family automobile so they are reasonably neat.
8. To provide the following housekeeping and house maintenance duties: *Daily* make the children's beds, assist them in cleaning their rooms and picking up in other areas of the house, clean the kitchen after every use, empty trash containers, empty dishwasher in the morning, fill dishwasher in the evening, do laundry for the family.

continued

Weekly vacuum the house (Tuesdays), take the dry cleaning in, shop for groceries.

Timothy and Marta Rodriguez agree:

1. To pay a salary of $250 a week, paid weekly. Overtime and extra baby-sitting is compensated at the rate of $6.50 an hour. Twenty-four-hour pay is $50 in addition to normal salary. A bonus of $500 will be paid after one year's employment.
2. To provide room and board plus specially requested food items up to $15 a week.
3. To provide an automobile, pay for all maintenance, gas, and insurance. There is a fifty-mile limit on personal use.
4. To allow Sally Mayer to take a two-week vacation after one year's employment. Sally will travel with family during their vacations and be paid twenty-four-hour pay during this time. If she does not travel with the family and remains home house-sitting, her normal wages are paid.
5. To recognize all federal holidays as days off. If Sally chooses to work these and the family needs her during this time, double wages will be paid or Sally may elect to take a substitute day off.
6. To pay for one-half the cost of medical insurance up to $45 a month.
7. To schedule extra hours needed as far in advance as possible and to give Sally first choice at working them. Additional hours are optional, unless it is a medical emergency, and Sally will not be penalized if she does not wish to work them.
8. To hold weekly meetings every Monday evening at 5:00 in order to discuss the job and the children. A formal performance evaluation and salary review will be conducted after ninety days and every six months thereafter.

Severance procedure:

Each party agrees to give the other three weeks' notice. Pay in lieu of notice may be given if it is the family's decision to terminate. No severance or notice period is needed during the thirty-day probation period.

Parents and Nannies Share Child Rearing Tips

During my interviews with parents and nannies, I received hundreds of hints, suggestions, and recommendations on every aspect of child rearing from how to get children to eat vegetables ("forbid them to eat anything green," one dad told me, "they'll beg to be given green peas as a snack") to ideas for birthday parties. I couldn't include them all and selected these useful and charming ideas from among them.

First Aid

COOPERATION IN TAKING MEDICINE

Several nannies and parents told me that the time to get children to be cooperative about taking medicines is when they are infants. If your infant requires medication, give it in a dropper very slowly and with lots of encouragement. Every time the baby takes a swallow say something like, "Good job. That's very good!" and look pleased. Show your approval in your voice and your face, exhibiting the same delight you will show when your child gets perfect scores on his or her college entrance exams.

Preface giving medicine to a child with a statement something to the effect that "this will make you feel better," or "this medicine will make the hurt go away from your ear." I have never called medicine "candy" out of fear the child will eat or drink some when I am not looking. But I do reassure that medicine is helpful and will taste good (most children's medicines taste as though they should be used as an ice cream topping).

ICE

" 'Magic' kisses and ice are wonderful healers for most bruises of childhood," one parent told me. "Kisses I used instinctively. The use of ice didn't start until my first child was old enough to walk and fall down. By then he refused to let me use ice. With subsequent children I started using ice at a much younger age. In fact, our second son—voted by our play group as the child most likely to get stitches—would yell out 'ice' when he fell rather than 'help.' "

Empty film containers, filled with water and then frozen, make wonderful ice holders. Give the injured child the canister to apply to the hurt area himself.

Frozen cans of juice or frozen juice boxes also function well as "ice" to reduce swelling of bruises.

Leaving Babyhood

ARRIVAL OF A SIBLING

When a new baby arrives, a parent will often view an older sibling as instantly more mature and capable. This can be especially tempting if the older sibling is close in age to the new baby. A parent may suddenly expect him or her to move out of a crib, give up a bottle, or become potty trained, just because the child is no longer the baby of the household.

One Super Nanny gently reminded the parents of a two-and-a-half-year-old and a newborn that they might be falling into the trap of mentally aging their toddler when they discussed taking his nighttime diaper away. "He's gone through a lot of change lately," she suggested. "Maybe you should let him keep his diaper for now."

ABOUT POTTY TRAINING . . .

For those of you with children who aren't potty trained, don't rush it. No one goes to college wearing a diaper. Eventually your child will no longer need diapers. It's a lot easier if the child comes to you and says, "Mom, all my friends are wearing underwear. Won't you *please* let me?" than to be frustrated trying to potty train a child who isn't motivated or ready.

PACIFIER WEANING

One parent told me about a technique for gradually weaning a child from a pacifier. He suggested putting a hole the size of a pinprick in the tip and waiting a week. The pacifier will be harder to suck with a hole in it. The next week put in a second hole. Each week add an additional hole until the child stops using the pacifier.

I was unable to double-check this tip. My children are thumb suckers. I tried to test the pinprick method on one of their thumbs, but it failed to work. Just kidding.

Cleaning

FINGER MARKS

To remove finger marks from wallpaper, rub some soft, slightly stale bread over the marks. This works like a charm.

INK

To get rid of ballpoint ink from fabric, spray the stain with hair spray and wipe it off with warm, sudsy water.

SILVER POLISH

Toothpaste works wonders as a silver polish. Put some on a damp cloth, rub it in, rinse, and pat dry. Regular toothpaste rather than a kid's toothpaste is best. The parents who told me this tip said they learned it from their Boss nanny who kept the silver baby gifts polished using this method.

They left their silver items unpolished and stored out of sight after the nanny left.

DIAPERS FOR TEENAGERS

Save your cloth diapers to use as cleaning cloths. They are terrific wood polishers. I gave one recently to our sixteen-year-old to use to polish his guitar. It's the only thing I saved from his babyhood that he considers worthwhile.

Food

PEANUT BUTTER AND KETCHUP

One nanny showed me the best way to store jars of peanut butter: upside down. Storing it this way enables the oil in the peanut butter to mix evenly with the peanut solids and prevents oil separation.

I adapted the upside-down method of storage to bottles of ketchup. It works best with the regular-sized plastic bottles, although you can use it with all ketchup bottles (you will just need to prop up the family-sized bottles or keep them on a shelf on the refrigerator door). Ketchup stored this way always comes out easily, and also makes getting out the last drops of the bottle a cinch.

FINGER JELL-O

Alphabet cookie cutters are great to use in making snacks for special occasions. You can use them to make edible letters, which are fun to hold and eat, out of gelatin. Either use commercial Jell-O and follow the recipe for jigglers (two packages of Jell-O mixed with two cups of ice-cold water) or if you want a less expensive, really homemade treat, follow the recipe below.

Use the alphabet cutters to cut out the letters in your child's name. Or, if you are feeding several children at once, cut out the alphabet, give them letters at random, and let them trade with each other so they can each spell their own names.

Really Homemade Jigglers

3 envelopes unflavored gelatin
1 12-ounce can frozen juice concentrate, thawed
12 ounces water

Soften the gelatin in the thawed juice. Meanwhile, bring the water to a boil. Add the juice/gelatin mixture to the boiling water and mix. Pour into a shallow greased bowl and refrigerate for two hours. Cut into shapes.

WOW-THEM-AT-PRESCHOOL-CHEESE SNACKS

Cookie cutters can also be used to make very attractive cheese snacks.

To make a sensational-looking cheese snack, you need to get American cheese slices that are individually wrapped. Get both white and yellow cheese. Then, partially unwrap one of the cheese slices and cut out a shape in the middle with a cookie cutter. Unwrap a cheese slice of the other color and cut out the same shape.

Next, you exchange the middle pieces. The yellow cheese slice will now have a white shape in the middle and the white cheese slice will have a yellow one. Rewrap both slices and proceed to do the remaining slices.

I have tried several brands of cheese slices and Kraft is the easiest to work with. It unwraps easiest and the cheese tends to break the least while you are lifting the middle out. In spite of the relative ease of working with Kraft cheese, I don't do this snack very often (to be perfectly frank, I only do it at the children's birthdays), but better moms than me—well, at least the mom who showed me this—vary the shapes and use this snack to celebrate the seasons. The mom who developed it uses a maple leaf cookie cutter in the fall, a bunny in spring, a flag for the fourth of July. You get the picture.

PRETTY FOOD

One nanny extended her love of color and art to meal preparation. She used food coloring in food to make it "pretty." The children were given blue mashed potatoes, pink milk, yellow noodles. The kids really enjoyed the novelty. They continued to request something "red" for lunch or something "blue" for snack. It taught colors and made mealtimes more fun. I don't know how healthy this trick is. If you suspect your child reacts poorly to food dyes, don't try it.

Other nannies shared with me their own tricks to making food attractive. Colored sprinkles were on several nannies' lists. I tried sprinkling celery stuffed with low-fat cream cheese with colored sprinkles and my kids loved it. I also got rave reviews when I topped cottage cheese and fruit with them.

Putting some Parmesan cheese in a shaker was one nanny's secret to getting her charges to love vegetables, pasta, and other foods. She said she let the children shake the cheese themselves. One parent extended this tip even further. She would tell her young children up front how many shakes they could have. It gave them experience counting as well as the feeling they have some control over food.

BIRTHDAY FOOD IDEAS

One of the Professionals I interviewed had participated in a number of birthday parties. She shared the following ideas.

Ice cream cones make great cake holders for young children. Fill each cone three-quarters full with cake batter and bake as long as directed for cupcakes. When the cake is done, each child can have his or her own cone filled with cake.

When using an ice cream cone as an ice cream holder (how novel!), put a hole through a cupcake liner and stick the cone through it. The cupcake liner helps to catch drips.

SUPER NANNY MISSY'S RECIPES WITH CANNED DOUGH

Missy, our first Super Nanny, performed wonders with Pillsbury roll dough, the kind that comes in a can and is usually stored near the dairy product case in the supermarket. The new cans are easier to open than the ones you used to have to hit on the countertop until they popped. Now you just have to peel the label off to get the can open. Some of the children's favorite meals used this dough.

Mini Pizzas

Separate the roll dough and flatten each piece. Spread some spaghetti sauce or pizza sauce on it. If you don't have either handy, ketchup seasoned with oregano can be used. I don't really care for this variation, but the children prefer it to all alternatives. Top with shredded mozzarella cheese and bake in a 450° oven for five minutes. Voilà! Homemade pizza.

Cinnamon Snacks

Separate the roll dough and flatten. Sprinkle with cinnamon and sugar. Dot with raisins and butter. Bake in a toaster oven for a few minutes.

Ghost Buns

She made these with the children for Halloween. Separate the roll dough and place on a toaster oven tray. If you don't have a toaster oven, you can use a cookie sheet, which will go into a 450° oven after the dough is decorated. Make ghost "faces" in the dough using raisins, candies, chocolate chips, or sprinkles. Bake according to the instructions on the package.

Wrapped Hot Dogs

Separate the roll dough. Wrap each hot dog in each section of dough. Bake in a 350° oven for ten minutes. If desired, you can wrap a slice of cheese around the hot dog before encasing the hot dog in dough. Ketchup and mustard for dipping can be provided in little cups.

FROZEN FRUIT BOXES

I wish serving juice in boxes was more ecologically sound. This innovation is so useful in myriad ways. In addition to its use as an ice applicator, which I mentioned in the first aid section, frozen fruit boxes, when added to a lunch box, can keep the food packed next to it cold for awhile.

ICE CREAM MADE IN A CAN

I didn't know whether to put this suggestion under food or activity. It's fun to do. You will need a 10-ounce-sized can and a 3-pound sized can, such as the one many shortenings come in.

In the small can, mix 1 cup heavy cream, 1 cup milk, 1/2 cup sugar, 1 teaspoon vanilla, 1/3 cup raisins or berries. These ingredients will yield 2 1/2 cups of ice cream. Put the lid on the can and place it in the larger can.

You will also need approximately 15 cups of crushed ice and 1 1/2 cups of kosher or rock salt. Layer one-half of the crushed ice alternately with one-half of the salt. Cover the large can. Save the remaining half quantities of ice and salt for a second application.

Go out to your driveway, patio, or any other hard surface where strangers can see you and comment on your insanity. (Actually, in testing this recipe, one time I did it on a hardwood floor, the other time my children rolled the can between them as they sat spread-legged on a carpet). Roll the can on the floor for ten minutes. Open it, empty the ice and water, lift out the small can, wipe its lid clean before opening it. Stir, scraping the ice cream from the sides of the can into the middle, then cover and return it to the larger can. Repack with the ice and salt you have saved, cover, and roll for an additional five minutes. Open and eat.

The original recipe called for a beaten egg, but I eliminated it to protect against possible salmonella poisoning from a raw egg. I didn't detect any taste difference.

VEGETABLES

Some children refuse to eat vegetables. This may come as a surprise to those parents whose children loved vegetables as babies.

Rather than fight with your child to eat vegetables, try cutting them into interesting shapes. Cookie cutters can be helpful in doing this; sometimes all you need is a sharp knife. Then you can coax your child into eating "shapes."

Activities

GOOP: THE MODERN MUD PIE

Do you need an activity to keep your toddler busy while you are busy composing a nanny ad? If it is a warm, sunny day, mix up some "goop," put it in a large plastic dishwashing bucket (or a water table if you have one), and let the child play outdoors. It's a great alternative to sand or water play, and appropriate for ages one year and up (I still love to play with it). Some parents also use bird seed. When the activity is finished, you can dump it on the ground for the enjoyment of the neighborhood birds. When the weather dictates indoor activities, use cornmeal in the bucket instead.

Goop (or Obleck)

Mix cornstarch with just enough water to make it into a runny clay consistency. A typical ratio would be 1 1/2 cups water to a package of cornstarch. Add it slowly until it feels right to you.

The mixture will run through your fingers, feeling slippery, yet leave your hands relatively clean. It's fun to squish, stir, and do all sorts of hand play with "goop." And if your toddler should taste it, no harm will be done.

STRAWBERRY BASKETS AND HOMEMADE BUBBLES

One nanny advised me to save strawberry cartons, the green, plastic kind. She said she would fill up a basin full of homemade bubbles and give each child a strawberry basket to use as a bubble blower.

Homemade Bubble Solution

2/3 cup liquid dishwashing detergent
Water to make one gallon
Optional: 1 tablespoon glycerin, which can be purchased at a drugstore (for longer lasting bubbles)

Combine, shake, and let sit for a couple of hours or even one day. Dip the baskets in the bubble solution and wave in the wind, or blow through the holes to make lots and lots of large bubbles.

Another use for the strawberry baskets is in conjunction with paint. Mix finger or tempera paints with some soap powder. This doesn't affect the paint and makes it a lot easier to wash color off clothes, hands, furniture, and other objects it ends up decorating. Dip the flat part of the basket into the paint and then onto a piece of white or colored paper. This can be repeated several times. It's a method of "painting" suited to toddlers, yet also fun for older children.

PLAY DOUGH

One nanny gave me a very good recipe for homemade play dough: Mix together 3 cups flour, 1 1/2 cups salt, and 1 tablespoon cream of tartar. Add 3 cups water, 2/3 cup oil, and 3 teaspoons food coloring. Cook over medium heat, stirring constantly until mixture forms into a ball. Remove and knead until dough is soft and has lost its stickiness.

On a personal note: Since ground-in play dough will not come out of carpets or the mouths of toddlers who think even the kind made with tons of salt tastes yummy, I suggest you put the play dough in a plastic bag and let your children manipulate it while it is enclosed.

And by the way, the only time I have actually made play dough was when I tested this recipe. My own recipe for play dough is as follows:

1. Get in the car,
2. Go to a discount store, and
3. Buy the cheapest brand.

ART THAT TASTES GOOD

Edible art is fun to make and then eat. Cheerios, Fruit Loops, or any other round cereal or candy, such as licorice with a hole in the middle, can be strung on a string or new shoelace to make edible jewelry. They also can be used to make towers, cemented together by water or spit. This edible art is especially useful to do on an airplane.

ART THAT TASTES GOOD . . . TO BIRDS

Another edible art project is to make a bird feeder out of a large pretzel. Coat the pretzel with a glue of cornstarch moistened with a bit of water, and sprinkle birdseed on it. Tie a ribbon on the pretzel and hang it outside during winter as an art/nature project to be consumed by the neighborhood birds.

Sharing

The use of a simple kitchen timer is a great way to impartially handle a situation in which children are vying for a possession. Establish a time limit for possession and set the timer appropriately. When the bell rings, the child must give the possession up to someone else.

TODDLER TIME MEASUREMENT

A timer is a good way to convey a time period for a toddler. It can be used to measure the amount of time a parent should be left undisturbed on the phone ("I'm going to be talking on the phone until the timer rings; please do not talk to Mommy until the bell rings"). It also can be used to time a punishment ("You cannot watch TV until the timer rings").

Farewells

One family told me about a favorite baby-sitter. They were impressed with how she handled farewells. They would tell their child they were going out, that they would return later, and that in the meantime the sitter would care for the child. When they were finished, the sitter would pick the child up, encourage him to wave bye-bye, and swiftly get him interested in an activity or object.

The first time she came, she turned him to a painting on the wall and said, "Oh, look at these pretty colors. And I also see a horse. Can you find the horse?" It worked like a charm. The child was soon so engrossed with what she was showing him that he forgot to cry about the parents' leaving. Other times she would turn to a special toy or treat she had stashed nearby.

Reconnecting with your child after a day spent apart

A single, working mom who didn't have a lot of spare time and was tired in the evenings when she returned home, came up with the practice of bathtub dinners. This is how she described them:

"I would come home, make a simple dinner like sandwiches, and we would eat dinner in the bathtub. It was fun, and relaxing; we could discuss the day, eat, and get clean all at once."

Time Out

One mom explained a variation of the "time-out" form of punishment where a child is told to sit down, be quiet, and take some time out to reflect on his or her misbehavior. The mother had explained to her new nanny that the family used time-outs to discipline. The nanny misunderstood her and gave "time out" to objects instead of to the kids. This worked very well; for certain situations, it was even better. For example, when their children started to hit each other with building blocks, the nanny gave the blocks "time out." She put them away out of reach and announced the blocks were in time out until the boys could play together better.

Balloons and Safety

Most children are fascinated by balloons. However, when a balloon pops, its pieces can be deadly if ingested. They can get stuck in a child's throat and cause suffocation.

Pop all balloons before allowing them in your house and dispose of the pieces in a garbage pail that is out of the reach of small children. Teach children at an early age that they can't play unsupervised with balloons.

Tape Recorders

Several families reported using tape recorders to entertain, document, and to soothe young children to sleep. Among the suggestions I received were:

- Record your children when they first start to speak. Play the tape back to them. They will love it and want to hear themselves again and again.
- Make it a family tradition to record your children at least once a year. One parent said she and her daughter baked the daughter's birthday cake the night before her birthday. While they baked, they discussed the previous year and taped the discussion. She plans to give the tapes to her daughter when her daughter has her first child.
- Several families tape record good-night stories to be heard when they have baby-sitters in the evening or when the parents are out of town. It is soothing to hear a parent's voice if the parent can't be there in person.
- In our family, from the time they were born, we started putting on a lullaby tape when we put our children to bed. The tape we used with our last two children was "Songs from Dreamland." After a while conditioning sets in, and a child will get sleepy just listening to the music.

  The only downside to this practice is that we also get heavy eyelids when we hear the music, so we can't play it while driving. We tried it once and everyone in the car started to fall asleep, including the driver.

Playpens

The only time our children would consent to use a playpen was when they were old enough to climb into one. The first Christmas we had a toddler, instead of protecting the tree and its ornaments by putting an unhappy child in the playpen, we put the Christmas tree inside the playpen instead. It worked great. Other parents offered the following suggestions for playpens:

- Playpens are great places to temporarily keep pets such as an unhousebroken puppy.
- A playpen is a good toy chest or a sports pen. You can throw all your sports equipment into it.
- Mom or Dad can climb into the playpen and do paperwork while watching toddlers, who are too young to know paper is not for eating, play outside the pen.

To All Readers

Do you have a nanny story you would like to share with others? Or are you a nanny with tales of her own to tell? Write to me and tell the highlights of your experience. I'd like to hear from you and perhaps include your story in another volume of *The Good Nanny Book.*

Write to: P. Michele Raffin
c/o The Berkley Publishing Group
200 Madison Avenue
New York, N.Y. 10016